Human Evolution

A Neuropsychological Perspective

John L. Bradshaw

Neuropsychology Research Unit, Department of Psychology, Monash University, Clayton, Australia

Psychology Press

a member of the Taylor & Francis group

Psychology Press, Publishers
27 Church Road
Hove
East Sussex, BN3 2FA
UK

British Library Cataloguing in Publication Data

A catalogue record for this book is available from the British Library

  ISBN 0-86377-504-7 (Hbk)

Typeset by DP Photosetting, Aylesbury, Bucks.
Printed and bound in the United Kingdom by Biddles Ltd, Guildford and King's Lynn

UNIVERSITY OF
WOLVERHAMPTON
KNOWLEDGE • INNOVATION • ENTERPRISE

Harrison Learning Centre
City Campus
University of Wolverhampton
St Peter's Square
Wolverhampton
WV1 1RH
Telephone: 0845 408 1631
Online renewals: www.wlv.ac.uk/lib/myaccount

1 2 FEB 2014		
		5

Telephone Renewals: 01902 321333 or 0845 408 1631
Online Renewals: www.wlv.ac.uk/lib/myaccount
Please return this item on or before the last date shown above.
Fines will be charged if items are returned late.
See tariff of fines displayed at the Counter.

WP 2117273 0

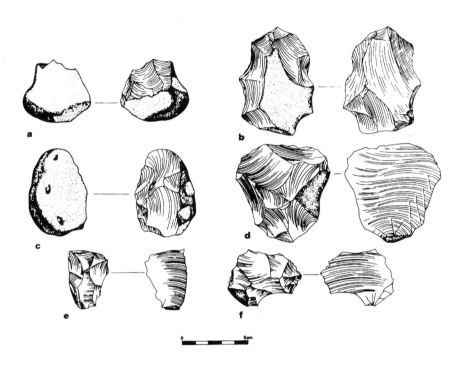

Sketches from a sample of the Gona artefacts, the oldest known tools from anywhere in the world: a, flaked pieces; b, discoid; c, unifacial side chopper; d–f, detached pieces. Reprinted with permission from Semaw, S., Renne, P., Harris, J.W.K. et al., 2.5-million-year-old stone tools from Gona, Ethiopia, *Nature*, 1997, *385*, 333–336. Copyright © 1997 Macmillan Magazines Ltd.

View of Jinmium rock-shelter (Northern Territory, Australia) and engraved pits (cupules) dated to older than 58,000 years and perhaps the world's oldest parietal (rock) art. Courtesy of Paul S.C. Taçon, Australian Museum.

Contents

Preface

Like many children, I was fascinated by fossils. In my case it stemmed from a holiday, when 11 years of age, on a coastline (why are all childhood vacations spent by the sea?) where there were dramatic exposures of the Jurassic Blue Lias (dialect for "layers", but now a geological division recognized world-wide and corresponding to the apogee, if that term is appropriate, of the dinosaurs). I never found a dinosaur, though I did eventually discover a "worteberry" (vertebra), and many pretty and aesthetically appealing ammonites and other fossils. I still have them.

At school, and for a while at university, I studied the classical languages, Latin and Greek, with a little Sanskrit (the Indo- side of Indo-European, the putative and reconstructed ancestor of many of the languages of Europe and parts of Asia). Languages do not strictly fossilize, but we can find something akin to a fossil in many everyday words. For instance, the words for "dog" (*hound* in English, *hund* in German, *can-* in Latin *gŵn* in Welsh, *kun-* in Greek) can take us on a fascinating journey through place and time. It is a game anyone who knows the elements of a few reasonably disparate languages can play.

As a university student I spent exciting weeks, with wonderful Welsh characters who possessed such evocative names as Mervyn Bevan-Evans and Trevor Pennant-Williams, scientifically excavating Iron-Age hillforts and Bronze-Age burials. We did not find (nor were we looking for) gold, and the work was often hard and uncomfortable. The rewards were the open moorland air and a few more pebbles in the mosaic of archaeological knowledge. I have since enjoyed amateur participation in "digs" in the Middle East and Oceania, to say nothing about photographing the magnificent aboriginal Rock Art, including the Kimberley "Bradshaw paintings", of Australia.

As a neuroscientist with a number of dedicated graduate students and colleagues, I have spent a fulfilling career studying the mechanisms, and clinical breakdown, of attention, movement, language, motor skill and praxis, object and pattern recognition. We have been fortunate in our access to many otherwise unfortunate but generous individuals with such disorders as focal brain lesions, Parkinson's, Huntington's, and Alzheimer's disease, Tourette's syndrome, schizophrenia, autism, and so on. From controlled experiments and the willing participation of such individuals we have learned much about how the brain mediates speech, language, thought, praxis, and conscious self-awareness.

In recent years there have been a number of books about human evolution. These have tended either to view it from the author's own personal experiences in often ground-breaking archaeological exploration and discovery, or to concentrate upon a particular aspect (the evolution of language, or of social intelligence, or of consciousness), or to elaborate a particular theoretical viewpoint. In the last respect, this book certainly subscribes to the view that all our cherished human attributes, so far from being unique, are grounded in our primate evolutionary history. Otherwise, however, it seeks to provide a comprehensive and fully referenced account, from the neuropsychological, molecular, anthropological, primatological, archaeological and palaeontological evidence, of what we are and how we have got here. Of course, it cannot be the last word on the matter; weekly, new finds in all these fields require reassessment and modification of the current picture. Unfortunately, in such a domain of interest, a book can never be wholly up to date. However, I hope my professional knowledge of one relevant area, and an amateur (and I hope not too uninformed) understanding of the others, will permit the painting of a picture not too unrepresentative of what may have happened.

I would like to express my profound gratitude to everyone who provided me so readily with illustrative material, often of their very latest finds, to Rosemary Williams, who provided the artwork often at short notice, and finally to my wife and colleague Judy, who typed and produced the manuscript.

Preamble

Although it may not strictly be politically correct to echo the old dictum "The proper study of Mankind is Man", it is nevertheless true that as intellectually the most "advanced" creatures on the planet, our own nature and origins fascinate us maybe more than any other subject. Mystics, religious leaders, and philosophers in many ages and places have proposed schemes of things and belief systems that are more or less internally consistent, and more or less coherent with daily empirical observation. Writers in Classical Greece and Alexandria were aware of our animal nature, whether or not a soul or psyche, however conceptualized, was also somehow to be accommodated. The idea of evolutionary development from "lower" life forms, though maybe with the Lamarckian transmission of features and characteristics acquired during an organism's life, has a long tradition in rationalist thought; even the great Charles Darwin was not unique in invoking the concept of chance variation and selective pressures. However, he, along with Wallace independently and contemporaneously, was the first systematically to develop the idea of evolution in contemporary form. Even now, however, debate continues on aspects of evolution, such as whether change is usually gradual and incremental, or whether major changes may come suddenly, in bursts, perhaps at the limits of a population's ecological equilibrium.

The idea of evolution in general, and of our own primate status and origins, has not always sat comfortably with the tenets of received religion. Nor, of course, have astronomical views of our place in the solar system, or, more recently, the claims of theoretical physics concerning the nature of matter, space, and time. However, the study of comparative religion, and the history of modern theological thought, indicate the plastic nature of such belief systems, which, in time, may adapt more or less successfully to accommodate whatever is the current empirical and political thought. Ultimately, of course, they are systems of belief and of faith, which by their nature cannot be verified, and contrast with the empirical scientific claims, which, in principle, though often not in practice, may be testable and falsifiable. However, even observation must be informed by theory, and few findings, whether in the initial observations or their later interpretations, can be totally value free. We usually see what in some way we expect to see, and we organize our observations according to some preconceived framework of thought. For this reason "paradigm shifts" in science are rare, and, similarly, certain approaches (evolution, to creationists; sociobiology and the measurement of individual differences to opponents of determinism) are rejected by some schools of thought.

The idea that humans are somehow unique is ancient and appealing. It is difficult, moreover, to conceive of such uniqueness (possession of a soul, of conscious self-awareness, of language, of the ability to manufacture and use tools) as incrementally appearing in our evolutionary history. What good is a partial soul (cf. questions such as whether a partially evolved eye could be of any further adaptive significance)? Does a chimpanzee, a monkey, or a kangaroo have a soul (or conscious self-awareness), however undeveloped or unelaborated? Yet many scientists, not necessarily religious believers, do see humans as somehow biologically special, set apart from the rest of creation (or evolution), and look for Rubicons between us and other species in the realms of language, thought, consciousness, tool behaviors, or even an upright, two-legged form of locomotion. Such areas of uniqueness may then be accommodated, if the theorist nevertheless accepts general biological theory, by invoking special genes, or sudden mutations, coinciding with the appearance of speech, Upper Palaeolithic art, or even of writing and the development of a historical tradition around the time of Homer.

Social scientists have for long recorded cognition and human behavior as exempt from Darwinian adaptive shaping. Only now, with a decline in popularity of Marxist approaches, has a coordinated search been made for the deep evolutionary roots for the mental mechanisms behind e.g. language, numeracy, the ability to assess bulk and quantity, skilled manual praxis, and even conscious awareness. Similarity alone, of course, does not prove an evolutionary link, as similar behaviors could always have evolved independently. However, to paraphrase an observation of Steven Pinker (1994), the fact that we instinctively fear snakes, but not far more dangerous fast cars, suggests our emotions are determined more by the built-in consequences of our evolutionary environment than by the environment within which we grew up (Williams, 1997).

The viewpoint adopted in this book is that our origins are firmly grounded, Darwinian fashion, in our primate ancestry, and that none of our behaviors, and none of the cerebral structures that mediate such behaviors, is devoid of prior primate precedent. Indeed, the chimpanzee, particularly perhaps the bonobo (*Pan paniscus*), if appropriately studied, can be shown to possess the roots of all our behaviors otherwise conceived of as uniquely human. Where, however, there *is* room for debate is the actual evolutionary trajectory or pathway taken between what we observe in our closest living relatives, and what we see in ourselves. Both species had a common ancestor, now extinct, and the bonobo may be as different in its way from that ancestor, as we are in ours. From living species (just as from extant language) we can only infer the characteristics of ancestral species (or languages), and there is room for much debate about the actual intermediate steps.

Those intermediate steps may sometimes (if they fossilize or otherwise preserve) survive in the palaeontological or archaeological record. In the last few years enormous advances in archaeology, palaeontology, and methods of dating have occurred. There have also been even greater advances in molecular biology, enabling us to calculate the likely degree of relatedness, and probable times of divergence, of extant lineages (between human populations, between humans and other primates, and so on). Primatology, ethology, anthropology, and the neurosciences have also made enormous strides. It is possible to put together an increasingly coherent picture of what we are and how we have become so. In the following chapters this picture will be developed.

CHAPTER ONE

Evolution to the advent of the mammals

When did the Universe, as we now know it, and the Earth come into being? When did life first appear on Earth, and when and how did it reach something like the level of multicellular complexity that we see nowadays in the various ecologies of our planet? What is the role of evolution, and how may that process operate in the continued unfolding of life forms? Is there a trend to an ever-increasing complexity, or is that an illusion when viewed from an anthropocentric standpoint? In this chapter we view evolution to the stage of the first mammals.

FORMATION OF THE UNIVERSE AND THE EARTH

The ultimate questions to be addressed by scientists and religious believers alike relate to the origin of matter and the universe, the origin of life, and the evolution and nature of thought and consciousness, which until recently have been viewed as essentially human. The *Universe*, according to cosmologists (e.g. Bolte & Hogan, 1995), may be about 16 thousand million (i.e. 16 billion) years old, though uncertainties about the exact age of Hubble's constant allow for a considerable margin of error (Maddox, 1995; Tyson, 1995). Hubble's constant enters into the equation linking an object's distance and its speed of recession, and therefore permits us to calculate when, at the beginning of time, all such objects everywhere in the Universe occupied a single point or singularity. It is possible, however, from features of our galaxy, called globular clusters, to estimate the age of the Universe independent of its age as estimated from its expansion as expressed in the Hubble constant. Chaboyer, Demarque, Kernan, and Krauss (1996) obtained a median age of 14.56 billion years. Other studies (Tanvir, Shanks, Ferguson, & Robinson, 1995), however, propose a lesser figure of between 8.4 and 10.6 billion years.

The difficulty in establishing the exact age of the *Earth* stems from the fact that there is no geological record for the time between its currently presumed origin (about 4.55 billion years ago), and the time represented by the oldest Earth rocks in the North West Territories of Canada, which have been fairly securely dated to 3.8 billion years of age (DePaolo, 1994), though individual zircon crystals have been dated to almost 4.2 billion years ago. Paradoxically, the best evidence for the exact age of our Earth may come from lunar rocks, the oldest of which is firmly dated at 4.44 billion years. Why should we turn to the Moon in order to date the Earth? The Moon was probably produced from a massive meteorite impact upon the Earth, so the latter must have been in existence when the Moon was formed, and its age must lie between that of the oldest Moon rocks, and that of the oldest meteorites, 4.56 billion years.

APPEARANCE OF LIFE

For living, sentient creatures capable of reflection on such matters, our own existence and that of the Universe we inhabit may nevertheless seem an implausible consequence of an unlikely combination of initial circumstances (Silk, 1997, reviewing Rees, 1997). Why were the density fluctuations in the early Universe of just the right range to permit the formation of galaxies? Why is the nuclear force of just the right strength to permit the formation of stars? Why is the weak force sufficiently weak to enable the formation of elements? Why is the neutron just 14% more massive than the proton, so enabling hydrogen to form? Why does the carbon atom, so essential for life, have an energy level of just the right value to enable its helium "constituents" to be captured before they dissociate in stellar cores? Why is the electron mass, relative to that of the proton, just large enough to permit the formation of larger molecules such as DNA? Is there perhaps an infinity of other, parallel, Universes, of which we clearly cannot be aware, where other constraints incompatible with life occur—or can sentience develop along totally different lines in such Universes?

It did not take long for life to appear on Earth. Fossils (see Fig. 1.1) have recently been discovered of microorganisms that had achieved a significant degree of complexity at least 3.5 billion years ago (Schopf, 1993). These filamentous microbes, measuring up to 20 microns in width and up to 90 microns in length, are linked together like beads on a string, and constitute at least 11 separate species. They occur in bedded chert from the Early

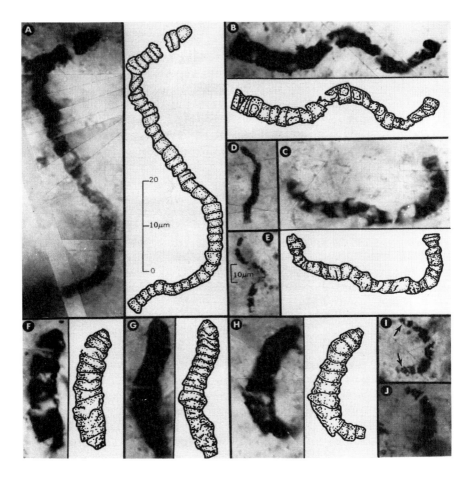

FIG. 1.1. Carbonaceous microfossil (with interpretive drawing) from the Early Archaean Apex Chert of Western Australia of 3465 million years ago. Such filamentous cyanobacterium-like microorganisms are among the oldest fossils known. Reprinted with permission from Schopf, J.W., Microfossils of the Early Archaean Apex chert: New evidence of the antiquity of life, *Science*, 1993, *260*, 640–646. Copyright © (1993) American Association for the Advancement of Science.

Archaean Apex basalt of northwestern Western Australia. They are described as prokaryotic, trichromic, cyanobacterium-like microorganisms, or single-celled blue-green algae, and suggest that oxygen-producing photosynthesis had probably evolved even at that early date. Indeed, until 3.9 billion years ago, continued impacts by asteroids may have rendered the Earth uninhabitable. Thus life must have appeared within the remarkably short window of around 400 milllion years, though we should note that the *past* 400 million years encompasses the entire evolutionary history of vertebrates, from fish to humans. Even that gap may be reduced if the claims of Mojzsis, Arrhenius, McKeegan et al. (1996; see also Balter, 1996, and Hayes, 1996) are substantiated. This group reported grains of apatite (calcium phosphate), containing graphite inclusions, from Akilia Island, the site of Earth's oldest rocks and dated to 3.87 billion years ago. The ratio of carbon-12 to carbon-13 is near to that typical of living organisms.

There is strong evidence that life on Earth divides into three primary domains, Archaea, Bacteria, and Eucarya, to the last of which we belong (Nisbet & Fowler, 1996). A phylogenetic tree of life has the noteworthy feature that all the most deeply rooted (i.e. earliest) branchings occur between (ancestors of) modern hyperthermophiles, organisms that can only grow at very high temperatures, such as are found in the vicinity of volcanic hydrothermal systems on the ocean floor. A hydrothermal origin of life is also consistent with the fact that metal-binding proteins, especially those involving iron-sulphur clusters and manganese, and those using copper, zinc, and molybdenum, participate in many crucial life processes such as photosynthesis; such elements are abundant in the vicinity of hydrothermal vents. While primitive Eucarya had no mitochondria, higher Eucarya may have incorporated them from purple bacteria, with the acquisition of chloroplasts by Eucarya at or before 1.9 billion years ago (Nisbet & Fowler, 1996).

By 1.9 billion years ago, multicellular algae may have evolved, judging by the appearance in the fossil record of what seem to be their reproductive cysts (Knoll, 1994). Hundreds of specimens of carbonaceous fossils shaped like leaves, tens of millimetres in length and more than a centimeter wide, have recently been found in north China, dated to around 1700 million years ago and resembling modern brown-algal seaweeds. The first well-documented multicellular animals may not have appeared until around 600 million years ago (Gould, 1994). Multicellular architecture then rapidly developed over the next 70 million years. The first such fauna, the Ediacaran, named after a type locality in South Australia, consisted of highly flattened fronds, sheets, and circlets composed of numerous slender segments quilted together. This controversial assemblage is widely held to have died out before the appearance of modern (invertebrate) life forms during the Cambrian explosion (530 to 520 million years ago, see Gould, 1995a). However, we shall see that the Ediacaran fauna did not disappear before the latter climactic event (Grotzinger, Bowring, Saylor, & Kaufman, 1995), but lasted through the basal Cambrian (544 million years ago) and may have contributed to the Cambrian explosion itself (Barinaga, 1995; Palmer, 1996).

Fully meiotic sexual reproduction, in which separate sex cells (egg and sperm) are produced via division and recombination of chromosomes, permits the reshuffling of genes and the potentiality for a vastly greater and faster evolutionary change. However, our impression that life evolves towards ever-greater complexity may be partly due to a parochial focus upon ourselves as lying at the top of the tree of evolution. Similarly our impression that we are somehow the inevitable culmination of evolutionary processes to date stems from a myopic view from our own particular standpoint. Natural selection locates the mechanism of evolutionary change in a struggle between organisms for reproductive advantage. We can only predict the *general trends* from such a continuing struggle ahead of time in evolution, not the specific details; the actual pathway is strongly undetermined, in that very slight chance changes in initial conditions will inexorably deviate the actual path taken ever further from what might otherwise have happened. Chaos theory makes similar statements, of course, about weather forecasting, the stock example being that the chance occurrence of a minor event ("a butterfly flapping its wings") in Peking may alter windspeeds days later in Melbourne; very small initial changes may rapidly amplify to ultimately quite major effects. Evolutionary theory can *explain* the trajectories taken, but cannot, except in very gross terms, *predict* them.

 Traditional evolutionary theory, moreover, has long held that a species changes gradually through millions of years of natural selection—Darwin's survival of the fittest—until it is so different that it constitutes a new species. Twenty or so years ago the theory of punctuated equilibrium was proposed (Gould & Eldredge, 1993), according to which a new species, especially if a small population is geographically isolated, may abruptly (within say 100,000 years) appear in the geological record after millions of years of apparent evolutionary stasis. Of course, both processes may occur, in different species at different times, and under different ecological circumstances (Kerr, 1995). Be that as it may, individuals die and only the species (itself an artificial and somewhat arbitrarily delimited taxonomic concept) survives, under the constantly changing adaptive pressures of natural selection. Whether the incremental changes which eventually result in the evolution of a mammalian eye or an avian wing occur gradually or abruptly, each adaptation along the way must have been viable and perhaps provided its transient and ephemeral owners with some extra advantage—and not necessarily the same kind of advantage as bestowed by the "final" end product. Thus structures which ultimately became wings, in insects, may have commenced as functional, mobile gills (Averof & Cohen, 1997).

There is, of course, a danger in ascribing all change, even incremental, to the forces of selection, as D'Arcy Thompson observed 80 years ago (see Gould, 1992, in his Foreword to an abridged edition of Thompson's classic work, *On growth and form*). Thus physical forces can directly shape organisms; and parts or wholes, even when not so shaped, may take the optimal forms of ideal geometries (e.g. the coil of a shell, the whorl of a sunflower head) as solutions to the problems of morphology. We are similarly cautioned against making up speculative stories about natural selection (and in the following chapters we shall encounter many such accounts attempting to explain the evolution of e.g. bipedalism, or an enlarged brain, and so on), just because gradual transitions may be apparent. The latter may merely reflect a changing set of external forces acting upon unaltered biological substrates. Similarly, some changes must be saltational rather than gradual, just as some geometries can only transform into others via a discontinuity or, as we would perhaps nowadays say, a cusp.

Darwin (1859) viewed evolution from the perspective of the differential survival of the individual organism, adopting a comparatively positive approach to the otherwise ruthless struggle for survival:

> There is a grandeur in this view of life, with its several powers, having been originally breathed into a few forms or into one; and that, whilst this planet has gone cycling on according to the fixed law of gravity, from so simple a beginning endless forms most beautiful and most wonderful have been and are being evolved. (p. 490)

In prose hardly less compelling, Dawkins (1995) views evolution from the alternative viewpoint of the gene. Our genes are selfish ones that ensured their own survival by enabling their hosts (bodies or organisms) to live long enough to reproduce—genes. However, his conclusion is bleak and profoundly pessimistic:

> In a universe of electrons and selfish genes, blind physical forces and genetic replication, some people are going to get hurt, other people are going to get lucky, and you won't find any rhyme or reason in it, nor any justice. The universe that we observe has precisely the properties we should expect if there is, at bottom, no design, no purpose, no evil and no good, nothing but pitiless indifference ... DNA neither knows nor cares. DNA just is. And we dance to its music. (p. 67)

The thread which links finite and mortal organisms, like beads upon a chain, is of course, whatever standpoint you adopt, their genetic information in the nucleic acids DNA and RNA. The nucleic acids code and specify the amino-acid sequences of all the proteins needed to constitute the living organism. The code consists of specific sequences of nucleotides, consisting in turn of a sugar (deoxyribose in DNA, ribose in RNA), a phosphate group, and most importantly, one of four different nitrogen-containing bases—adenine, guanine, cytosine and thymine in DNA, or uracil in RNA. These four bases constitute a four-letter alphabet, and triplets of bases (letters) form the three-letter words, or codons. There are therefore 4^3 (i.e. 64) possible permutations of the four bases, and as each

DNA codon encodes via RNA and amino acid, the building-blocks of the polypeptides, and, ultimately, the proteins that constitute each individual organism, it might be thought that there would be a corresponding number (64) of such amino acids. That number, however, does not exceed 20; some amino acids can be coded for by more than one codon, while each codon can only specify a single amino acid. DNA mutations are caused by substitutions of one base for another, or by deletions or insertions of bases or of whole stretches of bases.

If genes can influence behavior, they will do so either via the proteins for which they ultimately code, or by regulating the expression of other genes. Either way, at some point they or their consequences will interact with environmental events. There is an ongoing debate concerning the relative contributions of genes and environment to, for example, human abilities or "intelligence" (however defined, see Chapter 9). In general, and for complex functions, genes should not be seen as prescriptive, but along with environmental factors they can powerfully influence both form and function, structure and behavior. In a similar fashion we shall see (Chapter 8) that the size of a brain structure (itself partly under genetic control and partly under environmental influences) does not uniquely determine the extent to which a function, e.g. language, is represented or can be exercised. However, as increasingly indicated by brain-imaging studies, which measure metabolic activity during information processing in a range of tasks, we cannot afford to ignore the correlations that are emerging between form and function in the brain, between variations in the amount of tissue apparently devoted to a particular activity—processing space— and performance levels.

There is an as-yet-unresolved chicken-and-egg problem associated with the original emergence, at the dawn of life, of this system: Nucleic acids can only be synthesized with the help of proteins, and proteins can only be synthesized if a corresponding nucleotide sequence is present (Orgel, 1994). It is very improbable that these two complex structures both arose simultaneously and independently, though it is noteworthy that a protein has recently been built (Lee, Granja, Martinez, et al., 1996) that can in fact self-replicate unaided. This is the first hard evidence that life could have arisen purely from proteins, which in any case are among the best catalysts known. The protein that was constructed was a simple, self-replicating natural protein modeled on one from yeast; it acted as a template to accelerate the autocatalytic creation of another, which separated, with both pieces acting as templates for the next generation, and so on (Cohen, 1996; Kauffman, 1996). However, the original chicken-and-egg problem, and the very rapid appearance in the geological record of life so soon after the Earth's formation, has led some such as the astronomer Fred Hoyle (1981; see also Parsons, 1996) to propose an alien ("panspermic") origin of life from "seeds" throughout the Universe, though this "solution" merely shifts the problem back a notch. (In this context it might be noted that although the rain of asteroids and comets that pelted early Earth may have threatened primeval life, they may also have delivered key organic compounds and ingredients for living things, such as phosphorus, see e.g. Balter, 1996.) Nevertheless, it remains impressive that, so soon after the recently accreted and cooled Earth had stabilized to a point where life was possible, life did in fact appear. This meant that in addition now to the universal physico-chemical laws that governed at a micro scale the actions and reactions of atoms and molecules in gases, liquids and solids, and at a macro scale the orbits of the heavenly bodies, an additional set of processes emerged, involving competitive natural selection and genetic transmission (Freedman, 1995). Such selective-genetic principles came into their own with the appearance of the eukaryotes over 2 billion years ago, with their discrete nuclei containing DNA and specialist organelles like chloroplasts and mitochondria. The eukaryotes may themselves have undergone a major radiation around 1 billion years ago, according to molecular and palaeontological evidence, into a variety of more complex forms, which gave rise to the lineages that eventually led to the fungi, plants, and animals (Briggs, Erwin & Collier, 1994).

The two sets of principles, the physico-chemical and the selective-genetic, established and determined the realm that we inhabit, the biosphere. That realm, of course, has in the last few thousand years become subject to increasing modification, deliberate and otherwise, by newly emerging human activity. It is the psychology of these evolving and more or less uniquely human capacities, the third phase of the history of this planet, with which this book is partly concerned. However, it must be reiterated that although all life on Earth operates according to the same basic biochemistry of nucleic acids and adenosine triphosphate for energy storage, we do not know whether this is because it is the only possible chemistry, or because all Earthly organisms share a common descent from the same, single origin, Earthly or seeded from elsewhere in space. Did life inevitably appear via the physics and chemistry of abiotic self-organizing systems, here on Earth or elsewhere? Is consciousness the inevitable consequence of increasing complexity in living and maybe even in abiotic, artificial systems? Is it indeed the case that evolution necessarily tends, or even has tended towards ever increasing complexity? We still do not know exactly what consciousness entails, what are the adaptive advantages for its possession, whether it is unique to our species or present in some form even in other species, or where in the brain it is elaborated. Suffice it to say that consciousness clearly relates in a significant way to such (maybe nearly) unique human characteristics as language, aesthetics, and skilled manual praxis.

THE CAMBRIAN EXPLOSION OF DIVERSE LIFE FORMS

One of the most dramatic events in the fossil record is the apparently explosive diversification of marine invertebrates early in the Cambrian period (Bowring, Grotzinger, Isachsen et al., 1993). Following the appearance of simple organisms mostly lacking skeletons in uppermost Proterozoic rocks, shelly fossils (tiny cones, tubes, spines, and plates) rapidly appear in the basal Cambrian, with most of the currently extant phyla and classes of marine invertebrates soon in place. Evolutionary rates in the Cambrian have until recently been difficult to quantify accurately, because of a lack of precise dating. New uranium-lead zircon geochronology indicates that the Cambrian period began around 544 million years ago, not 570 million years ago as most wall-charts indicate, and that subsequent faunal diversification proceeded extremely rapidly, over a period (between 530 and 520 million years) of less than 10 million years. An often-proposed idea is that multicellular animals could not proliferate until there was sufficient atmospheric oxygen to support their metabolic needs; the first sizeable multicellular animals, however, appear in the fossil record around 575 million years ago, well before the beginning of the Cambrian explosion (Kerr, 1993). Alternatively, the animals' sheer simplicity may have held them back; until a certain level of physiological and anatomical complexity was attained, maybe organisms could not expand into available ecological niches. Once animals had passed a certain threshold of complexity, at the beginning of the Cambrian period, they might have exploded into existing and new ecological arenas, exploiting new resources, including each other. This would have resulted in spiralling ecological relationships, with ever more niches becoming available. It is, however, becoming increasingly clear (Davidson, Peterson, & Cameron, 1995) that large creatures (bilaterians, i.e. deuterostome and protostome metazoans, including flatworms) probably existed during the latest Precambrian (Vendian) period. The paucity or absence of such remains related to most modern taxa might simply be because they lacked the shells and exoskeletons so prominent in the Cambrian fossil assemblage (though see Briggs et al., 1994), or because many might have existed only as microscopic organisms similar to modern marine larvae. Either way, the Cambrian explosion would have to be seen at least partly as an explosion not of novel metazoan phyla, but of fossils (Davidson et al., 1995), even though the phylogenetic relationships of some of the groups appearing early in the Cambrian period, e.g. in the Burgess Shale, remain unclear (Briggs et al., 1994).

Whereas the traditional view of the origins of multicellular animals from the fossil record is that they appeared about 565 million years ago (and see Vermeij, 1996), new molecular evidence, on the basis of nucleotide sequences of 7 genes in living species from 16 phyla, supports an even earlier origin and diversification of the major phyla, in excess of 1000 million years ago (Wray, Levinton, & Shapiro, 1996). In a later chapter we shall review some of the assumptions underlying these new molecular-biological approaches, in the context of (the much later) human origins and diversi- fication. In both cases, however, there is the assumption of a roughly constant rate of substitution of nucleotides, an assumption that possibly may not be tenable (Morris, 1997).

Be such considerations as they may, mass extinctions followed in the Early Cambrian, Late Ordovician, Late Devonian, Late Permian, Early Triassic, Late Triassic, and, as everyone knows, with the demise of the dinosaurs, 65 million years ago at the end-Cretaceous (Benton, 1995). Most of these extinctions were experienced by both marine and continental organisms, and they occurred, contrary to popular belief, without evidence of periodicity. There may have been comparatively little evolutionary change between extinctions, with very rapid change immediately after such events. This scenario of punctuated equilibrium suggests rapid change followed by long periods of stasis.

THE FIRST CHORDATES AND VERTEBRATES

The Cambrian explosion, perhaps of only 10 million years' duration between 530 and 520 million years ago (Gould, 1995a), saw the attainment of full diversity of life forms, and the appearance of the first chordates (Chen, Dzik, Edgecombe et al., 1995), *Yunnanozoon lividum* (see Fig. 1.2), a cephalochordate like modern *Amphioxus*. The cephalochordates are one of the three major chordate lines, the others being the tunicates and the craniates, which include the vertebrates. All three lines may well have arisen during the Cambrian explosion. Cephalochordates possess a notochord, a rod of stiffened fibrous tissue supporting the animal's axis, and a tail fin supported by cartilaginous rods. They also have a series of V-shaped muscle bands along the body, dividing the tail into segments or somites (Long, 1995). Note, however, that Shu, Zhang, and Chen (1996) reinterpret *Yun- nanozoon* as a hemichordate, belonging to the phylum that possesses half the characteristic chordate features. (Chordates are characterized by the pos- session of a fluid-filled supporting rod, or notochord, which lies adjacent to the nerve cord that runs the length of the animal's body; from these struc- tures developed the cord and column of true vertebrates.) Shu, Morris, and Zhang (1996) report what they believe to be the earliest true chordate, the cephalochordate *Cathaymyrus diadexus*, a single specimen from the 535- million-year-old Lower Cambrian of Chengjiang, China. It resembles the lancelet, and appears to possess pharyngeal gill slits.

FIG. 1.2. *Yunnanozoon lividum* from Changjian, China, of 525 million years ago, variously described as a cephalochordate or a hemichordate, and providing an anatomical link between vertebrates and invertebrates. Reprinted with permission from Chen, J.-Y., Dzik, J., Edgecombe, G.D., Ramsköld, L., and Zhou, G.-Q., A possible Early Cambrian chordate, *Nature*, 1995, *377*, 720–722. Copyright © (1995) Macmillan Magazines Limited.

The oldest true and unambiguous vertebrate remains have been dated to 460 million years ago—ostracoderms, or small fish-like creatures that became extinct about 100 million years later (Forey & Janvier, 1994), but which beforehand gave rise to most of the vertebrate species extant, including ourselves. Ostracoderms resemble a cross between an awkward-looking fish and a horseshoe crab. Modern vertebrates are classified into two groups, the gnathostomes ("jawed mouths"), which appeared more than 400 million years ago in the Silurian, and the agnathans like the modern lampreys and hagfishes. Jaws seem to have evolved from the front set of gill arches in early relatives of lampreys and hagfishes. It now looks very likely that an agnathan *Anatolepis* may date to the late Cambrian period of 500 million years ago (Smith, Sansom, & Repetski, 1996).

The first legged creatures to leave terrestrial footprints in the fossil record were not quadrupeds, but creatures similar to modern centipedes and millipedes, living in shallow freshwater that dried up from time to time (Johnson, Briggs, Suthren et al., 1994) during the late Ordovician about 450 million years ago. The tracks indicate that the animals walked on several pairs of legs; the limbs had pointed ends and were strong enough to lift the body clear of the soft sediment substrate. The animals seem therefore not to have been soft bodied, but to have had hard external skeletons, like the arthropods. Indeed, they may have been early myriapod arthropods, similar to modern centipedes.

It has recently been determined that arthropods and chordates share a special family of genes, the homeotic or *Hox* genes, which are important in determining body pattern and morphological evolution (see e.g. S. B. Carroll, 1995). Thus in these extremely divergent groups of organisms there are common determinants of segmentation and structure, the *Hox* genes demarcating relative positions rather than specifying any particular structure. These findings may explain why vertebrates' hind and forelimbs are so remarkably homologous, despite their quite different evolutionary history—hind limbs from fish pelvic fins, and forelimbs (see later) from fish pectoral fins. Thus the long-axis morphology of most animals (nematodes, arthropods, vertebrates) is regulated by the *Hox* genes, which are expressed sequentially, in their chromosome order, over embryological time and along the main anterior–posterior axis (Weiss, 1994/95). The gene at one end of the cluster is expressed first, in the most anterior position of the embryo, followed by the gene second in line, which is expressed later and in more posterior cells, until the genes at the other end of the cluster are switched on in cells at the tail end of the developing embryo. *Hox* genes are therefore a basic and conservative set of genes that determine the anterior and posterior ends of an animal, and the location of any appendages. It is noteworthy that chordates have only one series of such genes, while the number increases to four with hagfishes and lampreys and all true vertebrates (Cooper, 1996). It should also be noted that the earliest vertebrates did not in fact possess bony vertebrae; instead, distinct heads with a bony braincase (but no jaws) evolved first, the creatures resembling the extant hagfishes and lampreys. Consequently, there are suggestions that the term "vertebrate" be replaced by "craniate".

The discovery of *Hox* gene commonalities between arthropods and chordates facilitates explanations of chordate and vertebrate evolution from arthropod forebears. Thus chordates share a common body plan with articulates (arthropods and annelids) (Nübler-Jung & Arendt, 1996), and, contrary to the common belief that the ventral nerve cord of insects and the dorsal nerve cord of vertebrates evolved independently and at opposite locations in the animal, they may instead have derived from the same centralized nervous system in a common ancestor (Arendt & Nübler-Jung, 1994). Because the nerve cord is located ventrally in insects (classifying as *Gastroneuralia*) and dorsally in chordates and vertebrates (classifying as *Notoneuralia*), with similar relative inversions of the direction of blood flow and of the relative positions of the gut, there may have been a 180° inversion or rotation of the dorsoventral axis early in chordate evolution.

THE FIRST TETRAPODS

The first tetrapods were terrestrial amphibians which derived from fish ancestors (see Fig. 1.3). The fish most closely related to amphibians are the osteolepiform sarcopterygians, especially *Panderichthys*, from the lower part of the Upper Devonian of about 375 million years ago (R. Carroll, 1995; see also Milner, 1996). *Panderichthys* was still a lobe-finned fish, of a group of which the coelocanth and lungfish are the sole survivors today, but possessed internal nostrils, like all terrestrial vertebrates, a slender tail, a skull resembling that of early amphibians (though the brain case was still primitive), and upwards- and backwards-located eyes (Ahlberg, Clack, & Lukševičs, 1996; Carroll, 1996). The best known basal tetrapods are *Acanthostega* (with 8 digits on the forelimb) and *Ichthyostega* (with 7 digits on the hindlimb) from the Upper Devonian of about 363 million years ago. They retained many aquatic features but possessed limbs, limb-girdles and brain cases like those of fully terrestrial vertebrates (Clack, 1994). Such rapid (12 million years or so) evolution is, as we shall see, comparable with that of apes and humans with respect to changes in brain size and loco-motion. Other species also, however, seem to have been transitional between true fish and the earliest tetrapods, so the transition may possibly not have occurred in a single lineage. There is nevertheless evidence of a mosaic pattern of primitive (old) and derived (newly evolved) characters indicative of different rates of evolution. Skeletal features once thought to be unique to

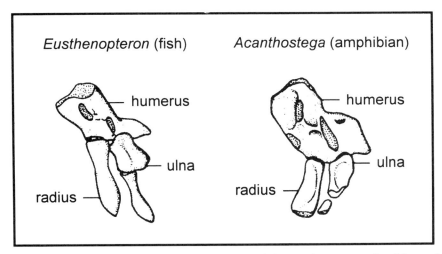

FIG. 1.3. Comparison between the front limb (arm) skeletons of crossopterygian fishes and early amphibians. Note the striking similarity in the features of the humerus. From Long, J.A., *The rise of fishes: 500 million years of evolution*, University of New South Wales Press, 1995.

land vertebrates now appear stepwise in a succession of aquatic, semi-aquatic, and semiterrestrial vertebrates, whereas features commonly associated with fish were retained in animals classified as amphibians. (As we shall see later, the term "amphibian" is loose and possibly should no longer be employed, but will be retained for convenience.) Profound structural, physiological and behavioral changes would have been needed for animals previously dependent on water for support, locomotion, respiration, and feeding to adapt to life on land. A complete transition from early osteole-piform sarcopterygians to primarily terrestrial tetrapods may have extended between 380 and 365 million years ago (R. Carroll, 1995), though the earliest trackways from an *Ichthyostega*-like animal in Western Victoria, Australia may date from between the late Silurian and early Devonian periods (Warren, Jupp, & Bolton, 1986). Coates and Clack (1995) note that early tetrapod remains coincide with a major extinction event involving massive depletion of the oxygen-content of marine surface waters. High faunal turnover, the adaptive advantage conferred upon air-breathers, and the possibility that early tetrapods occupied marine environments, suggest that this extinction could even have facilitated the evolutionary radiation of early or near tetrapods.

The lungs of amphibia are modified fish swim bladders, themselves outpouchings of the gut; their digits are the modified ends of the fins, which in osteolepiform fish already had a robust humerus, radius and ulna, whereas the skulls of amphibia and of *juveniles* of the osteolepiform fish *Eusthenopteron* show more features in common with primitive tetrapods than do adult fish (Long, 1995). Thus amphibians, like many other major higher groups of animals, including humans, probably evolved by retaining a number of juvenile features in their (here, fish) ancestors to bring about changes in adult morphology (Long, 1995). Retention of juvenile features into an adult stage (paedomorphosis) is a mechanism whereby tetrapods seem to have evolved from fishes, an evolutionary change termed "heterochrony".

While early amphibian labyrinthodonts somewhat resembled the crocodiles, it was not until the Early Carboniferous period of around 350 million years ago that the hitherto obligatory amphibian reproductive link with water was probably broken, with the appearance of the first amniotes and the appearance of the amniote egg. The latter is a collection of membranes allowing water to be contained within an egg (or uterus) while the embryo is developing. There is widespread (though not uniform) agreement that the Liss amphibia (the living amphibians) and the Amniota (the reptiles, birds, and mammals) are each monophyletic groups (Ahlberg & Milner, 1994). However, the exact evolutionary relationships are still a matter of debate, as is the time of divergence.

The archetypal tetrapod is commonly conceived of as pentadactyl, or as possessing five digits on each limb, though among extant species some have more and some less (Gould, 1991). With fewer than five we may never have developed the same capacity for manipulation and tool use, and there might have been further impacts upon cultural development. Thus wind and stringed instruments would have been radically different, though 6 fingers to the hand would probably have led to the far-more-flexible duodecimal (compared with the decimal) system; 2 and 5 divide into 10, but 2, 3, 4, and 6 divide into 12. Of course, manipulative capacity is unlikely ever to have been the only or even the major impetus for the evolution of larger brains or the development of culture. Large brains, even after correcting allometrically for body size, are possessed by both elephants and whales. The latter seem unable greatly to modify their environment or to learn how to avoid being caught by humans, despite an apparently complex system of acoustic communication. Elephants do manipulate objects with their trunks, using them during feeding, in social interactions, when bathing or even when scratching themselves with a trunk-held branch (Beck, 1980). However, it is now far from clear whether the oldest tetrapods did in fact possess penta-dactyly (Gould, 1991), as *Acanthostega* and *Ichthyostega* from the Devonian period apparently possessed, respectively, eight digits on the forelimb and seven on the hindlimb (Coates & Clack, 1990).

The embryogenesis of the tetrapod limb may be regarded as the consequence of interaction between three developmental processes: branching, segmentation, and condensation (Shubin & Alberch, 1986). Branching involves the production of two series from one; segmentation involves the generation of a series of further elements; and condensation is the opposite, or union between elements. In this context the forelimb is created outwards to the fingers from the shoulder; the humerus extends and then branches to form the radius and ulna, the next two paired elements (see Fig. 1.4). The fingers are a consequence of branching of the wrist bones (Gould, 1991), which ultimately derive from the ulna. The penultimate digit forms first and the thumb last, and the latter was in fact the first to be lost with the evolutionary reduction of the number of digits from pentadactyly. The next digit to be lost, with a reduction to three, was, similarly, the one normally forming next to last in a pentadactyl animal. Indeed, amphibia typically have four digits on their front limbs. Essentially similar processes operate in the embryogenesis (and, where relevant, evolutionary reduction in digit number) of the hind limb.

THE EARLIEST MAMMALS

In the middle to late Permian, around 260 million years ago, primitive synapsid reptiles gave rise to the mammal-like dicynodont therapsids, which in turn gave way to the cynodonts. The earliest true mammals were probably the triconodonts, tiny shrew-like creatures appearing more than 200

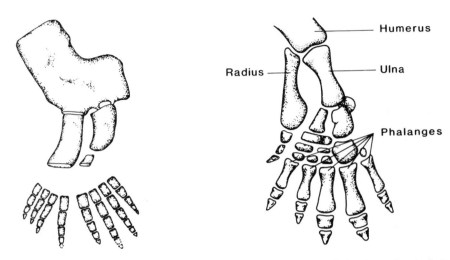

FIG. 1.4.   Forelimb of early tetrapod *Acanthostega* (left) has eight digits; the embryological development of a modern tetrapod hand (right) proceeds generally along the ulna-derived phalanges from left to right. Partly redrawn with permission from Coates, M.I., and Clack, J.A., Polydactyly in the earliest known tetrapod limbs, *Nature*, 1990, *347*, 66–69, copyright © (1990) Macmillan Magazines Limited; and from Gould, S.J., Eight (or fewer) little piggies, *Natural History*, 1991, *1*, 22–29.

million years ago during the Triassic (Novacek, 1994). They probably laid eggs, like the extant monotremes, the duck-billed platypus and echidna of Australia. During the succeeding Jurassic and Cretaceous, the triconodonts were joined by other mammalian lineages. Although many of these Mesozoic "experiments" failed to survive beyond the great extinction at the end of the Cretaceous 65 million years ago, which saw the demise of the dinosaurs, some did so and diversified into all the enormous range of mammals we see today. All however fall into three main lineages, the *monotremes*, which may have diverged from the main mammalian lineage near the beginning of the mammalian radiation, 200 million years ago, and the *marsupials* and *eutherians* (placentals), which parted company about 100 million years ago in the Cretaceous (Divac, 1995).

With our enormously evolved and developed brain (see later), we tend to see ourselves as lying in some sense on the culminating twig of the evolutionary tree, or, maybe even less appropriately, as having scaled the last rung of the evolutionary ladder. However, this viewpoint ignores the chronological sequence in which certain major evolutionary events occurred. The technique of cladistics, which groups organisms on the basis of shared features to create a hierarchical classification reflecting evolutionary relationships, permits classification of organisms in nested hierarchies based exclusively upon their chronological order of branching, though it tends to ignore or underplay unique features evolved by single lineages (autapomorphies) such as the hominid brain (Gould, 1995b). Thus a cladogram possesses major sequential branches defined by traits that arose since the previous branching point, and have been held in common by all subsequent lineages on this branch as shared-derived (newly evolved) or synapomorphic traits. A placenta is therefore a shared-derived character of all later mammals (placentals), in contrast to such pre-placentals as monotremes and marsupials. Thus a clade is a monophyletic group of animals that contains the common ancestor and all its evolutionary descendants, all of whom have inherited the particular advanced feature that arose first in the common ancestor. In this sense, the terms vertebrate, fish, and amphibian are cladistically inaccurate (Cooper, 1996); the first vertebrates, as we saw, did not possess vertebrae but rather a cranium as their distinguishing feature. Similarly, to be a clade, fishes would have to include all descendants of the first fish, such as amphibians, reptiles, and mammals. Similarly, the word "amphibia" is imprecise, as it lumps together animals that are not in fact closely related.

According to one possible cladogram of mammals (and we typically choose the cladogram that most economically explains the pattern of relationships between primitive and derived features or characteristics, see Fig. 1.5, and Gould, 1995b), there may be six branches, marked by:

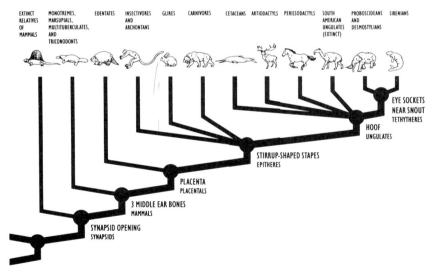

FIG. 1.5. A cladogram (here, of mammals) classifies organisms in nested hierarchies based upon their chronological order of branching. From Gould, S.J., Evolution by walking, *Natural History*, 1995, *3*, 10–15.

1. Possession of a synapsid opening in the skull behind the eye socket. Appearing more than 250 million years ago in certain reptiles, it is still possessed by some of the latter and by all mammals.
2. Possession of three middle-ear bones or auditory ossicles, malleus, incus, and stapes. Mammals differ from reptiles by possessing a chain of small bones, the auditory ossicles of the middle ear. They originally formed the hinge attaching jaw to skull, which, around 160 million years ago, moved back along the skull to what is now the middle ear, forming a unique sound amplifying system (Fischman, 1995a). This migration coincided with the emergence of the neocortex and may have been a consequence of a prolonged period of brain growth (Rowe, cited by Fischman, 1995a), though the whole transformation may have begun with the synapsids over 200 million years ago. However, the increasing cranial capacity resulted in an expanding arc between jaw point and inner ear, carrying the ossicles backward from the jaw.
3. Possession of a placenta, which evolved after the separation of marsupials and monotremes, and a derived character possessed by all subsequent mammals.
4. Possession of a stirrup-shaped or bifurcated (rather than rodlike) stapes, and possessed by carnivores, rodents, bats, and primates, for example, but not e.g. by edentates (like the armadillo). Thus the primates appeared fairly *early*.
5. Possession of a hoof from coalescing toes—perissodactyls or odd-toe ungulates like horses, rhinos, tapirs etc., and artiodactyls or even-toed ungulates like cows, goats, sheep, giraffe, deer etc.
6. Possession of eye sockets near the snout, as with elephants and sea cows.

Placentals, and possibly even primates, probably evolved from insectivores during a period marked by the spread of the angiosperms (flowering plants), which with nectar, fruit, berries, nuts, and associated insects provided a new ecological niche for rapid evolutionary change. The catastrophic extinction at the end of the Cretaceous period probably also provided a further impulse to refill now-empty niches. Without such extinctions about every 100 million years, like war in human history, change (biological or technological) would probably have been considerably slower and different; without the presence of Jupiter and possibly Saturn as giant interplanetary "vacuum cleaners", however, such extinctions arising from extraterrestrial impacts would probably have been far too frequent to sustain complex life forms.

SUMMARY AND CONCLUSIONS

The Earth may be about 4.55 billion years old, just over a quarter of the currently accepted age of the Universe of around 16 billion years. Life on Earth only took a further billion years to appear, or rather less than half that figure from when conditions were first permissible. Two billion years ago marked the advent of multicellular algae, though modern invertebrate forms of animal life, and the first chordates, may date from just over half a billion years ago. The basal tetrapods appeared 380 million years ago, and the earliest true mammals less than 180 million years later. However, the geological record is partial and incomplete with numerous discontinuities, and repeated catastrophic extinctions totally changed the apparent evolutionary trajectories. In any case there is nothing "necessary" in the route eventually taken, and "winners" and "losers" took their places as a result of chance contingencies. Not only can we not predict, except in the most general terms, future evolutionary trends, but it is still far from clear at what level we should impute the occurrence of evolutionary forces—the gene, the cell, the "organism", or maybe even an ecological unit, however defined or delimited—or the mode of evolution, gradual or punctuated.

FURTHER READINGS

Ahlberg, P.E., & Milner, A.R. (1994). The origin and early diversification of tetrapods. *Nature, 368*, 507–514.

Allégre, C.J., & Schneider, S.H. (1994). The evolution of the Earth. *Scientific American, October*, 44–51.

Benton, M.J. (1995). Diversification and extinction in the history of life. *Science, 268*, 52–58.

Bolte, M., & Hogan, C.J. (1995). Conflict over the age of the Universe. *Nature, 376*, 399–402.

Bowring, S.A., Grotzinger, J.P., Isachsen, C.E., Knoll, A.H., Pelechaty, S.M., & Kolosor, P. (1993). Calibrating rates of Early Cambrian evolution. *Science, 261*, 1293–1298.

Chaboyer, B., Demarque, P., Kernan, P. J., & Krauss, L.M. (1996). A lower limit to the age of the Universe. *Science, 271*, 957–961.

Forey, P., & Janvier, P. (1994). Evolution of the early vertebrates. *American Scientist, 82*, 554–565.

Gould, S.J. (1994). The evolution of life on earth. *Scientific American, October*, 63–69.

Gould, S.J., & Eldredge, N. (1993). Punctuated equilibrium comes of age. *Nature, 366*, 223–227.

Grotzinger, J.P., Bowring, S.A., Saylor, B.Z., & Kaufman, A.J. (1995). Biostratigraphic and geochronological constraints on early animal evolution. *Science, 270*, 598–604.

Orgel, L.E. (1994). The origin of life on the earth. *Scientific American, October*, 53–61.

Schopf, J.W. (1993). Microfossils of the Early Archean Apex Chert: New evidence of the antiquity of life. *Science, 260*, 640–646.

Tyson, N.D.G. (1995). The size and age of the Universe. *Natural History, 2*, 72–75.

CHAPTER TWO

Primates to hominids and the advent of bipedalism

We belong to the Primates, an order with a respectable ancestry back into the Mesozoic. As hominids, we are very closely related to the pongids—indeed the chimpanzee is our closest relative—and some authorities even prefer a nomenclature that includes the African apes, with us, in the family Hominidae. Our own lineage, with very recent finds, is extending rapidly backwards in time, and there is currently considerable uncertainty about the exact details of our lineage. In addition to these issues, this chapter deals with the evolution of bipedalism and its impact upon obstetrics and the pelvis.

THE PRIMATES

The order Primates is closely related to three other orders, Scandentia (tree shrews), Dermoptera (flying lemurs), and Chiroptera (bats), and is characterized by its (often arboreal) agility, dexterity, good binocular vision, increased relative brain size, and enhanced parental care. Rooted in the Cretaceous period before 65 million years ago, the order Primates is divisible into the two suborders Strepsirhini (e.g. lemurs and lorises) and Haplorhini (tarsiers, New and Old World monkeys, apes, and humans). The New World platyrrhine (Ceboidea) and Old World catarrhine (Cercopithecoidea) lineages separated more than 35 million years ago. The higher (anthropoid) primates include the New and Old World monkeys, apes and humans, giving rise to the Hominoidea (apes—Pongidae, and humans—Hominidae).

Most of our own evolutionary trajectory, at least as far back as 35 million years ago, is conventionally thought to have occurred in Africa, though *Catopithecus* from Fayum (Egypt) has been dated to 37 million years ago (Simons, 1995) and linked to extinct lemurlike adapids. However, an Asian challenger, *Eosimias*, from China is now emerging, dated to 40 million years ago (Culotta, 1995a). As Kay, Ross, and Williams (1997) observe, the origin of the anthropoids continues to be hotly debated, and the Adapidae are probably a sister taxon, belonging to the strepsirhines, rather than ancestral to the Anthropoidea.

THE HOMINOIDS

The anthropoids, whose origins more than 45 million years ago are, as we saw, still shrouded in mystery (Beard, Tong, Dawson et al., 1996), were the first primates to develop a postorbital septum (Pickford, 1986) to isolate the eyes from temporal muscles that bulge during mastication and would otherwise interfere with fine stereoscopic vision. This feature is first apparent in the Oligocene fossil *Aegyptopithecus* of 35 million years ago, which may have been the ancestor of the east African Miocene genus *Proconsul* (23–17 million years ago). *Proconsul* possessed many features of modern apes, though its posture was pronograde. In the last few years, dated to around 10 million years ago, several candidates have emerged as possible last common ancestors of African apes and humans (Begun, 1992, 1994). These include *Dryopithecus*, *Ouranopithecus*, and an unnamed Hungarian fossil. A recent find in Spain of *Dryopithecus* from 9.5 million years ago (Moyà-Solà, & Köhler, 1996) indicates that orthograde posture (suspension) and locomotion (brachiation) was more prominent than in African apes; its relationship with the (Asian? African) ape and/or possibly human clade is a matter of debate (Andrews & Pilbeam, 1996; Benefit & McCrossin, 1995). Even more recently, Alpagut, Andrews, Fortelius et al. (1996) report the discovery of a new and nearly complete specimen of *Ankarapithecus meteai* from the Upper Miocene Sinap formation of central Turkey (see Fig. 2.1), dated to around 9.8 million years ago. Earlier discoveries of more fragmentary remains had suggested affinities with the Asian hominoids *Sivapithecus* and *Pongo* (orangutan); this new specimen possesses features that the authors claim support its placement as a stem member of the great ape and human clade.

   Molecular biology provides an alternative to palaeontology and physical taxonomy in tracing the relatedness and time of divergence of such extant and apparently closely related species as humans, chimpanzee and gorillas. There are several molecular approaches, but all essentially measure the degree of differentiation of nuclear or mitochondrial DNA in individuals from any two target species, and assume a known rate of change over time.

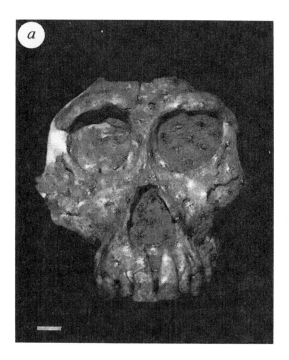

FIG. 2.1.   Face of *Ankarapithecus mateai*, an Upper Miocene hominoid now thought to be a stem member of the great ape and human clade. Reprinted with permission from Alpagut, B., Andrews, P., Fortelius, M., Kappelman, J., Temizsoy, I., Celebi, H., and Lindsay, W., A new specimen of *Ankarapithecus meteai*, from the Sinap formation of central Anatolia, *Nature*, 1996, *382*, 349–351. Copyright © (1996) Macmillan Magazines Limited.

In this way the likely time of divergence of the two species can be calculated. Such techniques indicate that the ancestor of the South-East Asian gibbons split off at least 17 million years ago (Harrison, Tanner, Pilbeam et al., 1988); then a split occurred between the Asian *Pongo* (orangutan) and African *Pan* (chimpanzee) lineages around 12 million years ago, followed by the gorilla divergence between 7 and 9 million years ago. The chimpanzee-"human" split probably occurred between 5 and 8 million years ago (Ruvolo, Disotell, Allard et al., 1991). Thus chimpanzees may be even more closely related to us than to gorillas (Gibbons, 1990), despite the fact that gorillas and chimpanzees look more alike; both are hairy, walk on all fours or knuckle walk, have short legs and long arms, brachiate, are less manually dextrous than ourselves, and have smaller brains. However, these apparent chimpanzee–gorilla similarities may not necessarily reflect closeness of kinship, or even perhaps convergent evolution, so much as perhaps retention of ancestral traits that we have lost, though the problem of knuckle-walking remains unresolved. One possibility is that our common ancestor with the African apes was a knuckle-walker (Begun, 1994), and that they retained this trait while we lost it. Alternatively, our common ancestor may have been a suspensory, arboreally brachiating climber (and see Savage-Rumbaugh, 1994); we would then have evolved bipedal gait, while the chimpanzee and gorilla independently evolved knuckle-walking. Perhaps the most likely hypothesis is that after the split from our arboreal-climbing ancestors, we became bipeds, while the African apes evolved knuckle-walking as a specialized adaptation to terrestriality before diverging into different ape species. The specialized characteristics unique to knuckle-walking are all relatively subtle and restricted to the forelimb, while the specializations of our own upright bipedal gait affect most post-cranial and even some cranial bones. Humans share with African apes many skeletal adaptations and other characteristics, including behavioral ecology and social structure, e.g. group formation, omnivory, culturally diverse technologies in food acquisition, habitation of a wide range of environments, and cooperative ventures from defence to hunting (Begun, 1994).

Confirmation recently that chimpanzees and humans are more closely related to each other than either is to gorillas comes from sequencing of the Y-linked DNA for testis-specific protein Y in the three species and the hamadryas baboon (Kim & Takenaka, 1996). From humans, the chimpanzee differed by 1.9%, the gorilla by 4.0%, the orangutan by 8.2%, and the baboon by 16.8%. In a later chapter we shall further discuss the use of molecular-biological techniques in the study of our own origins. Suffice it to say that, given the close genetic similarity between ourselves and the African apes, it is probable that mutations in the regulatory mechanisms that control how genes are expressed underlie our biological differences. Biological factors, of course, also underlie our cultural differences, our ability to pass on information across the generations by teaching and learning. Genetic and cultural factors, and their interplay, account for the rapid "evolution" of human societies.

THE HOMINID LINEAGE

Traditionally, the term pongid has been applied to the great apes and hominid to the human clade, the two clades being grouped as the hominoids. Some authorities (Andrews, 1995) prefer the term hominine to hominid, so that the family Hominidae may now include the African apes with humans. Alternatively, humans and African apes may be classed in the subfamily Hominae, and orangutans (and their ancestors) in the subfamily Ponginae. We shall, however, for convenience adhere to the traditional taxonomy.

Until very recently, the hominid lineage was seen as commencing with *Australopithecus afarensis* around 3.8 million years ago, and moving (perhaps via *Australopithecus africanus*, at 3 to 2.6 million years ago) to *Homo habilis* (2.2 to 1.5 million years ago) and *Homo erectus* (1.9 to 0.5 million years ago) before reaching *Homo sapiens*. A new species (*Australopithecus anamensis*) has been described (Leakey, Feibel, McDougall, & Walker, 1995) from Lake Turkana in northern Kenya, dated to between 4.2 and 3.9 million years ago. From its tibia it seems to have been bipedal and may be the ancestor of *Australopithecus afarensis*. From Aramis in Ethiopia, however, a slightly older (4.4 million years ago) species (*Ardipithecus ramidus*) has also now been described (White, Suwa, & Asfaw, 1994, 1995), which, though also apelike, may too have walked upright, judging by the apparently forward position of the foramen magnum. It is unclear whether a linear trajectory can link *Ardipithecus ramidus, Australopithecus anamensis* and *Australopithecus afarensis*; however *Australopithecus afarensis*, from skeletal and cranial evidence, and from the dramatic footprint tracks found at Laetoli in Tanzania and ascribed to that taxon (Boaz, 1988), almost certainly was at least partly bipedal. Moreover, its minimum age has now been put back to before 4 million years ago (Kappelman, Swisher, Fleagle et al., 1996) (see Fig. 2.2).

Indeed, other taxa may both precede (*Homo rudolfensis*) and follow (*Homo ergaster*) *Homo habilis*, the taxon conventionally thought of as following *Australopithecus afarensis* and constituting the first true *Homo* (Lieberman, Wood, & Pilbeam, 1996). Moreover, the integrity of *Homo habilis* has recently been questioned, and neither that taxon nor *Homo*

Possible nodal events in the hominid lineage

Ardipithecus ramidus	4.4	million years ago
Australopithecus anamensis	4.2	.. .. ..
Australopithecus afarensis	4.0	.. .. ..
Australopithecus africanus	3.0	.. .. ..
Homo rudolfensis	2.5	.. .. ..
Homo habilis	2.2	.. .. ..
Homo ergaster	1.9	.. .. ..
Homo erectus	1.9	.. .. ..
Homo heidelbergensis	0.7	.. .. ..
Neanderthals	0.23	.. .. ..
Homo sapiens	0.20	.. .. ..

The above dates are currently the likely earliest appearance. It is not clear yet through how many of the above taxa our lineage actually passed, and whether or how they should be differentiated.

FIG. 2.2.   Possible nodal events in the hominid lineage.

erectus (conventionally the taxon succeeding *Homo habilis*) may lie directly upon our evolutionary trajectory, and *Homo heidelbergensis* might precede both the Neanderthals and *Homo sapiens* (Fischman, 1994; Rightmire, 1995; Wood, 1992, 1994). There has even been debate as to whether specimens ascribed to *Australopithecus afarensis* belonged to a single species, though it now seems probable that it was a single, if highly variable, species exhibiting considerable sexual dimorphism (White, Suwa, Hart et al., 1993; Gee, 1993). Moreover there are suggestions (Bromage & Schrenk, 1995) that whatever the later trajectory of *Homo*, *Homo rudolfensis* evolved from *Australopithecus afarensis* and *Homo habilis* from *Australopithecus africanus*. It may be some time before the lineages are resolved, owing to the paucity of critical specimens and unresolved debate about sexual dimorphism versus speciation, though *Australopithecus afarensis* does seem still to occupy a more or less privileged position at or near the base of the trajectory of *Homo*. Nevertheless, rather than a relatively uncomplicated linear progression, as was proposed until comparatively recently, the human evolutionary "tree" may well possess many more branches and extinct species than was previously thought (Rightmire, 1995). Indeed, our ancestry should perhaps rather be conceived of as a bush, with its branches representing a number of more or less humanlike bipedal species that evolved along differing evolutionary lines, and which survived, with varying degrees of success and for various periods of time, before becoming extinct.

THE ADVENT OF BIPEDALISM

Human evolution over the past 4 million years seems, for many characteristics, to have followed the general model of punctuated equilibrium (Gould & Eldredge, 1993) of prolonged stasis followed by a brief burst of rapid change; for other characteristics, the more traditional Darwinian mode of phyletic gradualism may also have operated, where some change continues to occur, somewhat more slowly, away from speciation events. Thus our extinct cousins the Neanderthals changed considerably between their early and late manifestations. Generally, the pattern of morphological lineage was mosaic in form, with different structures evolving at different times and at different rates; as we shall see, adaptations essential to bipedalism tended to appear early, with other features appearing later (McHenry, 1994). Early stages of human evolution seem to have had their origin in climate change, which resulted in a progressively more fragmented or mosaic habitat. The latter could more easily have been exploited by a more efficient bipedal form of locomotion than knuckle-walking. If we can characterize the unique qualities of *Homo*, compared with its immediate australopithecine precursors, we see an increase in brain size, a propensity for tool use and culture, reduced mastication in food preparation, and bipedalism;

conversely, *Australopithecus* retains a small, ape-sized brain, large post-canine dentition, and a probable propensity for climbing as well as bipedal locomotion. The major early event, however, in hominid evolution, is not so much an initial increase in brain size, but the advent of bipedalism; the latter preceded any substantive increase in cranial capacity and the development of a lithic tool-manufacturing tradition, and, subsequently, language.

In many ways bipedalism is likely to be the foundation on which all subsequent and apparently quintessentially human attributes were built (Jablonski & Chaplin, 1993). Brain size, corrected for body mass, slightly increased (from the African-ape level) during the evolution of the australopithecines, and expanded significantly with the appearance of *Homo*, but within early *Homo* remained at about half that of current levels for about 1 million years. From *Australopithecus afarensis* to anatomically modern *Homo sapiens* cranial volume doubled in relative (body-mass-corrected) terms, and tripled in absolute terms (McHenry, 1994). Early specimens of *Homo erectus* often demonstrate a small brain for such a large body, averaging around a 200 cm^3 increase over that of *Homo habilis*, with *relative* volumes nearly equivalent. Moreover, for its first 1 million years the cranial capacity of *Homo erectus* increased only gradually. On the other hand archaic *Homo sapiens* showed a rapid increase over time, with specimens nearly half a million years old lying within the modern range. Following that, of course, there may have been (possibly substantial) changes in organization, locally or at large.

While apes, dogs and bears may sometimes adopt a bipedal stance or even mode of locomotion, this is habitual only in our own species, with its characteristic cycle of heel strike followed by stance phase and then push off from the toes. In living primates other than great apes and humans, the foot is placed in a heel-elevated (semiplantigrade) position when moving on arboreal or terrestrial substrates (Gebo, 1992). Plantigrady in chimpanzees and gorillas involves the heel contacting the substrate at the end of the swing phase, especially during terrestrial locomotion, such that these species are adapted for both arboreal and terrestrial substrates. These species also share several lower-skeletal features relating to plantigrady and terrestrial locomotion with early hominids, further indicating that hominid locomotion passed through a quadrupedal terrestrial phase. It is commonly held that bipedalism deprives us of speed and agility, and limits our ability to climb trees through redesign of the upper femur and foot. Recent analyses, however, of the bioenergetics of bipedalism (Jablonski & Chaplin, 1993) indicate that it is far from inefficient, except perhaps during standing, though it is not, as has been previously suggested, particularly suited for long-distance endurance pursuit. In fact, the efficiency of bipedalism in humans seems to approximate to that of quadrupedalism in quadrupeds. Steudel (1996) reviews the cost of human bipedal walking and running, comparing it with quadrupedal data. She concludes that increased energetic efficiency could not have accrued to early bipeds, though improvements may have occurred once the transition was made. Just as the anatomical functions selected throughout human evolution seem to have favored greater flexibility, rather then narrow specialization (Rightmire, 1995), so too we are not particularly highly adapted as walkers, runners, climbers, or indeed swimmers; we can do all of these things, though none perhaps individually as well as animal specialists. Striding perhaps is where we excel.

Bipedalism has necessitated major redesign of the lower spine, pelvis, femur, knee-joint, foot and musculature, including the gluteus maximus; the latter adaptation secondarily permits us to engage in lifting, levering, digging, clubbing, and throwing. Indeed, bipedalism is a major factor in freeing up the hands for other purposes, and thereby preadapting our ancestors for tool use. Circulatory constraints during bipedal standing may also have resulted in changes in venous drainage, which would have improved cooling and heat dispersal (see later); bipedal locomotion, moreover, required pelvic adaptations with obstetric consequences during the birth of large-headed infants (see later). However, many evolutionary accounts for the adoption of bipedalism partake of "just-so" explanations, and underline the dangers in seeking single-factor explanations in the complex multifactorially interacting worlds of ecology, evolution, or medicine. Nevertheless, various single-factor explanations have been proffered for hominid bipedalism. Brachiation, or hanging by the forelimbs from branches, certainly would have preadapted apes for an orthograde posture upon the hind limbs, as essentially similar postures and muscle systems are involved. The last common hominoid ancestor of African apes and hominids seems to have possessed long arms, a modified shoulder anatomy, an orthograde-adapted trunk, a comparatively large body, and arboreal adaptations; it would probably have been a frequent climber and a quadruped quite capable of brachiating. As this arboreal hominoid ancestor began exploiting a rapidly changing and fragmenting terrestrial environment, a plantigrade foot would have evolved. As its arms were longer than its legs, its trunk would have adopted a considerably more vertical posture than that of other quadrupedal primates, and its body weight would have been redistributed progressively more towards the rear limbs and thus to the heels (Gebo, 1992). Knuckle-walking requires that the long, flexible fingers designed for climbing be folded back to support the semi-erect body. Chimpanzees and gorillas have feet adapted for both arboreal locomotion and later-evolved terrestrial knuckle-walking; African apes and especially humans uniquely have feet adapted for plantigrady and terrestriality. Thus our last common ancestor with the African apes seems to have possessed a plantigrade foot adapted for terrestrial locomotion.

Gebo (1996) takes these ideas further, noting that African apes, when arboreal, are good vertical climbers, and that evidence from the hand and foot points to a quadrupedal phase in hominoid evolution before the adoption of bipedalism. Thus, he argues, the evolution of stance and locomotion from early hominoids to hominids may have commenced with an arboreal quadrupedal-climbing phase and proceeded through an ortho-grade, brachiating, forelimb-suspensory phase, which was in turn followed by *arboreal and terrestrial quadrupedal phases* prior to the advent of hominid bipedalism. It was during the terrestrial quadrupedal phase, he suggests, that ancestral African apes developed a foot morphology associated with heel-strike plantigrade footfalls, a weight-bearing wrist, and perhaps knuckle-walking fingers. While *Australopithecus afarensis* did not possess a grasping big toe, but resembled ourselves in this respect, in other respects its lower and upper limbs evidenced traces of retained arboreality while in evolutionary transition to full bipedalism.

If brachiation preadapted our hominoid ancestors for bipedalism, what might have been the evolutionary pressures that selected for the latter's adoption, bearing in mind the aforementioned proviso that a number of factors are likely to have acted in concert? Feeding behavior in one form or another has often been proposed, e.g. hunting, scavenging (Blumenschine & Cavallo, 1992), foraging, or the hypothesis (Lovejoy, 1988) of a division of labor between the sexes. This proposal envisages spatially oriented hunting or scavenging for occasional high-protein food sources by the male parent, while the female forages for vegetable staples nearer the home base and develops the offspring's social and communicatory skills. There is indeed evidence that modern males may be slightly superior in spatial and inferior in verbal abilities to females (Halpern, 1986; McGlone, 1986), and that language and manual praxis may be differentially localized in and mediated by male and female brains (Kimura & Harshman, 1984; Shaywitz, Shaywitz, Pugh et al., 1995).

A related idea (Hunt, 1994) stems from the observation that in chimpanzees about 80% of bipedalism is postural and relates to feeding, specifically upwards for fruit, whereas only about 4% of bipedalism relates to locomotion and is relatively inefficient. Indeed, the considerable width of the hips (pelvis) of *Australopithecus afarensis*, our putative ancestor, would have provided good support for feeding from an upright posture, but would have been less suitable for sustained walking and running. Moreover, higher-ranking chimpanzees more frequently adopt a bipedal stance, an observation that neatly meshes with the idea (Jablonski & Chaplin, 1993) of bipedal posture as part of threat and appeasement behavior in the peaceful resolution of intraspecific conflicts; thus chimpanzee, gorilla, and human all engage in similar bipedal threat displays, and it is therefore likely that their common ancestor did likewise.

Whether or not bipedalism was at least partly selected for in the context of thermoregulation (see earlier), it is certainly true that more efficient thermoregulation removed a physical constraint on further increase in brain size (Falk, 1993). Thus a comparatively small rise in temperature can threaten the brain, the organ that in humans, though representing only 2% of the body mass, consumes 18% of the energy budget. A consequence of heating is hallucinations, convulsions, permanent brain damage, and death. A shift from shaded arboreal to open terrestrial habitat was probably accompanied by the loss of body hair, increase in numbers of sweat glands, an upright posture (with hair retained on the head), which itself greatly reduces body surface area exposed to the equatorial sun's rays (Wheeler, 1993), and perhaps a change in cerebral venous drainage effectively to function as a radiator. Thus we possess a network of veins originating in the scalp and face, which can return blood to the heart either directly via the *external* jugular vein, or indirectly via the meningeal veins and sinuses of the dura mater covering the brain, exiting via the *internal* jugular vein. The latter route may cool the brain via blood itself cooled by surface skin sweating. Thus when hot one's face flushes and sweats. Apes and *Australopithecus afarensis* lack this modern human venous radiator (Falk, 1990). Specifically, by 3 million years ago, there may have been a change in venous drainage by occipital and marginal sinuses, instead of or additional to the previous lateral or transverse-sigmoid drainage system, together with alternative routes for blood delivery to vertebral venous plexuses via a host of emissary foramina, especially parietal and mastoid. Such cooling would have released possible thermal constraints on further increases in brain size.

In summary, many factors, individually or in concert, may have selected for an upright bipedal posture, including locomotion, feeding and dominance behaviors, and cooling. We should not, of course, lose sight of the advantages, in terms of increased range of view and ability to threaten potential predators, that such a posture provides. Moreover, if it was pre-selected for from earlier arboreal brachiation, it would have continued to provide an increased ability to retreat up a tree when threatened (Tattersall, 1995).

Trackways with numerous footprints of three bipedal hominids have been found preserved in hardened ashfall at Laetoli, Tanzania, dated to 3.6 million years ago (Leakey & Hay, 1979). They indicate fully fledged bipedalism at least 1 million years before the earliest humans emerged with the advent of stone tools, and have fairly confidently been attributed to *Australopithecus afarensis* (Tuttle, 1990); indeed, the Laetoli prints and strides are well within the range of modern Peruvian Indians, who are used to walking without footwear. Nevertheless, debate (Gibbons, 1994a) continues as to whether, and to what possible extent, the bipedalism of

Australopithecus afarensis (or possible ancestors such as *Ardipithecus rami-dus* and *Australopithecus anamensis*) might have been kinematically and energetically different from modern humans. In this context we should remember the subtle differences in the *afarensis* pelvis, hand, and possibly femur and foot, perhaps associated with a retained arboreal or tree-climbing capacity (Berge, 1994). Abitbol (1995) examined the lower spine and pelvis of "Lucy", the best-known and most complete *afarensis* specimen, and concluded that "she" would have had to adopt postures never seen outside of pathology in modern humans; "her" erect posture is unlike that seen in modern humans, but is still apparently a mystery, he says, with insufficient fossil data yet available to make a final judgement.

Four articulating hominid foot bones (Clarke & Tobias, 1995), dating perhaps to 3.5 million years ago and probably belonging to an early australopithecine, indicate human features in the hindfoot and apelike traits in the forefoot. Thus, although the creature was clearly bipedal, it still apparently included arboreal-climbing activities in its locomotor repertoire (see also Lewin, 1995a; Oliwenstein, 1995).

A new slant on this general question has come from a study of the inner-ear bones of apes, modern and fossil humans (Spoor, Wood, & Zonneveld, 1994, 1996) by high-resolution computed tomography (CT scan). These images focused on the bony labyrinth, fluid-filled canals of the inner ear that help us maintain our balance. Modern humans and our probable close ancestors *Homo erectus* have vertically oriented canals, whereas chimpanzees and other apes have more horizontally aligned canals. The labyrinths of the two nearest descendants of *Australopithecus afarensis* (the latter's configuration is as yet unknown) most closely resemble the ape pattern, suggesting that *afarensis* would also have done so. However, it is far from clear how these conclusions mesh with the Laetoli prints, always assuming that the latter were indeed made by *afarensis*, and the conclusions themselves have been disputed by Graf and Vidal (1996).

Further light on this issue is thrown by McHenry (cited by Shreeve, 1996) in an analysis of lower-limb bones of *Australopithecus africanus*, often thought, because of its expanded brain, less projecting muzzle and smaller canines, to lie between *Australopithecus afarensis* and ultimately ourselves. The new data make *Australopithecus africanus* look much more apelike and arboreal, with big arms and small legs, though with a humanlike bipedal pelvis. Does this mean that (earlier) *Australopithecus afarensis* was somehow a failed bipedal "evolutionary experiment" and lay off our lineage? Or do we conclude, in accordance with the traditional viewpoint, in favor of an *afarensis* to *africanus* to *Homo* trajectory, but with an evolutionary reversal in *africanus* to a (temporarily) more arboreal mode? Bipedalism, of course, does not necessarily preclude arboreality, and the route to bipedalism, and to *Homo*, may be less simple than previously imagined.

OBSTETRICS AND THE PELVIS

Posture and locomotion, as we have seen, are affected by, and impact upon, the evolution of the shape of the pelvis. The latter, in turn, has major obstetric consequences. The pattern of human childbirth is unique among mammals (Bunney, 1993; Rosenberg, 1992) (see Fig. 2.3), involving a tortuous rotating pathway as the sacrum and other pelvic bones are arranged for an upright posture, and because the baby's head is large compared with the rest of the body. In all nonhuman primates the birth canal is basically a straight tube that throughout its width is wider front-to-back than side-to-side; there is ample room for the baby's head, which in apes enters the birth canal with its long axis aligned with the mother's pelvis, and passes down and out without rotation (though see Culotta, 1995b). In humans, however, there is a tube of varying cross-section; at the pelvic inlet it is wider side-to-side, while half way down (i.e. at midplane) it is deeper from front to back but less wide laterally, while it is nearly circular at the outlet. Circumference is smallest at midplane. However, the long axis of the baby's head is larger than the front-to-back diameter of the pelvic inlet; consequently, the head must start by facing the mother's side, and rotate at midplane usually 90° to face the mother's back. Thus birth has important implications for pelvic morphology, especially in the female, and for size and maturity of the offspring at birth. Growth continues after birth for 1 year in humans, so that our gestation is effectively 21 months. Other primates, including the apes, do not have this extra period of brain growth following birth.

The modern human pattern of birth probably evolved in a mosaic fashion, with some unique features appearing early in evolution, and others later. A humanlike entry of the fetal head into the birth canal was already present in *Australopithecus afarensis*, according to conventional thinking, as shown by well-preserved fossil evidence. However, the obstetric constraints in a small-brained but habitually bipedal creature meant that *afarensis* birth was almost certainly considerably different from that of both humans and apes. Rotation of the head and body within the birth canal, and emergence in the occiput-anterior position, would have been a late human modification, when increased encephalization had placed further selective pressures on both pelvic form and the timing of birth. Indeed, Ruff (1995) claims that rotational birth, along with increased cranial capacity which it permitted, appeared as recently as late *Homo erectus* or archaic *Homo sapiens*.

We might incidentally note that although it is conventionally held that the famous *Australopithecus afarensis* skeleton (and pelvis) of Lucy was that of a female, this is now being questioned (Hausler & Schmid, 1995), the pelvis possibly being too narrow to accommodate even an australopithecine baby. However, such an analysis has itself since been brought into question,

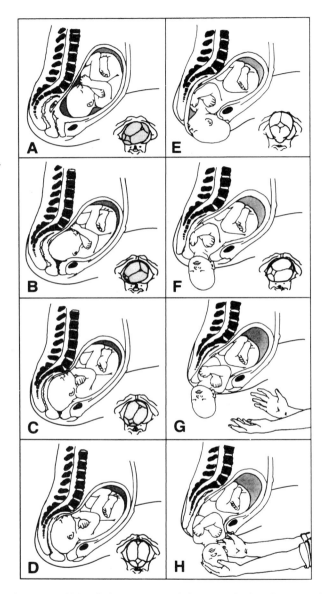

FIG. 2.3. The stages of labor in humans. In each box, a sagittal section through the maternal body during labor is shown. The maternal pubic bone and vertebral column appear in black. Also shown is a "midwife's eye" view of the foetus as it rotates within and emerges through the birth canal. From Rosenberg, K.R., The evolution of modern human childbirth, *Yearbook of Physical Anthropology*, 1992, *35*, 89–124. Copyright © (1992, Wiley-Liss), reprinted with permission of Wiley-Liss, Inc., a subsidiary of John Wiley & Sons Inc.

Wood and Quinney (1996) concluding that Lucy (AL 288-1) should still be regarded as a female of *Australopithecus afarensis*.

The Neanderthals (in Europe from 200,000 to 30,000 years ago) had brains comparable in size with our own and probably were born like us, as probably also was true of the smaller-brained *Homo erectus*. Rosenberg and Trevathan (1996) note that the Neanderthal pelvis is consistent with a birth canal that falls within the modern female range, and because of the emergence of the baby's head in an extended, backward-facing position, birth is likely to have been a social, cooperative process requiring assistance probably at least from the time of archaic *Homo sapiens*.

SUMMARY AND CONCLUSIONS

Although the order Primates precedes in origin the terminal Cretaceous catastrophe of 65 million years ago, most of our evolutionary trajectory, at least as far back as 35 million years ago when the Old World catarrhine lineage (Cercopithecoidea) separated from that of the New World platyrrhines (Ceboidea), probably took place in Africa. The anthropoid primates (monkeys, apes, and humans) may, however, extend back more than 45 million years. Molecular biology nowadays provides an alternative to palaeontology and physical taxonomy in determining the relatedness and time of divergence of extant species; it suggests a chimpanzee–"human" split between 5 and 8 million years ago, with chimpanzees probably even more closely related to us than to gorillas, though the problem of knuckle-walking in a putative common ancestor remains unresolved.

The traditional hominid lineage of *Australopithecus afarensis*, *Australopithecus africanus* (?), *Homo habilis*, *Homo erectus* and *Homo sapiens* is now being modified with recent discoveries. We may instead have to propose some or all of the following: *Ardipithecus ramidus* (4.4 million years ago), *Australopithecus anamensis* (4.2 million years ago), *Australopithecus afarensis* (4 million years ago), *Homo rudolfensis* (2.5 million years ago?), *Homo habilis* (2.2 million years ago), *Homo ergaster/Homo erectus* (1.9 million years ago) and archaic *Homo sapiens* or *Homo heidelbergensis* (0.7 million years ago). Nor, indeed, may the evolutionary pathway have always passed *directly* through such taxa, and it is often unclear whether specimens ascribed to a given taxon do belong to a single sexually dimorphic species.

Many single-factor explanations have been advanced for the advent of bipedal locomotion, just as for language. While climate change and an increasingly mosaic ecology is likely to have played a major role, as so often in biology we should probably seek a multifactorial-interactive explanation. Bipedalism is far from inefficient as a generalist form of locomotion, though it has involved major skeletal redesign, including that of the pelvis, with major obstetric consequences. Perhaps preadapted for by brachiation, it has freed up the hands for many other purposes and permits better thermo-regulation, thereby perhaps removing a physical constraint on further increases in brain size. There is clear (fossil trackway) evidence for biped-alism 3.6 million years ago, though it may not have been kinematically identical to that of modern humans, and some form may even predate *Australopithecus afarensis* to around 4 million years ago. The obstetric consequences of bipedalism, including headsize and rotation during child-birth, and subsequent altriciality and prolonged maternal care, are still being worked out.

FURTHER READINGS

Begun, D.R. (1992). Miocene fossil hominids and the chimp–human clade. *Science, 257,* 1929–1933.

Begun, D.R. (1994). Relations among the great apes and humans: New interpretations based on the fossil great ape *Dryopithecus. Yearbook of Physical Anthropology, 37,* 11–63.

Benefit, B.R., & McCrossin, M.L. (1995). Miocene hominoids and hominid origins. *Annual Review of Anthropology, 24,* 237–256.

Berge, C. (1994). How did the australopithecines walk? A biomechanical study of the hip and thigh of *Australopithecus afarensis. Journal of Human Evolution, 26,* 259–273.

Foley, R. (1995). *Humans before humanity.* Oxford: Blackwell.

Gebo, D.L. (1992). Plantigrady and foot adaptation in African apes: Implications for hominid origins. *American Journal of Physical Anthropology, 89,* 29–58.

Hunt, K.D. (1994). The evolution of human bipedality: Ecology and functional morphology. *Journal of Human Evolution, 26,* 183–202.

Jablonski, N.G., & Chaplin, G. (1993). Origin of habitual terrestrial bipedalism in the ancestor of the Hominidae. *Journal of Human Evolution, 24,* 259–280.

Jones, S., Martin, R., & Pilbeam, D. (Eds.) (1992). *Cambridge encyclopedia of human evolution.* Cambridge: Cambridge University Press.

Kay, R.F., Ross, C., & Williams, B.A. (1997). Anthropoid origins. *Science, 275,* 797–804.

Larick, R., & Ciochon, R.L. (1996). The African emergence and early Asian dispersals of the genus *Homo. American Scientist, 84,* 538–551.

Lewin, R. (1993). *Human evolution: An illustrated introduction* (3rd Edn). Oxford: Blackwell Scientific.

Rosenberg, K.R. (1992). The evolution of modern human childbirth. *Yearbook of Physical Anthropology, 35,* 89–124.

Ruff, C. (1995). Biomechanics of the hip and birth in early *Homo. American Journal of Physical Anthropology, 98,* 527–574.

Smith, B.H., & Tompkins, R.L. (1995). Toward the life history of the hominidae. *Annual Review of Anthropology, 24,* 257–270.

Steudel, K. (1996). Limb morphology, bipedal gait, and the energetics of hominid locomotion. *American Journal of Physical Anthropology, 99,* 345–355.

Tattersall, I. (1993). *The human odyssey: Four million years of human evolution.* Englewood Cliffs, NJ: Prentice Hall.

Tattersall, I. (1995). *The fossil trail.* Oxford: Oxford University Press.

CHAPTER THREE

Evolution of the genus *Homo*

Homo habilis is conventionally regarded as the first true "human", giving way to *Homo erectus* and in turn to two subspecies of *Homo sapiens*—ourselves and our extinct Neanderthal cousins. In this chapter we review what is known about these taxa, whether *Homo habilis* and *Homo erectus* are true unitary taxa, whether they really lie directly upon our lineage, and whether additional intermediaries should also be included. In particular, we discuss archaeological and molecular-biological conclusions about the origin—recently in Africa, or earlier and more or less simultaneously in many parts of the world—of anatomically modern people.

HOMO HABILIS

Homo habilis probably appeared around 2.2 million years ago at a time of global cooling (Harrison et al., 1988; Hill, Ward, Deino et al., 1992), around the time of the appearance of the oldest stone tools. Debate continues as to whether it constitutes one sexually very dimorphic species, or more than one, and as to its correct location upon our evolutionary trajectory. Assuming that it does constitute one of our ancestors, it should be noted that this first species of the genus *Homo* has a larger brain (700–750 c.c.) than any australopithecine (*afarensis*—400 c.c.; *africanus*—460 c.c.), though smaller than that of *Homo erectus* (900 c.c., see e.g. Holloway, 1995), and a less massive dentition, associated perhaps with a new reliance on tools; indeed, its hands were essentially modern, though its skeleton was small, with relatively long apelike arms and large teeth. *Homo habilis* represents the first real increase, allometrically, in brain size from the apes, attaining about 50% of the level of *Homo sapiens*. The expansion of the habiline brain was largely one of broadening and, to some extent, of an increase in height, without noticeable lengthening (Tobias, 1987). Increase was especially marked in the frontal and parietal lobes, regions intimately connected with our intrinsic "humanness". The sulcal and gyral patterns of the frontal lobe of the habiline brain, left impressed upon the inner surface of the cranium, seem very similar to our own and distinct from those of the pongids; this is particularly true of regions corresponding to our own two major speech areas, Broca's and Wernicke's (Tobias, 1995). Articulate speech, if perhaps rudimentary, remains therefore a distinct possibility for *Homo habilis*. Although the posterior parietal growth would have also subserved the multimodal processing of visual, auditory, and somesthetic information and permitted visuospatial integration, frontal development would have furthered strategic planning and goal-directed behavior (Bradshaw & Mattingley, 1995; Holloway, 1995). Given the very small genetic differences between apes and humans, such changes are likely to have been wrought by regulatory genes governing the timing and rates of growth of regional cortical areas (Holloway, 1995). Thus the lunate sulcus, which is absent in humans but prominent in apes, marking the forward boundary of the occipital lobe has, along with the growth and downward rotation of the parietal cortex, been effectively pushed to an inferior-mesial location.

The first regular manufacturer of stone tools was probably *Homo habilis* (see Fig. 3.1), though currently the latter's remains are dated to slightly later than the commencement of the Oldowan industry (after Olduvai, in east Africa) more than 2.5 million years ago (Klein, 1989). In a preliminary report, Kimbel, Walter, Johanson et al. (1996) describe the discovery of a maxilla of *Homo* (of indeterminate species) closely associated with Oldowan stone tools from Hadar, Ethiopia, dated to around 2.3 million years ago, the earliest actual association of hominid remains with stone tools. In the adjacent Gona River drainage, Semaw, Renne, Harris et al. (1997) report Oldowan assemblages securely dated to more than 2.5 million years ago, the oldest known artefacts from anywhere in the world. They show surprisingly sophisticated control of stone-fracture mechanics, equivalent to much younger Oldowan assemblages, and indicating an unexpectedly long period of technological stasis in the Oldowan of around 1 million years. In the Oldowan industry, stone cores seem to have been transported some kilometers from their likely sources, and to have either served as tools in their own right or to have had sharp flakes struck off them, by direct if clumsy percussion. There are suggestions from microscopic analysis of wear that flakes may have been used for cutting plant and animal material (indicative of carnivory, whether by scavenging or hunting), and wood. Thus they may

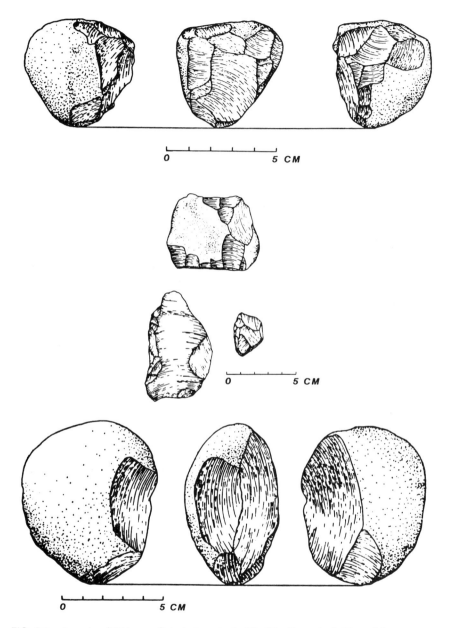

FIG. 3.1. Sample of Oldowan flaked stone tools. Modifications via flaking of the core were apparently designed merely to provide a cutting edge; there is little apparent attempt to achieve an overall shape. From Wynn, T.G., and McGrew, W.C., An ape's view of the Oldowan, *Man*, 1989, *24*, 383–393.

have been used to manufacture new tools like digging sticks (Harrison et al., 1988). Scattered and aggregated tools, with and without animal bones often possessing cut marks, have been found as in the camp sites of modern hunter-gatherers near streams and lakes. Thus there are already indications of food sharing, division of labor, reciprocity, and cooperation, all of which may have further contributed to our early evolution.

HOMO ERECTUS

Homo erectus was first described a century ago by Eugene Dubois in Java, though it, or a very similar creature, is also known from China, Africa, and Europe. Rightmire (1995) notes that there is little agreement about *Homo erectus*, whether there is really more than one species under that name, whether it (or maybe instead its African "equivalent" *Homo ergaster*) lay on our direct lineage, when it first appeared and where and so on. He opts for the conventional view that the African, Asian, and European specimens all constitute a single *Homo erectus* taxon, which was originally African and from which (instead of *Homo ergaster*) *Homo sapiens* derives. It is characterized by a tall, lean build with long legs (thereby perhaps facilitating its migrations), and a long, low cranium with an endocranial capacity of around 1000 cm^3, still considerably below our own. There is also debate as to whether or not there was a general increase in capacity during its long history of more than 1 million years; some see *Homo sapiens* as evolving locally from separate populations of *Homo erectus*, with a gradual increase in cranial capacity, while others see a more-or-less universal *replacement* of aboriginal *Homo erectus* populations by anatomically modern *Homo sapiens sapiens*, with an abrupt increase. Suffice it to say that the two taxa are generally seen as distinct (Rightmire, 1990), with *Homo erectus* a real species rather than just an arbitrary grade or stage in the evolution of *Homo sapiens*; the latter perhaps only in Africa evolved into *Homo sapiens sapiens*, eventually replacing all other more archaic forms of *Homo* everywhere else (see later). Thus in Europe, *Homo erectus* may have been replaced by bigger-brained hominids which themselves evolved into Neanderthals, later themselves to be replaced by African-derived anatomically modern *Homo sapiens sapiens*. However, human remains have now been dated to more than 780,000 years ago in the caves of Gran Dolina, Sierra de Atapuerca, Burgos (Spain), which cannot be accommodated in any of the defined *Homo* species (Carbonell, Bermudez de Castro, Arsuaga et al., 1995). This extremely early settlement of Europe was apparently made by a creature with many primitive traits and a pre-Acheulian technology that lacked hand axes, picks, cleavers etc. (The Acheulian technology, see later, roughly equates with later *Homo erectus*.) For those who hypothesize *Homo heidelbergensis* as a possible ancestor of the Neanderthals (see Rightmire, 1995, for discussion), the Spanish find may have been a primitive form thereof. In any case, it was distinct from other contemporary Asiatic remains of *Homo erectus*, possibly more closely resembling *Homo ergaster*, the hypothetical east African "equivalent" of Asiatic *Homo erectus*. (*Homo ergaster*, if adopted as the African equivalent of Asiatic *Homo erectus*, flourished in east Africa around 1.7 million years ago, and is seen as less specialized than its Asiatic counterpart, especially in cranial anatomy; with a larger brain and smaller teeth than its predecessor *Homo habilis*, its skeleton approached ours in size, except for a narrow pelvis.)

In Africa, sometime after the appearance of *Homo erectus* (or *ergaster*, see below) new stone tools appear (see Fig. 3.2), especially the symmetrical

100 millimetres

FIG. 3.2.   Two Acheulian bifaces (handaxes), from between 500 and 300 thousand years ago. Courtesy of Martin Williams.

and larger biface (teardrop) handaxe forms (Harrison et al., 1988), in the Acheulian tradition, which initially nevertheless retained many older Oldowan features. (The reason for the pleasing symmetry of this "Swiss Army Knife" of the Lower Palaeolithic is unclear—maybe pure bravado!—though it certainly suggests the presence of some form of mental template; nor do we know exactly what it was used for, except that this probably included cutting, hacking, scraping, and digging, see Tattersall, 1995.)

In China, the Acheulian is absent, and few stone tools are found in Java. It used to be thought that the absence of stone tools in Southeast Asia was because hard, otherwise suitable, but nevertheless perishable bamboo artefacts were instead employed; alternatively as we shall see *Homo erectus* may have left Africa before developing Acheulian lithic technology. The Acheulian industry was not replaced by the Mousterian (typically Neanderthal) in Europe until 200,000 years ago. Nevertheless, *Homo erectus* may have been the first hominid to leave Africa for colder climates, indicating adaptive capacities, though as we shall see there are hints of a possible earlier migration also by *Homo habilis*. *Homo erectus* was also associated with the first true home bases, the first indication of an extended childhood, and the first possible use of fire at 500,000 years ago in northern China, although there is no evidence of elaborate cooking arrangements. Unlike the later Neanderthals, however, *Homo erectus* may never have reached really cold regions. Thus frost heaves and the clumping of rock piles could have naturally produced what otherwise might have been interpreted as shelters or dwellings (Klein, 1989). Microscopic analysis of edge wear indicates a more sophisticated use of tools, to cut, shred, butcher, or whittle meat, hide, bone, antler, wood and plant material. However, the tools seem not to have been transported any great distance from source, and bone, despite its good preservation, seems to little have been used. Though bones from large game animals are evident, we cannot unequivocally conclude that *Homo erectus* engaged in coordinated hunting, ambushing, or trapping, or transported meat in large quantities any distance. Nevertheless, increased carnivory, reduction in the size of the jaw, and an enlarging brain all probably increased the reliance upon tools—even though the tools were very slow to change—and led to a further acceleration in growth of the brain.

Until very recently it was believed that *Homo erectus* (or *Homo ergaster*) first appeared in Africa between 1.8 and 1.9 million years ago, true *Homo erectus* appearing in Eurasia (China and Java) at about 1.25 million years ago, and in western Europe at 0.5 million years ago or less. However, in 1994 there were reports (Swisher, Curtis, Jacob et al., 1994) of Javan specimens assigned to *Homo erectus* being radiometrically dated to between 1.6 and 1.8 million years of age. This finding resolves two questions: Why did *Homo erectus* apparently stay in Africa so long before leaving for other parts (it did not), and why was there apparently no Acheulian tradition associated with *Homo erectus* in South-East Asia? The answer to the latter question may simply be that the Acheulian tradition (with its earlier African date of 1.4 million years ago) had simply not yet been developed, when *Homo erectus* left for Asia at or before 1.8 million years ago, shortly after the first appearance of *Homo erectus* in Africa (Holloway, 1994). A further possibility is that the taxon first evolved in Asia, not Africa, from an earlier-departing *Homo ergaster* or even *Homo habilis*, returning to Africa (and venturing to Europe?) around 1.2 million years ago, to give rise to archaic *Homo sapiens*. This speculation has now received empirical support (Wanpo, Ciochon, Yumin et al., 1995) from finds dated to around 1.9 million years ago in the Longgupo cave in the Sichuan Province of south-central China; these resemble the (dental) remains of both *Homo habilis* and *Homo ergaster*, together with transported stone tools, rounded pieces of igneous rock showing signs of repeated bashing and resembling the basic Oldowan choppers of African *Homo habilis*. This would suggest an evolutionary trajectory (direct or indirect) via *habilis, ergaster, erectus*, and *sapiens*, with *Homo* commencing to travel and use tools soon after first appearing. The only problem is that contemporaneous occupation of Asia by two different hominid species, true *erectus* (?) in Java around 1.7 million years ago (Swisher et al., 1994) and *ergaster/habilis* (?) in Sichuan around 1.9 million years ago, might be unrealistic. If so, the Longgupo find may be "merely" an early true *erectus*. Moreover, if there were two *erectus* populations nearly 2 million years ago, one in Asia and one in Africa, which of them gave rise to *Homo sapiens*? Rightmire (1995) as we saw believes that the name *Homo ergaster* is unnecessary, and that there is only one taxon for *Homo erectus*, which evolved in Africa, later spreading to Asia—a return to a more traditional view.

We shall shortly note that there is another ongoing debate, concerning whether anatomically modern *Homo sapiens sapiens* evolved everywhere (except in the Americas and Australia) in parallel from pre-existing *Homo erectus* populations (the multiregional hypothesis), or first appeared probably in Africa and, migrating, replaced earlier, aboriginal *erectus* populations 100,000 years ago (the out-of-Africa hypothesis). The new Javan and Chinese finds and dates are far more compatible with the latter hypothesis, as if human ancestors in Asia 2 million years ago had not been replaced by *Homo sapiens*, they would have had more than enough time to evolve quite differently from what we see today (Gibbons, 1994b; Holloway, 1994).

Not only do we now have Javan and Chinese *Homo* species radiometrically dated to nearly 2 million years ago, but also in 1994 there were reports (Dean & Delson, 1994; Gabunia & Vekua, 1994) of a fossil hominid mandible dated by three independent methods to 1.8 million years ago in Dmanisi, Georgia, i.e. comparable in age with the Javan find. We must now ask why *Homo erectus* did not move to western Europe too. However, anatomically modern *Homo sapiens sapiens* seems not to have reached western Europe, from western Asia, until after 50,000 years ago, perhaps because of the extreme cold. Archaic forms of *Homo sapiens* (perhaps to be identified with *Homo heidelbergensis* and that may well have given rise to the Neanderthals by about 230,000 years ago) are known from much of Europe from 500,000 years ago, possibly earlier in Africa and southern Europe (a reasonably firm figure of 780,000 years is given for Atapuerca, Spain, see e.g. Dennell, 1997). There was an overlapping period of maybe 200,000 years between archaic *Homo sapiens* and late-surviving *Homo erectus* (maybe until 250,000 years ago in China, and as late as perhaps 100,000 years ago in Java, see e.g. Jones, Martin, & Pilbeam, 1992; indeed, according to Swisher, Rink, Antón et al., 1996, *Homo erectus* survived in Java until between 27,000 and 53,000 years ago, thus spelling further trouble for the multiregional hypothesis, which proposes that Asian *Homo erectus* was ancestral to modern humans in Asia and Australia, who were certainly present then). All this speciation is probably the result of geographical or behavioral isolation. We shall see that anatomically modern *Homo sapiens sapiens* almost certainly had a separate, African origin.

ARCHAIC *HOMO SAPIENS* AND THE NEANDERTHALS

Archaic *Homo sapiens* emerged in Africa and Europe between 0.5 and 0.7 million years ago (Klein, 1989). A skull dated to at least 200,000 years ago has been reported from Jinniushan in China (Tlemel, Quan, & En, 1994), almost as old as the latest Chinese *Homo erectus*, raising the possibility that the two species may have coexisted in that region. Archaic *Homo sapiens* possessed a larger cranium than *Homo erectus*, and merged progressively into the Neanderthals via (in Europe) the "pre-Neanderthals". The Neanderthals appeared around 230,000 years ago or later, depending upon the distinguishing criteria adopted (and whether or not a prior *Homo heidelbergensis* is postulated), arriving perhaps 130,000 years ago in Europe, and lasted as late as 34,000 to 31,000 years ago in western Europe. They were largely limited to Europe and the Middle East, adapting there to climate extremes and overlapping with anatomically modern *Homo sapiens sapiens* in the Middle East for many tens of thousands of years; there is debate as to whether interbreeding may or may not have occurred.

Pre-Neanderthal skulls have recently been reported from near Burgos in northern Spain (Arsuaga, Martinez, Gracia et al., 1993), and at around 300,000 years old they represent that intermediate stage in Europe of archaic *Homo sapiens* which may lie between *Homo erectus* and Neanderthals proper. They already had many Neanderthal characteristics, and the cranial volume of one individual at 1390 cm^3 made it larger than the brain of *Homo erectus* and bigger even than that of many a *Homo sapiens*. Another recent pre-Neanderthal find, not yet properly described, comes from southeastern Italy (Altamura), and has been provisionally dated to around 400,000 years ago (Dorozynski, 1993).

The Neanderthals were the last truly "primitive" members of the genus *Homo*. However, they resembled anatomically modern humans in many ways, and were undoubtedly more sophisticated then *Homo erectus*. In Israel and probably elsewhere (Simons, 1989) they even shared with our ancestors the same toolkit during the Middle Palaeolithic of 50–100,000 years ago. Nevertheless, the two groups probably evolved independently, in mutual isolation, modern *Homo sapiens sapiens* having entered Eurasia from Africa relatively recently. Like the earlier *Homo erectus*, whom they resembled, despite possessing a more massive build, the Neanderthals are noteworthy for their dense skeletons (though perhaps only in proportion to their muscle mass, see Ruff & Trinkaus, 1996, reported by Gibbons, 1996), short limbs (which may have been adaptations to cold), projecting brow ridges, and thick skulls. The face was markedly prognathous, with massive jaws and front dentition, which seem from patterns of wear to have been employed as a vice or clamp. The nose was large, perhaps again an adaptation to warm cold air, and the cranium, which was globelike in cross section, was lower and longer than nowadays, a configuration that is compatible (though the evidence is disputed) with a high larynx and reduced phonological control. However, the internal configuration of the cranial cavity indicates that speech-related areas similar in size and location to our own may have been present. Indeed, the volume of the brain may even have exceeded our own, though relative frontal reduction could have been disadvantageous in terms of behavioral flexibility and planning capacity.

The width of the Neanderthal birth canal also exceeded modern dimensions. Thus their babies, like the adults, may have been large, or there may have been a longer gestation. The latter, another possible adaptation to cold, would have resulted in more independent and precocial offspring, and slightly slowed population growth—another slight selective disadvantage relative to our ancestors.

A recent study (Schwartz & Tattersall, 1996; see also Laitman, Reidenberg, Marquez, & Gannon, 1996) finds that Neanderthals differed from anatomically modern humans in their skeletal anatomy in more ways than had been previously recognized, enough perhaps for them to be seen as possessing sufficiently unique derived characters (autapomorphies) as to warrant their being assigned to their own species (*Homo neanderthalensis*) rather than these characters merely reflecting race differences within normal *sapiens sapiens* limits. In particular, Schwartz and Tattersall (1996) describe important new aspects of the functional morphology of the upper respiratory tract. Previous emphasis, to which we shall return in a later chapter, had been less on respiratory requirements than on the vocal-tract component; it should of course be noted that the area's main functions were respiration (and food ingestion), and that it did not evolve for the sole purpose of vocalization. We should also remember the many problems in reconstructing respiratory, digestive, and nervous systems—all largely soft tissue—from bony remains. The main conclusion of Schwartz and Tattersall is that the Neanderthals seem to have relied more heavily on the nasal than on the oral route for respiration than do modern humans; this may reflect the rigors of their environment, and the need to warm and humidify cold dry air.

To judge from the killing and butchering sites (Kozlowski, 1990), big-game hunting was a common Neanderthal practice, with microwear analysis of middle-Palaeolithic Mousterian tools indicating butchery and working of hides and of wood (Anderson-Gerfaud, 1990). Compared with the Acheulian, the number and size of bifaces decreased, the lithic technology now consisting largely of flakes. As we shall see in a later chapter, there was evidence of hafting of implements, and during the terminal Mousterian Châtelperronian, when anatomically modern people arrived in western Europe and briefly coexisted with the Neanderthals, the latter may have borrowed new technologies. Nevertheless, as again we shall shortly review, there was little evidence of carving or polishing ivory, antler, bone, or shell, or of art in general. Fire was employed, probably for warmth, cooking, and personal protection, with burial of the dead either for spiritual or hygienic purposes. Although there is little evidence of substantial dwellings (Klein, 1989), Kozlowski (1990) describes the construction of dwellings from mammoth bones in Russia (Molodova) and elsewhere.

It is not known why the Neanderthals disappeared, though reproductively and linguistically they may have been at a competitive disadvantage with the newcomers. While the two groups may have coexisted for a thousand or more years during the western European Châtelperronian around 35,000 years ago, in southwest Asia they may have coexisted, or alternated during cyclical climatic changes, for very much longer, from between 90 and 40,000 years ago (Tillier, 1989). Why, when both groups had such a similar, comparatively simple toolkit and culture, were they able to coexist for so long, apparently without hybridizing (Stringer, 1990a,b)? Were they so different genetically or even behaviorally that they remained isolated, and, if so, why were their cultural artefacts at that point in their two developments so similar? Or was there in fact some hybridization?

Why, also, did the anatomically modern peoples continue to use old technologies for so long in the Levant, yet when they suddenly appeared in western Europe it was with a newer and far more sophisticated culture? What drove this technological and cultural transition—a sudden mutation or attainment of a critical social mass? The appearance of a more efficient language or communicatory system? Changes in social organization? All we know is that at the beginning of the Upper Palaeolithic in Europe around 35,000 years ago, there was the seemingly sudden appearance of advanced culture, the manufacture of sophisticated, highly standardized tools, routine long-distance transport of raw materials indicative of social networks, substantial dwellings, sophisticated hearths, tailored clothing, rituals and other innovations (Klein, 1993).

Where did the Neanderthals of southwest Asia in fact come from? One possibility (Bar-Yosef & Vandermeersch, 1993) is that they came from western Europe during a period of very severe climate change which drove them from their frozen lands; it is even possible that at the same time and for similar reasons the gracile anatomically modern *Homo sapiens sapiens* also left the Levant (for which the more massive Neanderthals were better cold adapted) for warmer north Africa, the two groups oscillating back and forth, in and out of phase with each other, during the climate oscillations, or maybe briefly coexisting and possibly even interbreeding.

Although not everyone excludes the possibility (or evidence) of such intermingling, we may also note that the extinction of the Neanderthals need not have been catastrophic (Lewin, 1993); it could have occurred locally, over perhaps 1000 years or 30 or more generations, and this scenario would have needed only a slight competitive advantage (perhaps around 1%) by *Homo sapiens sapiens*. Language superiority might be one such possibility; another might be birth rate. A third possibility (see Lewin, 1991) relates to pelvic shape and running. A Neanderthal pelvis has in fact been fully reconstructed from fragments in the Kebara cave. Sockets for the hip joints were found to be backwards, relative to our own. Thus the line of the center of gravity of the trunk passed through the hip joints and down the legs in a single, straight vertical line. In us the line forms a zigzag in the pelvis; the line through the trunk hits the pelvis behind the position of the hip joints, moves horizontally forward within the pelvis, then vertically down through the hip joints and legs. Not only does this configuration result in a canti-levered shock-absorber, but it permits a bounce-back effect during pro-gression in some ways analogous to that of the kangaroo. The Neanderthal hip joint may even have been superior to our own with respect to resultant back alignment (Hale, 1991), though our own energy-efficient design may be an adaptation for striding or jogging.

A related observation (Trinkaus, 1996, reported by Gibbons, 1996) is that the femoral necks of Neanderthals are more sharply bent than those of contemporary early moderns, indicating that they were more active as children; perhaps the Neanderthals moved as a group in pursuit of food, while our ancestors could split up, leaving the young with care-givers while other adults hunted and returned with food. Indeed, there is other skeletal evidence of behavioral differences between the two taxa; Neanderthals' upper-arm bones record more vigorous exercise, perhaps because they were less efficient in tool use or other behaviors, maybe relying on brawn rather than on brain. Allopatric differentiation is the process of divergence of sibling groups that have been geographically isolated from each other and have come to share a habitat only after the occurrence of such differentiation. Such groups may come to exploit different aspects of the environment, and such resource polymorphism, known to have occurred in a variety of vertebrate species, may result in unique patterns of development, growth, morphology, and behavior (Campbell, 1996). Ultimately, this may result in reproductive isolation sufficient to stop interbreeding, and, by definition, the evolution of separate species. One may speculate whether a similar process could have operated with the Neanderthals and anatomically modern humans.

THE MORPHOLOGY AND ORIGIN OF ANATOMICALLY MODERN *HOMO SAPIENS SAPIENS*

Compared with our likely immediate predecessors, on or off our actual lineage, our skeleton is less bulky, the skull is now more rounded, the face flatter, the front dentition smaller (perhaps now being used less as a vice or tool), and the cranial base more fully flexed (Harrison et al., 1988); although the brain volume is largely unchanged, there may now be subtle changes in proportions of the different regions, with more emphasis perhaps on frontal regions involved in strategic aspects of forward planning and sequencing. Concomitant changes in shoulder, elbow, wrist, and hand are perhaps associated with more efficient limb and weapon use, and a more successful dependence on manufactured tools (Simons, 1989). All kinds of new tools and weapons for killing at a distance appear at the start of the Upper Palaeolithic cultural explosion in western Europe around 35,000 years ago, together with nets, snares, improved hearths and clothing, and better dwellings differentiated into areas for living, food preparation, and sleeping. Burials are elaborate, with grave goods, and elaborate personal decoration now appears, along with rock art and cave paintings, and other indications of a sophisticated system of linguistic communication.

Three models have been proposed for the appearance of anatomically modern *Homo sapiens sapiens* (Ayala, Escalante, O'hUigin, & Klein, 1994). According to the "candelabra" account, the evolution to *Homo sapiens* from *Homo erectus* (if indeed that latter taxon were our immediate progenitor), which had much earlier migrated from Africa to Eurasia, occurred several times in different places at different periods. However, this strong theory, which is probably no longer held in precisely that form, is weakened by the very low probability that the *same* species (and we can all interbreed, so we *must* all belong to a single species) would independently evolve more than once. The "multiregional" account is a weaker version of the above; it still emphasizes regional continuity from *Homo erectus*, and the (questionable) maintenance (over 1 million years) of very ancient morphological features in modern races (e.g. the shovel-shaped incisors of east Asians, and the prominent brow ridges of Australian aboriginals) with roots back in *Homo erectus*, nevertheless some migration and/or hybridization is allowed (Stringer & Gamble, 1993; Wolpoff & Caspari, 1996).

According to the out-of-Africa model (and see Stringer & McKie, 1996), anatomically modern *Homo sapiens sapiens* first arose in Africa maybe up to 200,000 years ago, migrating there from maybe 100,000 years ago and replacing prior archaic aboriginals. An extreme version of the above model, though one for which there is increasing support, argues that this transition to anatomically modern people occurred with a very narrow population bottleneck consisting of very few individuals, all ancestors of all the extant populations. As we shall see, this viewpoint is supported by mitochondrial DNA (mtDNA) studies showing that the diverse mtDNA sequences found in modern individuals of all races coalesce to a single ancestral sequence, the "mitochondrial Eve", in Africa, of around 200,000 years ago.

If we were to accept the multiregional evolution account, we would see the operation of long-term trends in human evolution, occurring mainly through the resorting of the same genetic material in similar fashions in different regions, rather than by evolution and radiation of novel genetic material and morphologies. *Homo sapiens* is not therefore seen as a significant speciation event, i.e. the appearance of a new *species*, in relation to *Homo erectus*. Indeed, we would have to abolish the taxon *Homo erectus* as it would not be sufficiently different from *Homo sapiens*, and the latter would now include hominids with brains ranging in size from 850 cm^3 to 2,000 cm^3, and would probably lump together *Homo habilis, Homo erectus* and anatomically modern *Homo sapiens sapiens*. In theory, the fossil record should be able to test between the multiregional theory and out-of Africa replacement, as the replacing population should always be the same everywhere, and always different from the replaced population (Thomson, 1992); however, the fossil record is poor, and differences and similarities are disputed. A recent study (Lahr, 1994) examining various modern populations found that the regional features claimed by the multiregional model to characterize east Asian and Australasian evolutionary lines were not exclusive to these regions, either spatially or temporally, and that many of the traits were functional, and therefore subject to selective pressures. Indeed, characters marking specific population lineages, and surviving over hundreds of thousands of years, are very likely to have conferred some kind of selective advantage. At the same time, there would have to be enough gene flow involving advantageous new mutations to keep all the populations evolving toward modern *Homo sapiens* in lockstep. Thus, selection and gene flow would make human populations more like each other, whereas selection and *lack* of gene flow would keep them differentiated—an unlikely balance to be maintained for almost a million years (Sarich, 1992).

In summary, the multiregional account argues that archaic and modern humans belong to the same species, and that human evolution following the dispersal of *Homo erectus* from Africa during the Lower Pleistocene was a combination of local evolution in large regions of the Old World (Africa, Australasia, Europe, and North Africa) and gene flow between these regions (Lieberman, 1995). It predicts sets of unique features linking archaic and modern peoples in each of these regions, together with transitional fossils. Any similarities between living peoples in diverse regions should be a consequence of shared recent genes and retention of ancient regional characteristics. Conversely, according to the alternative "out-of Africa" approach, the evolution of modern humans is the result of a speciation event from a single population of archaic *Homo* probably in Africa, with distinctive regional features of archaic taxa of *Homo* in other areas failing to be incorporated into the modern populations that eventually replaced them; any regional characteristics are therefore seen as probably recent. Most of the cranial, mandibular, and dental characters that can test between the two competing hypotheses tend to support "out-of-Africa" (Lieberman, 1995). Indeed, there may be no unique African regional characteristics, suggesting that all modern people belong in a monophyletic group with archaic *Homo* from Africa. As we shall shortly see, the molecular evidence also supports such a conclusion, as all existing people are remarkably similar, far more so than are populations of chimpanzees or gorillas. The multiregional hypothesis would have to invoke implausibly high levels of gene flow among all regions of the world in all directions, given the distances and geographical barriers during the Late Pleistocene.

EVIDENCE FROM MOLECULAR BIOLOGY

According to the molecularly derived version ("African Eve") of the out-of Africa account, all mtDNA types in contemporary populations trace back to a single (necessarily female) ancestor, who probably lived in Africa around 150,000 to 200,000 years ago. This ancestor was *not* the only female alive, as the popular misconception seems to hold; it is just that her contemporaries *ultimately* (maybe thousands of generations later) left no offspring to contribute to modern populations, or left only males. Nor was she the first woman on the scene; she merely represents the point at which all contemporary mtDNA types coalesce. Generally, two sets of data, phylogenetic analysis (in terms of degree of relatedness of different extant populations, expressed as a tree), and the relative degree of overall DNA sequence divergence between those populations, both support an African origin for the human mtDNA ancestor (Gibbons, 1995a; Stoneking, 1993). Indeed, most studies, however they resolve the phylogenetic analysis, find that African populations have accumulated the greatest number of mutations, compared with all other populations, and therefore are likely to be the *oldest* population—assuming that all populations have the same rate of mtDNA evolution, and selective pressures have not been operating.

The new molecular (*genetic*) approach to the study of human ancestry is complementary to the palaeontological evidence, which depends upon *phenotypes*. Genes are units that replicate, with or without modification, and are less ephemeral than phenotypes. Phenotypes may be subject to multi-gene modifying influences and to the environment itself, whereas genes, if nuclear, are subject to genetic recombination through mating in each generation. Above all, genes in living individuals clearly must have ancestors, while dead fossils may have left no descendants. The fossil record is patchy, incomplete, and replete with dating and interpretational problems, while the genome contains all the inherited biological information of an individual (Wilson & Cann, 1992), in the form of the linear sequencing of the four nucleotide components of DNA, adenine, cytosine, guanine, and thymine. As many mutations, substitutions of one nucleotide by another, may be selectively neutral, neither being eliminated from the genome if injurious nor being favored, retained and accumulating, if advantageous, such selectively neutral genes may become fixed or spread in a taxon at a constant rate. They may therefore be used as a stochastic molecular clock to time divergences between two lineages from a common stock (Ayala, 1995). However, recent evidence questions this assumption of a constant rate of neutral mutations, like radioactive decay, suggesting that longer-lived animals may have a greater ability to repair their DNA than shorter-lived animals, thereby reducing mutation rates and slowing the molecular clock (Gibbons, 1995b).

In deriving quantitative information about the times of divergence between different species, molecular biologists can study nuclear genes (around 100,000), or instead mtDNA. In nuclear DNA (nDNA) mutations accumulate comparatively slowly, and as nuclear genes are inherited from both parents, mixing or recombining in each new generation, individual histories cannot easily be followed. However, with only 37 genes (or 16,500 base pairs of DNA), mtDNA gives a much clearer picture (Cann, Stoneking, & Wilson, 1987), as mutations occur much faster and, being haploid, mtDNA is clonally inherited via the *maternal* line, without recombination. Of course, nDNA, via the Y chromosome, must be examined to follow the males of a lineage. As we shall see, however, both approaches indicate a recent African origin of modern humans.

Mitochondria are cytoplasmic organelles, which are involved in energy production (Spuhler, 1988). Quite independently of nDNA, they may have originated in pre-Cambrian times as free-living bacteria, which, like chloroplasts in plants, established a symbiotic relationship with host cells. A basic assumption in using mtDNA to determine lineages and divergence times is that mutations are not influenced by natural selection, are not repaired, and occur at a constant rate. Sequences known as "junk" DNA, which appear not to affect the phenotype, fulfill such requirements (Stringer, 1990a,b). Knowledge (archaeological, or from physical dating techniques), independently derived as to when two branches diverged, can be used to calibrate the molecular mutation-clock, and so ascertain the time of occurrence of *other* divergences (Gibbons, 1995a). In practice, however, there are many disputes about the regularity and rates of change, the calibratory times of divergence, and how most parsimoniously to interconnect all sampled populations in a single phylogenetic tree. Many of these problems may be resolved by the Human Genome Diversity Project. However, as indicated earlier, the fact that the highest levels of mitochondrial and nuclear DNA diversity for any living human group are found in populations from sub-Saharan Africa, irrespective of disputes about parsimony in phylogenetic trees, strongly supports Africa as our center of origin.

The most consistent molecular evidence puts an African mtDNA ancestor at around 200,000 years ago, a figure that fits well with the archaeological evidence of 100,000 years ago for the appearance of anatomically modern people in Africa, and a subsequent spread elsewhere (Stoneking, 1993). Because the non-African populations predating the mtDNA ancestor apparently did not contribute mtDNA to contemporary populations, there must have been little or no admixture with old non-African residents elsewhere, otherwise contemporary human populations would be far more divergent in mtDNA; in fact, divergence is far less than in chimpanzees (Morrell, 1994; Ruvolo, Pan, Zehr et al., 1994). Thus Ruvolo et al. (1994) performed a mtDNA analysis of humans, chimpanzees, gorillas, orangutans, and siamangs, estimating the spontaneous mutation (substitution) rate as 0.8% per million years; they concluded that gorillas separated from human/chimpanzee stock around 9 million years ago, with humans and chimpanzees splitting about 6 million years ago. They also noted that whereas the apes are genetically diverse and are therefore descended from large ancestral populations, modern humans are *very* much less diverse, genetically, and the two most different humans on the face of the Earth are less different than the two lowland gorillas from the same forest in west Africa.

Horai, Hayasaka, Kondo et al. (1995) analyzed the complete mtDNA sequences (16,500 in humans) from three humans (African, European, and Japanese) and four apes (common and pygmy chimpanzee, gorilla, and orangutan) in an attempt to estimate the substitution rates and divergence times of hominoid mtDNAs. With the assumption that orangutans and

African apes diverged 13 million years ago, a divergence time for humans and chimpanzees was found of 4.9 million years, and the age of the last common ancestor of the human mtDNAs was inferred to be 143,000, plus or minus 18,000 years ago. They concluded that the shallow ancestry of the human mtDNAs, together with the observation that the African sequence was the most divergent among humans, strongly supports the recent African origin of anatomically modern *Homo sapiens sapiens*.

Cavalli-Sforza and colleagues (Gibbons, 1995c) used *nuclear* DNA from 30 Africans and 120 individuals from 4 other continents, examining repeating series of nucleotides from chromosomes 13 and 15. They also found more diversity within the African samples, and concluded that Africans and non-Africans split around 112,000 years ago. An almost identical figure (115,000 years ago, or 156,000 years ago, depending upon estimated generation time, see Nei, 1995) is obtained by Goldstein, Ruiz-Linares, Cavalli-Sforza, and Feldman (1995) using microsatellite DNA polymorphisms. Similarly, a figure of 100,000 years is given by Tishkoff, Dietzsch, Speed et al. (1996) who analyzed two markers at the CD4 gene locus on chromosome 12 from 42 different populations. Sub-Saharans exhibited the most variability, and the northeast corner of Africa was indicated as the origin of humans, populations losing diversity as they went.

The extreme genetic similarity of all modern humans suggests that a small ancestral population may have passed through a "bottleneck" sometime in our recent past, with an effective population size of perhaps only 10,000 (Gibbons, 1995a). A genetic bottleneck involves the successive loss of genetic diversity owing to local extinction events, which prevent the transmission of all but a few alleles (nuclear loci) or maternal lineages (mtDNA). Indeed, a *series* of bottlenecks may have occurred, one in each of several different populations in various parts of the world, each followed by subsequent explosions (Gibbons, 1993a; Harpending, Sherry, Rogers, and Stoneking, 1993). These last findings may possibly support a *weak* out-of-Africa hypothesis, modern humans appearing first in a subpopulation (rather than a separate species) that survived the African bottleneck of 80,000 years ago, and then slowly spread around the old world over tens of thousands of years, mating at a *low* rate with pre-existing aboriginals.

Whatever the conclusions from the last study, the popular idea must be rejected of a single African mitochondrial Eve from whom all modern individuals are descended. Rather, all mtDNA variants now present in human populations are derived from an ancestral molecule borne by a female who lived maybe 200,000 years ago (depending on the study); that is, the extant mtDNA alleles coalesce to a single ancestral molecule then extant (see Fig. 3.3), perhaps in a population bottleneck such that her contemporaries provided no descendants surviving down to present time (Klein, Takahata, & Ayala, 1993). It should, however, be noted that there

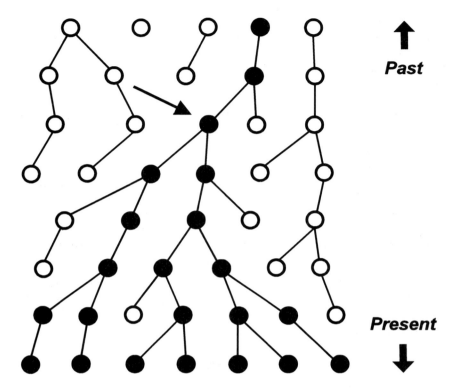

FIG. 3.3 An illustration of the principle that all contemporary mtDNA types must trace back to a single ancestor. The solid circles indicate the path of descent from the ancestor (arrow) to the present generation (or, alternatively, the path of coalescence from the present population of mtDNA types to the ancestor). Empty circles represent mtDNA types that went extinct. Though the contemporary mtDNA types ultimately trace back to a single ancestor, note that other individuals coexisted with the mtDNA ancestor, and that the mtDNA ancestor also had ancestors. From Stoneking, M., DNA and recent human evolution, *Evolutionary Anthropology*, 1993, *2*, 60–73. Copyright © (1993, Wiley-Liss), reprinted by permission of Wiley-Liss, Inc., a subsidiary of John Wiley & Sons, Inc.

are occasional dissenting voices who deny the occurrence of population bottlenecks (Ayala, 1995) or who support the idea of multiregional evolution (Wolpoff, 1989). Nor is it clear whether, if there was replacement of an existing archaic population by new "modern" arrivals, such replacement was "clean", or whether some interbreeding might still have occurred; such a possibility is perhaps most probable in Australasia (Cavalli-Sforza, Menozzi, & Piazza, 1994).

If there was in fact a mitochondrial Eve, was there perhaps also a (nuclear) Adam? Dorit, Akashi, and Gilbert (1995) sequenced part of a gene on the Y chromosome, which determines maleness and is transmitted only through the paternal line. It offers molecular anthropologists the equivalent of mtDNA for males (Lewin, 1995b). They concluded that modern humans originated recently, around 270,000 years ago, a figure fitting well with the mtDNA values (and see also Pääbo, 1995). A somewhat more recent figure (around 190,000 years ago) was obtained from an analysis of the Y chromosome by Hammer (1995).

In summary, four lines of genetic evidence seem to support a recent out-of-Africa model (and see also Relethford, 1995):

- the relative degree of *among-group* variation in human species today is comparatively low;
- many traits show higher levels of *within-group* variation in populations from sub-Saharan Africa;
- genetic distances show sub-Saharan African populations are the most genetically divergent;
- the estimated average effective population size of human species over the past 100 to 200 thousand years is very small.

The molecular-biological study of human origins and diversity (see Fig. 3.4) has until now depended upon analyses from living individuals drawn

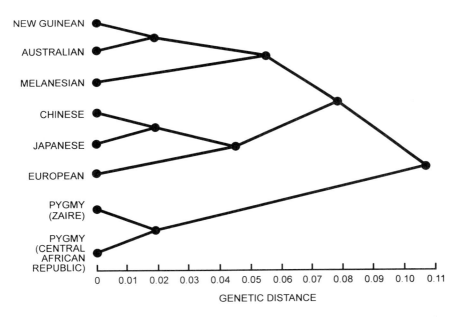

FIG. 3.4. Family trees derived from gene frequencies constructed for various populations of the world, based on the work of Joanna Mountain and colleagues at Stanford University. From Renfrew, C., World linguistic diversity, *Scientific American*, 1994, *1*, 104–110. Copyright © (1994) by Scientific American, Inc. All rights reserved.

from various populations. Clearly, sample material contemporary with archaeological finds would greatly expedite research. Soon after the polymerase chain reaction made it possible to amplify tiny samples of DNA, spectacular reports appeared of DNA tens of millions of years old (Williams, 1995). DNA, of course, degrades, via hydrolysis and loss of purines, one of the building blocks of the molecule. How long can DNA samples last, even when encased in materials such as amber, which will enormously reduce but may not totally eliminate oxidative damage? To date, compression fossils of leaves from Idaho have yielded DNA dated to around 17 million years, whereas insects in Dominican amber have provided material dated to between 25 and 30 million years of age. A weevil from Lebanese amber yielded DNA dated to around 135 million years, and there are reports of dinosaur DNA of more than 65 million years. Whether or not this material is authenticated and validated, it is likely that before too long we shall be able to sequence DNA from archaeological specimens of at least some of our more immediate ancestors.

MIGRATION AND EXPANSION

Migrations and expansions have many driving forces, apart from climate change during a period of Pleistocene instability (Cavalli-Sforza, Menozzi, & Piazza, 1993). They may stem from innovations—biological, technical, or cultural. Increasing availability of food may lead to population increase, the need to expand, new opportunities, and so to new growth. The radial rate of population expansion depends on population growth rate and migration rate; 1 kilometre (km) per year may not be uncommon. Populations differentiate genetically from their neighbours because of divergence, owing to random genetic drift as well as natural selection to different environments. Ancient migrations can often be detected in the patterns of genetic variation in modern populations. There may often be rapid change in a given locus, owing to new arrivals and new opportunities, followed by long periods of stasis. This, of course, is the classic picture of punctuated evolution. In the past 60,000 years, rafts, boats, and navigation have been used to populate Australia and the islands of the Pacific. (A date between 53 and 60 thousand years ago seems secure, see Roberts, Jones, Spooner et al., 1994, for arrivals in Australia.) On the whole, the genetic evidence favors the idea that *people*, rather than *ideas*, diffuse and spread (Cavalli-Sforza et al., 1993; though see also Renfrew, 1994).

SUMMARY AND CONCLUSIONS

Homo habilis, the first species of the genus *Homo*, had a larger brain two million years ago than any prior australopithecine, and was probably the first hominid to rely extensively on tools. Brain expansion was particularly marked in prefrontal "strategic" and "executive" regions, and in temporo-parietal regions that were at least subsequently involved in speech. Expansion continued two million years ago through *Homo erectus* and/or its possible African "equivalent" *Homo ergaster*, though debate continues about the existence, unity, and relatedness of all three taxa, and where they lie on our evolutionary trajectory. Nor is it clear that *Homo erectus* was the first to leave Africa. Indeed, three waves of emigration now seem feasible, culminating with *Homo sapiens sapiens*. The Acheulian lithic assembly came to replace the Oldowan associated with *Homo habilis*, itself to be replaced with the Mousterian of the later Neanderthals, who appeared a quarter of a million years ago. The latter were the first to penetrate the truly cold regions of Eurasia, and to provide evidence of a complex society and culture; they may have developed from an archaic form of *Homo sapiens* perhaps to be identified as *Homo heidelbergensis*.

Archaic *Homo sapiens* emerged in Africa between half and three-quarters of a million years ago, and may have been the common ancestors of the Neanderthals and *Homo sapiens sapiens*. The latter, anatomically modern humans, emerged in Africa (according to a majority out-of-Africa viewpoint supported by molecular genetics) between one and two hundred thousand years ago, spreading to much of the rest of the Old World around the latter date. According to the other minority (multiregional) viewpoint, the roots of all modern peoples lie much deeper in local *erectus* populations. Neanderthals and moderns seem to have coexisted, or alternated (though maybe not interbred) with each other for a very long time in the near East, though in western Europe replacement, when it came around 35,000 years ago, was relatively rapid. Superior technology, culture, and perhaps even language may have been responsible.

FURTHER READINGS

Ayala, F.J. (1995). The myth of Eve: Molecular biology and human origins. *Science, 270,* 1930–1936.

Ayala, F.J., Escalante, A., O'hUigin, C., & Klein, J. (1994). Molecular genetics of speciation and human origins. *Proceedings of the National Academy of Sciences, 91,* 6787–6794.

Bar-Yosef, O., & Vandermeersch, B. (1993). Modern humans in the Levant. *Scientific American, April,* 64–70.

Cavalli-Sforza, L.L., & Cavalli-Sforza, F. (1995). *The great human diasporas: A history of diversity and evolution.* Reading, MA: Addison-Wesley.

Cavalli-Sforza, L.L. Piazza, A., & Menozzi, P. (1994). *The history and geography of human genes.* Princeton, NJ: Princeton University Press.

Foley, R. *Humans before humanity.* (1995). Oxford: Blackwell.

Harpending, H.C., Sherry, S.T., Rogers, A.R., & Stoneking, M. (1993). The genetic structure of ancient human populations. *Current Anthropology, 34,* 483–496.

Lahr, M.M. (1994). The multiregional model of modern human origins: A reassessment of its morphological basis. *Journal of Human Evolution, 26,* 23–56.

Lewin, R. (1993). *The origin of modern humans.* New York: Freeman.

Mellars, P. (1996). *The Neanderthal Legacy: An archaeological perspective from Western Europe.* Princeton, NJ: Princeton University Press.

Relethford, J. H. (1995). Genetics and modern human origins. *Evolutionary Anthropology, 4,* 53–63.

Ruvolo, M., Pan, D., Zehr, S., Goldberg, T., Disotell, T.R., & von Dornum, M. (1994). Gene trees and hominid phylogeny. *Proceedings of the National Academy of Sciences, 91,* 8900–8904.

Shreeve, J. (1995). *The Neanderthal enigma: Solving the mystery of human origins.* New York: Morrow.

Stoneking, M. (1993). DNA and recent human evolution. *Evolutionary Anthropology, 2,* 60–73.

Stringer, C. B., & Gamble, C. (1993). *In search of the Neanderthals: solving the puzzle of human origins.* London: Thames & Hudson.

Stringer, C.B., & McKie, R. (1996). *African exodus: The origins of modern humanity.* London: Cape.

Tattersall, I. (1995). *The fossil trail.* Oxford: Oxford University Press.

von Haeseler, A., Sajantila, A., and Pääbo, S. (1996). The genetical archaeology of the human genome. *Nature Genetics, 14,* 135–140.

Wilson, A.C., & Cann, R.L. (1992). The recent African genesis of humans. *Scientific American,* April, 22–33.

Wolpoff, M., & Caspari, R. (1996). *Race and human evolution.* New York: Simon & Schuster.

Wood, B. (1992). Origin and evolution of the genus Homo. *Nature, 355,* 783–790.

CHAPTER FOUR

Art, culture and prehistory

Art, like language, is seen as a quintessentially human attribute and activity, though, as with so many other supposedly uniquely human characteristics, we can probably detect its precursors in the chimpanzee. When did a truly aesthetic sense first emerge? In this chapter we discuss the evidence for *Homo erectus* and Neanderthal art, the "cultural explosion" of the European Upper Palaeolithic, evidence for art and culture among anatomically modern humans elsewhere and possibly earlier, why we engage in art, and what are the psychological principles that may operate during such activities.

THE ART AND CULTURE OF THE MOUSTERIAN AND ACHEULIAN

From a human perspective it is often difficult to avoid imputing aesthetic sensibilities to the behavior of certain nonhuman species. In Australia, the male bower-bird (of various genera) collects colorful objects (typically blue) such as shells, petals, and pieces of paper or plastic, and with them decorates a "bower", a construction of vegetation, with which to woo passing females. If we view art and aesthetics as being ends in themselves, rather than (as here) means to an (reproductive) end, clearly the two forms of behavior, avian and human, have little in common. Even human decoration of course can be functional, to designate membership of a tribe, clan, or even football team. On the other side of the coin bodily decoration such as painting or tattooing, which may seem to serve a purely aesthetic purpose, may leave little trace in the archaeological record; the presence of ochre in an inhumation may suggest such decoration, and, very occasionally, as with natural mummification through aridity, actual tattooing may be preserved. Bodily distortions, such as foot- or head-binding, or the wearing of neck rings, do of course leave skeletal traces.

There is a reluctance among many archaeologists to accept evidence for an aesthetic sense among humans prior to the (western European) Upper Palaeolithic "creative explosion" of rock art and artefacts between 35,000 and 40,000 years ago; this date coincides with the apparently sudden appearance of anatomically modern humans in that region, and a technology of considerable sophistication. Why, then, is there so little evidence of comparable activity among apparently similar anatomically modern humans in central Europe, the Near East, Africa, or the Mediterranean during the preceding tens of millennia? Many would reject the idea of symbolic activity occurring before the appearance of anatomically modern people in the Upper Palaeolithic (Chase & Dibble, 1987), while accepting that there is evidence of an *aesthetic* sense in the Lower Palaeolithic; this is apparently indicated in the pleasing symmetry, which far surpasses functional requirements, of biface tools in the Acheulian, the apparent use of haematite and ochre, the various manuports, *objets trouvés* and so on of rock crystals, fossils, and pebbles naturally shaped to resemble other objects.

What, then, is the evidence for artistic, aesthetic, or even symbolic precedents in the earlier cultures of the Neanderthals, archaic *Homo sapiens*, or even *Homo erectus*? Acheulian flint hand axes have been found constructed around Cretaceous fossils that have been preserved in a prominent and aesthetically pleasing location (Oakley, 1981). A scoria pebble (see Fig. 4.1) from an Acheulian occupation site of Berkhat Ram on the Golan Heights has been found in the naturally occurring shape of a female figure (Goren-Inbar & Peltz, 1995) with the possible addition of lines and grooves to accentuate its likeness (Schepartz, 1993). Nevertheless most evidence is nonrepresentational, and other explanations are possible (Noble & Davidson, 1996).

Ochre seems to have been collected (and therefore perhaps used for personal or object decoration) 300,000 years ago in the Acheulian of several regions in Europe (Marshack, 1989a). From the same period beautifully shaped and carved spears of fire-hardened wood have been reported, as also have bones apparently intentionally engraved with geometric designs (Bahn & Vertut, 1988). Microwear analysis of tools seems to indicate that they had been used to work skins and for boring and reaming (Marshack, 1991).

In the Middle Palaeolithic (the Mousterian culture of the Neanderthals, see e.g. Mellars, 1996, though we should note that the people of the Middle Palaeolithic were not inevitably Neanderthals, and not all Neanderthals

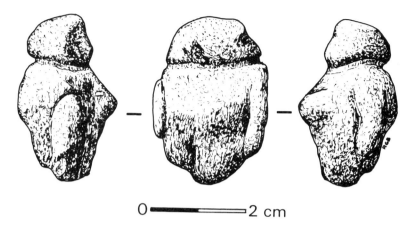

0 ⟺========⟹2 cm

FIG. 4.1. A scoria pebble figure (female) from the Acheulian site of Berekhat Ram, Israel. Courtesy of Robert Bednarik.

belonged to the Middle Palaeolithic) the archaeological record becomes richer and more evocative; however, we do not know to what extent this reflects better preservation of more recent material, despite the tendency still to dehumanize this taxon as incompetent at language and symbolic thought, incapable of anticipating expediency, lacking in society, aesthetics, symbolism, or culture. There is nevertheless a swing nowadays to accepting that the Neanderthals may not have been so very different from ourselves in their genetic capacity for cultural behavior, and that they may well have enjoyed significant levels of symbolism, language, social structure, conceptual ability, technology, and maybe even art (Bednarik, 1995; Hayden, 1993). They were effective hunters, and the fact that they hafted their tools itself indicates foresight and the possession of mental templates of tool design. (Boëda, Connan, Dessort et al., 1996, report a probable Mousterian scraper and Levallois flake at the Umm el Tlel site in Syria, and dated to more than 36,000 years ago, with remains of bituminous hafting adhesive that had been subjected to very high temperature—the earliest example of such use or treatment.)

Composite use by Neanderthals of different materials shaped to predetermined specifications, and their patterns of procurement, similarly suggest planning, organization, and economic rationalization. There are now numerous records of bone points, awls, oval-ochered bone plaques, finely incised lines and zig-zags, and pendants drilled and prepared from teeth and phalanges (Hayden, 1993; Marshack, 1989a) (see Fig. 4.2). In many respects their tool-making standards cannot easily be achieved today, and the comparatively infrequent finds nowadays may merely reflect the

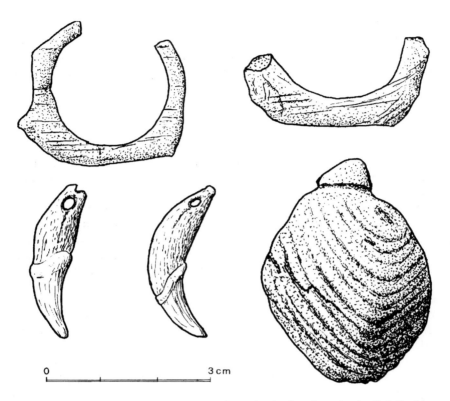

FIG. 4.2 Two ivory ring fragments, two perforated animal teeth, and a fossil shell with an artificial groove for attachment. Châtelperronian, Grotte du Renne, Arcy-sur-Cure, France. These objects were used, and almost certainly made, by Neanderthals. Courtesy of Robert Bednarik.

comparatively infrequent needs of the time (though see Davidson, 1990, 1991). Rare discoveries of preserved *wooden* objects resembling modern domestic implements (Carbonell & Castro-Curel, 1992) are tantalizing suggestions of what might have been lost.

An even earlier indication of technological and cognitive sophistication comes from a fragment of a polished plank of willow wood from the Acheulian deposit of Gesher Benot Ya'aqov, dated between 240 and 730,000 years ago, perhaps the earliest known, probably utilitarian artefact of its kind (Belitzky, Goren-Inbar, & Werker, 1991). Also present, presumably as pleasing nonutilitarian objects (a useful definition of art and aesthetics, perhaps), were two beadlike crinoid fossils with naturally occurring central perforations, and some quartz crystals (Goren-Inbar, Lewy, & Kislev, 1991). At the time of writing, Thieme (1997; and see commentary by Dennell, 1997) reports the oldest known (at 400,000 years) complete hunting weapons yet found, from the Middle Pleistocene Reinsdorf Interglacial, in Schöningen, Germany. These are a set of wooden throwing spears of sophisticated design and patterned like modern javelins, with the maximum thickness and weight at the front, and long tapering tails, indicating their use as projectiles rather than as thrusting spears. Their association with butchered horse remains, a possible hearth, and with wooden "handles"(?) cut with diagonal grooves as if to take flint flakes and so constitute a composite tool, all suggest systematic hunting and butchering, and the application of foresight, planning, and appropriate technology: We may well have to revise our current thinking about early human (and especially pre-Neanderthal European) behavior and culture.

A similar reassessment may be indicated by the recent report (Waters, Forman, & Pierson, 1997; see Holden, 1997, for commentary) of Lower Palaeolithic artefacts at Diring Yuriakh, Siberia, 61° North, and dated to more than 260,000 years ago. Whoever these early people were—and in northern China *Homo erectus* was certainly intelligent enough to survive 400,000 years ago in a cold climate with the aid of fire—they again must have been far more intelligent and resourceful than previously thought.

Neanderthal use of ritual is hotly debated (Chase & Dibble, 1987; Gargett, 1989), and evidence comes mostly from burials. Much of the taphonomic controversy relates to whether such burials were intentional or the result of natural processes, and, if deliberate, whether they took place for spiritual, religious, or ritual reasons, or merely for purposes of hygiene; after all, many species of mammal, for example horses and rabbits, naturally defecate only in certain set regions of their home ranges. There are, of course, many anecdotal and poorly documented accounts in the animal literature of chimpanzees displaying expressions of horror at the sight of a dead conspecific, of undergoing apparent depression and grief on the loss of a close relative (Goodall, 1989), and of elephants covering their dead with earth and boughs, and appearing to display behaviors reminiscent of mourning (Douglas-Hamilton & Douglas-Hamilton, 1975; Joubert, 1991). Burial with flowers, reported from the Mousterian at Shanidar cave (Iraq), may just be wind or animal transport of plant material. Apparent stone arrangements may be accidental or the result of the organizing power of the observer's perceptual system. Although some would regard as at best tenuous the evidence so far proffered for deliberate ritualistic Neanderthal burials (Gargett, 1989), or for Mousterian care for the infirm or injured on the basis of the apparently prolonged survival of so many previously lamed, crippled, blind, toothless, aged, or malformed individuals (Dettwyler, 1991), others (Hayden, 1993) do see ritual as then beginning in the human record. Thus burials (with a characteristic sex ratio) do seem to have taken place in deliberately constructed and preferentially oriented (east–west) depressions, along with grave goods of food offerings, ochre, skulls and tusks. The discovery (Akazawa, Muhesen, Dodo et al., 1995) of a Neanderthal infant apparently deliberately buried at the Dederiyeh cave in Syria sheds further light on this issue. The infant was found *in situ* in the Mousterian deposit, lying on its back with arms extended and legs flexed, indicating intentional burial. A subrectangular limestone slab at the top of the head and a small piece of triangular flint just on the heart completed the picture (see Fig. 4.3).

The adoption of fire by hominids originating from the tropics clearly assisted colonization of colder, higher latitudes in Eurasia, especially during global cooling, though evidence described in previous chapters might suggest a very early arrival in these regions, when fire was unlikely to have been utilized. Fire, in addition to providing warmth, protection against predators, and the ability to modify and detoxify food, would have had a major social impact. Thus in the daytime (smoke) and at night (light) it would have permitted signaling, and at night the campfire may well have provided a major impetus for language development, the transmission of cultural knowledge, and the manufacture of artefacts.

James (1989) critically reviews the archaeological evidence for the deliberate use of fire by early hominids. Natural processes (burned tree stumps in a clay soil from a bush fire, followed by local mineral deposition) can simulate a hearth, and earlier sites can be revisited and occupied by later

FIG. 4.3 Burial of Neanderthal (Dederiyeh) infant. Note limestone slab (top right) at top of head, and artefactual flint (above position of heart) to right of vertebrae. Courtesy of Takeru Akazawa.

visitors. While a securely dated hearth to confine or enhance the fire is clearly the best evidence we can hope for, often all we have to go on are burned soil layers, ash, fire-cracked rocks, and the charred remains of bones, shells, and tools, all of which may be adventitious. Initially, natural ground fires, which are common after lightning strikes in savannah country, may have been opportunistically captured. Fairly convincing evidence for deliberate use of fire has been reported from several sites in China between 400,000 and 500,000 years ago (James, 1989), though claims of 1,000,000 or more years ago have been made for Southeast Asia (Pope, 1991) and South Africa (Sillen & Brain, 1990), presumably by *Homo erectus*. However, Rigaud, Simek, and Thierry (1995) argue that few of these finds stand up to modern scrutiny, the source of the burning being equivocal and the integrity of the site being generally questionable. The earliest European findings, again without hearths, may also date to around 400,000 or more years ago (and see also Bolter, 1995; Patel, 1995; Thieme, 1997). However, Rigaud et al. (1995) are happy that modern methods confirm intentional use of fire at least as early as the Mousterian Middle Palaeolithic.

Debate also continues concerning the paucity of evidence for structured patterns of occupation by Neanderthals. Mostly, shelters appear to be simple windbreaks, or to consist of posts leaning against a rock wall, with a brush or hide covering. Structures made of mammoth bones and of reindeer antlers have been reported from the Ukraine dating to 40,000 or more years ago (Bahn & Vertut, 1988). Otherwise, there is evidence of rock circles with a central post hole, and suggestions of paving in wet areas of caves, dry stone walls separating living or occupation areas, pits on lake shores, constructed hearths, bone dumps on the periphery of habitation zones, etc. (Hayden, 1993).

In summary, there does seem to be something intangibly different about the behavior of Neanderthals, but it is biologically subtle (Hayden, 1993); they show evidence of planning, forethought, abstraction, learning, and human characteristics at least to a basic level. They are associated with bone tools, blades, sewn clothing (as indicated by awls), mobile art, an aesthetic sense, burials, and community living. However, their lifestyle was spartan, primitive, and basic. These aspects may have been apparent quite early, in the contrasting lifestyles of the two populations, Neanderthal and anatomically modern *Homo sapiens sapiens*, who inhabited the Levant region of the eastern Mediterranean between 120,000 and 45,000 years ago (Trinkaus, 1994). Superficially, the two populations left very similar cultural remains, both using similar stone tools, perhaps burying their dead and processing their food in apparently similar ways. The two groups may have alternated occupation in the region, as a function of climate changes. During periods of intense cold, Neanderthals may have escaped south from frozen Europe to the relative warmth of the Levant, while *Homo sapiens sapiens* may have migrated to north Africa during such periods, both groups returning to their places of origin during periods of warming (Bunney, 1994). However, the culture of the modern people in the Levant was subtly more complex, and they may have spent longer periods in their home bases, whereas the Neanderthals seem to have been more energetically active in foraging patterns, as indicated by skeletal remains, especially the femoral neck-shaft angle, and the relative abundance of commensal rodents during cave occupation by one or other group. Indeed, the frequency of healed fractures in Neanderthal skeletons certainly testifies to a level of activity and risk-taking (or incompetence?) that exceeded that of *Homo sapiens sapiens*; it might or might not also indicate a capacity for care and nurturing of injured individuals as shown by modern humans.

THE ART OF THE EUROPEAN UPPER PALAEOLITHIC

A particularly rapid transition from older forms of culture is evident in Europe, a transition that is clearly compatible with the arrival 40,000 years ago of anatomically modern peoples. Seasonally migrating herds of horses, bison, aurochs, ibex, woolly mammoths, and rhinoceros along a fertile network of richly grassed valleys may have provided the necessary hospitality, in a largely hostile Ice-Age world, for the development of a critical cultural mass for ushering in the Aurignacian Upper Palaeolithic revolution of western Europe. In this region the transition indeed seems abrupt (though see White, 1992), and until very recently the appearance of new technologies like prismatic blade cores, specialized bone tools, etc., were only known from the beginning of the Upper Palaeolithic in Europe and perhaps, to a lesser extent, in central Asia, Siberia, and the Near East between 40,000 and 30,000 years ago. However, Yellen, Brooks, Cornelissen et al. (1995) report evidence in the Western Rift Valley of Zaire of a well developed bone industry of 90,000 years ago or older, including barbed points (see Fig. 4.4), and evidence of complex subsistence specialization and behavioral competence consistent with Upper Palaeolithic *Homo sapiens sapiens*. Moreover, McBrearty (cited by Gutin, 1995) reports long, thin blades (10 cm in length, less than 1 cm thick) from the Kapthurin formation near Kenya's Lake Baringo, which she dates to 240,000 years ago. The Middle Stone Age artefacts, though not as complex as those of the European Upper Palaeolithic, nevertheless seem worthy precursors. Were these made by anatomically modern *Homo sapiens*? Early members of the species have been found in Ethiopia and South Africa from at least 130,000 years ago. Could they have been around 100,000 years earlier?

Straus (1995) also questions the abruptness of the replacement of the Mousterian Middle Palaeolithic by the innovative Upper Palaeolithic in

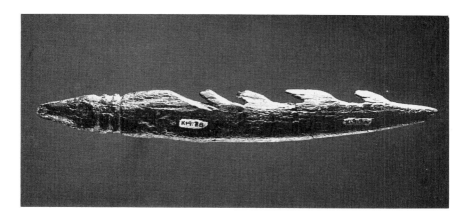

FIG. 4.4 Worked-bone artefact dated to around 90,000 years ago from Zaire (Upper Semliki River). This barbed figure indicates a behavioral competence consistent with the much later (European) Upper Palaeolithic. Figure courtesy of J.E. Yellen and Chip Clark.

Europe, opting for a more mosaic scenario, with significant production of true blades, considered to be characteristic of the Upper Palaeolithic, in Middle Palaeolithic contexts, some of considerable antiquity. Thus burins, endscrapers, perforators, backed and truncated flakes and blades are regular components of many Mousterian assemblages. There is apparent continuity, moreover, between Middle and Early Upper Palaeolithic in Europe in long-distance transport of lithic raw materials, indicating mobility and advance planning. Nor did the classic characteristics of the Upper Palaeolithic (blades, endscrapers, burins, and other light-weight lithic tools; ivory, bone, or antler tools and weapon tips; stone, tooth, or shell beads, and other objects of ornament and art) erupt perhaps quite as abruptly as often is thought during the latter part of the Würm Interpleniglacial (the Würm Interstadial), between 40 and 30,000 years ago, under conditions that were intermediate between full glacial and interglacial ones. (Increased cooling occurred after 30,000 years ago, to the Last Glacial Maximum around 18,000 years ago. Around 13,000 years ago, at the outset of the Bölling oscillation, temperatures rose abruptly, though the Ice Age was not truly over until about 10,000 years ago, Straus, 1995.)

Nor in this context should we ignore the indigenous cultures of Australia, where the quality, quantity, and antiquity may also rival that of Europe (see Fig. 4.5). Indeed, humans arrived in Australia at least 60,000 years ago, and were using the natural-pigment haematite and red and yellow ochres from the very beginning (Roberts, Jones, Spooner et al., 1994; see also Morrell, 1995). Palaeoecological evidence suggests human colonization of Australia before or coincident with the Last Interglacial 125,000 years ago, either by

FIG. 4.5   Parietal (rock) art from near Laura, north Queensland, Australia.

modern or archaic humans, and there are now reports (Fullagar, Price, & Head, 1996; see also Holden, 1996) of stone artefacts at Jinmium rock shelter, Northern Territory, from sediments dated by thermoluminescence to greater than 116,000 years ago, with artistic activity inferred from ochre dating between 75,000 and 116,000 years ago, and rock engravings (cupules) preceding 58,000 years ago. If confirmed, these findings would imply either a very early arrival of anatomically modern humans in Australia, or a previously unsuspected capacity for sea travel, technology, and culture in archaic precursors. Nor indeed do we know whether the new Cro-Magnon arrivals in western Europe, who anyway had probably previously coexisted, or at least alternated, with pre-existing Neanderthals for tens of millennia in the Middle East, sharing apparently similar cultural traditions with them, exchanged ideas with indigenous European Neanderthals (Marshack, 1989a) during the disputed Châtelperronian period.

Hublin, Spoor, Braun et al. (1996) throw further light on the question of Neanderthal–CroMagnon interactions in the Châtelperronian, the early Upper Palaeolithic industry known from northern Spain and central and southwestern France, which is so important for understanding the transition from the Middle Palaeolithic. At the French site of Arcy-sur-Cure a skull dated to 34,000 years ago, and representative of the youngest known Neanderthal populations, was found in an archaeological context of a rich bone industry and personal ornaments that included pierced teeth and ivory rings. The semi-circular canals in the labyrinth were found to be typically Neanderthal, smaller and of a different configuration from that of coexisting anatomically modern humans. The strikingly derived nature of the Neanderthal labyrinth and the complete absence of such traits in the modern populations of that time argues against interbreeding and in favor of a species distinction and a reproductive barrier between the two groups. However, the Neanderthals do seem during the Châtelperronian to have acquired cultural elements and ornaments similar to those of the Aurignacian, perhaps by trading rather than by imitation, suggest Hublin et al. (1996), who see the Châtelperronian as resulting from an acculturation process during the two groups' overlapping coexistence.

An interest in cave art and engraved objects first developed in the 19th century, and since then archaeologists, art historians, devoted amateurs, and developmental psychologists have all imposed their own idiosyncratic interpretations, from a largely Eurocentric viewpoint; the Magdalenian galleries of Lascaux received far more attention than the Aurignacian flowering 15,000 years previously, an interval at least as long as from Lascaux and Altamira to Picasso (White, 1992). The earliest fully credible art in Europe dates to more than 43,000 years ago, and by 35,000 years ago (see Fig. 4.6) the Aurignacian was well established. It includes pierced or drilled ivory, bone and soft stone beads, fossil coral, fossil belemnites, jet, haematite, pyrite, and shell, and often is very beautiful, indicative of the attainment of a modern aesthetic "sense". Material is frequently highly standardized and labor intensive. Though teeth and shells were perforated for use as pendants, rotational drilling was far less common than preliminary gouging, thinning, or pecking followed by pressure piercing.

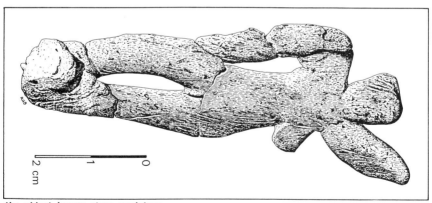

the oldest known stone sculpture

FIG. 4.6. "Venus" of Galbenberg from near Krems, Austria, *c.* 32,000 years before present. Courtesy of R. Bednarik.

Utilitarian and ornamental objects were cut, sawn, ground, carved, polished, perforated, and grooved. Figurative three-dimensional images of ivory, steatite, or schist were reduced by gouging, grinding, and polishing, being finished with fine metallic abrasives of haematite powder. These represented a variety of animals or, more rarely, the human form, or occasionally even "therianthrope" (half-human, half-animal) creatures associated perhaps with cults or ritual (Marshack, 1988).

Sculptures tended to be tucked away in the back of caves or along one wall, and to include only the largest and strongest animal species (mammoth, rhino, bison, lion, bear), and only the adults. Individual slabs were often prepared by abrasion, with representations applied by engraving, pecking, chiselling, and gouging, and marks created that were suggestive of animal spoor, hoof marks, and human vulvae. It is of course easy to invoke sexual or fertility explanations where none may in fact apply, for these and other manifestations, including the increasingly numerous (in the later Gravettian) "Venus" figures, which emphasize breasts, buttocks, hips, and thighs. Indeed, not all the Gravettian Venus figures glorify maternity and fertility, and they may simply be about "womanhood" (Bahn & Vertut, 1988), though as ancient erotica they seem less than successful nowadays. McDermott (1996) discusses their possible role in fertility rituals and as obstetrical and gynaeological self-portraits by women themselves. Flutes made from drilled bird long bones have been reported, indicative of ancient music, and calendrical or notational markings have been suggested (Marshack, 1988); these, if upheld, imply a knowledge of seasonal events, though it must be admitted that such interpretations are hotly debated.

Though, as we saw previously, the classic Magdalenian galleries of Lascaux and Altamira are thought to have long post-dated the early Aurignacian cultural flowering, Clottes (cited by Patel, 1995) and Chauvet, Deschamps, and Hillaire (1996) have reported sophisticated rock paintings (e.g. of rhinoceros and bison) created between 30,000 and 33,000 years ago—images that dispel the idea that the first art was simple and crudely drawn, and only later evolved into more sophisticated images. Cruder paintings were probably made by people without talent. The Chauvet-cave images are noteworthy for the techniques used to represent motion and perspective. Many of the drawings interact, and natural convexities on the rock wall are exploited to convey a three-dimensional impression. Indeed, the cave is noteworthy for the range of species previously unknown in the region's Ice-Age art, and rarely depicted with such flair. How many more such examples await discovery? Can we in fact completely discount the possibility of Neanderthal involvement in very early parietal art? Why is there so little evidence of such art, even by anatomically modern peoples, earlier than 35,000 years ago, in other parts of the world? Did such art evolve slowly but suddenly manifest at the right place (caves, where it might be preserved) and the right time (a critical cultural mass or concentration of appropriately oriented individuals)? Why was it done—art for its own sake, as a form of graffiti, as a personal record of events and experiences, as a rite of passage, for religious significance, shamanism, fertility magic, or for several or all of these reasons? Can we answer these questions by analogy with similar, recent practices of cave art in Africa and Australia? Meighan (1996) addresses these issues from an analysis of contemporary "geoglyphs" in Hawaii, and identifies the following themes:

- an "I was here" message;
- recording of clan symbols—a form perhaps of territorial marking;
- commemoration of events or of the death of notable or loved indiviuals;
- doodling, to while away the time, a form of graffiti, which nevertheless involves some effort and brings some aesthetic satisfaction, at least to the artist. Quite independently, Mulvaney (1996) records the reminiscences of elderly aborigines in the northwest of Australia; they apparently created considerable bodies of such art in rock-shelters while detained during prolonged periods of monsoonal rain—something to do on a rainy day! However, the effort and inconvenient inaccessibility of many of the European Upper Palaeolithic sites, coupled with the eerie quality of the likely experience, does suggest a religious, mystic, or ritual contribution.

What can we learn from the psychology of art?

THE PSYCHOLOGY OF ART, ANCIENT AND RECENT

It is easy, and not always helpful, to invoke commonalities between art and language in terms of abstraction, symbolism, imagery, and visual categorization (Marshack, 1989a,b); such a metaphor or analogy is reminiscent of the equally facile equation that is often made between language and tool use, where commonalities of syntax and recursive embedding are often erroneously invoked. As we saw earlier, and will discuss in further detail later, though similar (but not identical) brain regions do indeed mediate language and manual praxis, skilled manual praxis is far better represented as involving chained, sequential activities without the convoluted and recursive syntactic embedding of language. (Both language and praxis do of course share the commonality of sequence generation.) The enormous and widely admired Franco-Cantabrian parietal paintings of Lascaux and Altamira, dating generally to around the Magdalenian of about 15,000 years ago, clearly represent ideas and may be metaphorical to the extent, for example, of a mammoth signifying strength. However, again, we should be wary of making interpretations based upon modern concepts (White, 1992); nor should we assume that the historical development of art is mirrored in the development of (modern) *children's* art, as a sort of phylogenetic recapitulation. Thus just as Piagettian stages of intellectual development in children have from time to time been invoked in the context of ape intellect (Parker & Gibson, 1979) or of the lithic industries of the early hominids (Wynn, 1989), we should note that not everyone accepts Piagettian theory. However, Gestalt principles of form and closure, adopted from the experimental psychology of visual perception, may not be irrelevant (Halverson, 1992a).

Magdalenian works were created on unprepared rock surfaces by painting, engraving, or low-relief carving on the natural walls, ceilings, or floors of caves and overhanging shelters (parietal art), or on portable (and often easily perishable) material such as bone or ivory or stone plaques (mobiliary art): Much of this will undoubtedly have been lost. Suggestive natural features were often incorporated, such as a curved ridge (for a spine) or a protuberance (for an eye). Indeed, caves, with their convoluted, complex surfaces that can be accentuated by the lighting employed, offer endless opportunities for the perceiver to impose his or her own interpretative meaning (Halverson, 1992b), just as we see images in clouds, frosty window panes, fire, or grained wood panels. Thus, a natural rock feature recalling the back of an animal might lead to the observer-artist completing the image, from memory—an image of a prototypical *concept* of that general animal, rather than a *particular* animal engaged in a *particular* activity. Thus, subject matter (overwhelmingly animal, some humans, few plants, and mostly large edible herbivores like horses and bison, less commonly ibex, mammoth or rhinoceros, and rarely felines, bears, fish, birds, or reptiles) generally represented individuals rather than groups or herds. Situations were typically static rather than dynamic, without scenic background, with the animals usually in profile and mostly in outline. Representations were very economical, and suggestive with a minimum of strokes—cartoon-like, and naturalistic but lacking in photographic realism. Thus an outline generally served as surrogate for a three-dimensional representation. Gestalt principles of figure–ground distinction, closure, grouping, and good continuation tended to be observed, with images represented in standard or canonical form or orientation, so as to reveal the most salient information, with emphasis of distinctive features. Redundancies of color, texture, linear perspective, or completeness of representation all generally were avoided (Halverson, 1992b). Relative size differences, for example between an ibex and a horse, tended to be ignored; linear convergence perspective was absent, and figures were often abbreviated or truncated, perhaps portraying heads without bodies. Though the *production* of representational art, like spoken language (but perhaps not tool use), is an evolved, adaptive human trait that has been transfered to a cultural context, we cannot claim a unique capacity to *comprehend* such material; thus the higher primates can recognize and discriminate between well-executed line drawings, which is not perhaps surprising as such drawings share with three-dimensional objects access to the same receptor mechanisms that are sensitive to luminance differences, boundaries, and changes. Indeed, there is therefore even less evidence that Upper Palaeolithic humans differed perceptually or cognitively from ourselves.

It has of course long been known that apes take a strong and spontaneous interest in playing with painting, though little systematic study seems to have been done, especially in the context of the evolution of a human aesthetic sense. Lenain (1995) notes apes' capacities for introducing variations that appear to be formally relevant and aesthetic, their sense of order and of relevant formal variations, evidence for their form, rhythmicity, and balance, their taste for color contrasts, and their general evidence of visual thinking while engaging in a free and intelligent activity. Similarly Boysen, Berntson, and Prentice (1987) note that chimpanzees do not mark randomly, but pay particular attention to the boundaries of the paper and to the boundaries of predrawn squares. Clearly, at least 5 million years ago the seeds were sown for an artistic sense.

An artist, ancient or modern, in representing an object, typically three-dimensional, must somehow create another, typically two-dimensional, object (unless the latter is sculpted "in the round") that is conceptually equivalent. This is best achieved by representation of a canonical form from a characteristic angle of view (Deregowski, 1995). Thus not all views of an object are equally recognizable. Indeed, with visual agnosia subsequent to brain damage, objects seen from an unusual viewpoint may be particularly hard to recognize (Bradshaw & Mattingley, 1995). Hence artists, ancient or modern, usually choose a predominant, salient, or typical aspect. More than one perspective may be combined so as to include all relevant information, whether it is an ancient engraving on a European rock surface, an Australian aboriginal rock painting, or a modern Picasso (see Fig. 4.7). Thus an Australian crocodile may have, for reasons of typicality, the body as viewed from above, and the head from the side, leading our eyes to a feeling of torsion or unreality, although clearly the salient crocodilian features are well preserved. Though the most informationally economical representation involves boundaries, contours, and transitions (Deregowski, 1995) via outlines, especially at points of directional change or transition, inclusion within these contours of color or texture adds verisimilitude. Such verisimilitude, however, comes at a price; movement or action is more easily represented via the posture of "stick" or "pin" figures, though clearly the *identity* of such figures is then lost. The latter, ultimately, is best represented by three-dimensional sculptures "in the round"; thus Upper Palaeolithic "Venus" figurines are intrinsically capable of representing a particular

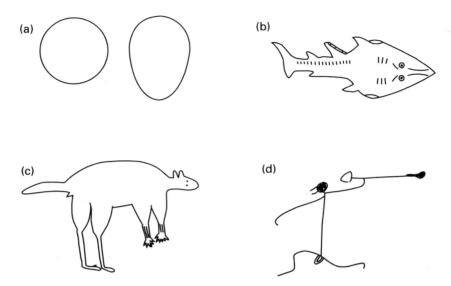

FIG. 4.7.   Typicality and representation in art.
   (a) Two equally legitimate but not equally typical, canonical or meaningful representations of an egg
   (b) Australian aboriginal rock painting from Arnhemland of a shark, with component elements as seen from their own most significant viewpoint (head from above, body from side).
   (c) Redrawn realistic rock painting from near Laura, north Queensland.
   (d) Stick or pin figure of a hunter from the Arnhemland region of northern Australia depicts action.

individual, though there is no evidence that they actually did so. Of course, outline-drawn cartoon sketches in the hands of an expert can achieve the same result in two dimensions.

SUMMARY AND CONCLUSIONS

Prior to the "creative explosion" of art and artefacts in the (western European) Upper Palaeolithic of around 35,000 years ago, there is a relative dearth of evidence for such activity, either in the earlier assemblages of artefacts from (supposedly) anatomically modern *Homo sapiens sapiens*, or from the Neanderthals or *Homo erectus*. Nevertheless, the pleasing symmetry of Acheulian bifaces, the apparent use of haematite and ochre, and the various manuports and *objets trouvés* suggest an aesthetic sense perhaps extending back half a million or more years. In the Neanderthal Mousterian, the record becomes richer and more evocative, and there is a recent tendency to see these peoples as being not so very different from ourselves in their genetic capacity for cultural behavior. In many respects, their tool-making standards cannot easily be achieved today. However, debate continues on their use of ritual. Possession and use of fire would have produced a major cultural impetus, and, though the Neanderthals may have been the first to have constructed hearths, fire has been reported from sites older perhaps than half a million years. Nevertheless, life seems to have been fairly spartan and basic until the European Upper Palaeolithic, and equivalent cultures elsewhere, when there appears to have been an explosive and self-sustaining take-off of culture, artefacts, and art. To what extent do the natural physical properties of matter, and the inherited mechanisms of primate perceptual systems constrain and determine representational art? Can such physical remains tell us anything about the appearance of language? What has the symbolism of art to do with that of language?

FURTHER READINGS

Chase, P.G., & Dibble, H.L. (1987). Middle Palaeolithic symbolism: A review of current evidence and interpretations. *Journal of Anthropological Archaeology, 6*, 263–296.

Chauvet, J.M., Deschamps, E.B., & Hillaire, C. (1996). *Chauvet cave: Discovery of world's oldest paintings.* London: Thames & Hudson.

Deregowski, J.B. (1995). Perception–depiction–perception and communication: A skeleton key to rock art and its significance. *Rock Art Research, 12*, 3–10.

Halverson, J. (1992a). The first pictures: Perceptual foundations of Paleolithic art. *Perception, 21*, 389–404.

Halverson, J. (1992b). Paleolithic art and cognition. *The Journal of Psychology, 126*, 221–236.

Hayden, B. (1993). The cultural capacities of Neandertals: A review and re-evaluation. *Journal of Human Evolution, 24*, 113–146.

Lenain, T. (1995). Ape painting and the problem of the origin of art. *Human Evolution, 10*, 205–215.

McDermott, L. (1996). Self-representation in Upper Paleolithic female figures. *Current Anthropology, 37*, 227–275.

Mellars, P. (1996). *The Neanderthal legacy: An archaeological perspective from western Europe.* Princeton, NJ: Princeton University Press.

Strauss, L.S. (1995). The Upper Paleolithic of Europe: An overview. *Evolutionary Anthropology, 4*, 4–16.

Trinkaus, E., & Shipman, P. (1993). *The Neanderthals: Changing the image of mankind.* New York: Knopf.

White, R. (1992). Beyond art: Toward an understanding of the origins of material representation in Europe. *Annual Review of Anthropology, 21*, 537–564.

CHAPTER FIVE

Language and communication

Language, even more than art, is commonly seen as uniquely human, though the expressive (by nonverbal channels) and receptive (even for speech) communicative capacities of nonhuman species are beginning to pose some very intriguing questions. Languages differentiate and evolve in surprisingly parallel ways to races, as defined in genetic terms, and molecular-biological and linguistic evidence can provide complementary information about our various origins and migrations. In addition to these issues, in this chapter we ask whether there are evolutionary commonalities between propositional speech and primate systems of communication, how language may have evolved, ontogenetic aspects in speech perception, communication by apes with ourselves, the role of gesture, and why apes may be unable to produce articulate speech.

THE COEVOLUTION OF GENOTYPE AND LANGUAGE

The evolutionary or phylogenetic tree of a set of human populations, constructed on the basis of genetic data as described in an earlier chapter, and representing a large part of the world, turns out to resemble very closely a tree based upon linguistic classification (Cavalli-Sforza, Minch, & Mountain, 1992) (see Fig. 5.1). We see a coevolution of language and genes, with similar mechanisms in both for differentiation and diversification. Thus geographic and behavioral isolation that led to different genetic lines seems

population   language group

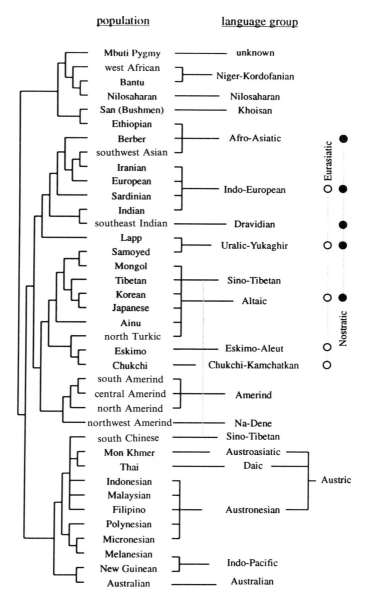

FIG. 5.1. Association between linguistic families of languages spoken by a set of 38 populations, and an evolutionary tree of the same populations derived from genetic data. Reprinted
with permission from Cavalli-Sforza, L.L., Minch, E., & Mountain, J.L., Coevolution of genes
and languages revisited, *Proceedings of the National Academy of Sciences*, 1992, *89*, 5620–5624.

also to have resulted in the development of different linguistic groups. Of course, language transmission from parent to offspring is less clear cut, as we can learn new languages from immigrants or invaders—horizontal transmission, as opposed to the necessarily *vertical* transmission of genes. Thus language replacement can reduce or even eliminate the amount of linguistic–genetic correlation. Conversely, new genetic input is also possible, without language replacement, when immigrants, whether or not they adopt the language of aborigines, nevertheless alter the latter's genes by interbreeding. Generally, however, linguistic differences seem to have tended to act as isolating mechanisms or reproductive barriers, maintaining or even accentuating genetic differences between adjacent populations. In another difference from genes that are constrained to the reproductive cycle via the genome, words can be acquired or modified during an individual's lifetime, and, slang or new technical terms especially, can spread throughout an entire population within a single generation.

THE PREHISTORY OF SPOKEN LANGUAGE

We have seen that all mtDNA types in contemporary populations may be traced back to a common origin, a divergence point that can be dated from a knowledge of substitution rates. We have also seen that linguistic and phylogenetic trees can be constructed that overlap remarkably, and that language "inheritance" obeys similar principles to those operating in the molecular realm. Can we therefore similarly trace the ancestry of language, from the babble (and Babel) of extant tongues back to a common, dateable origin? Psammetichus (Psamtik) the 7th-century BC Egyptian pharaoh, according to the 5th-century BC Greek historian Herodotus, conducted the first empirical study to determine the answer, with a procedure that would not get past a modern ethics committee. He had two newborns reared in isolation until the first word they uttered was heard, "bekos", or "bread" in Phrygian, an Anatolian language. He concluded that Phrygian was the world's first language (Renfrew, 1994). However, by the 19th century, speculation on the origins of language had become so interminable that the Société de Linguistique de Paris banned further discussion in 1865 (Kendon, 1991). However, in the same way that extant populations may be studied using the techniques of molecular genetics, so may living or recorded languages be analysed to determine commonalities and lines of descent from a common ancestor. In 1786, in British India, Sir William Jones noted affinities, which he recognized as indicating common descent between Sanskrit (the classical language of India), Persian, Greek, Latin, and Gothic. His observations laid the groundwork for the reconstruction of ancestral Indo-European, from which are derived most European languages and many spoken in western and central Asia, and whose speakers number nearly half the world's population. Affinities are also evident between other (non-Indo-European) tongues, leading to the recognition of more superfamilies similar and parallel to Indo-European, though the latter, with speakers of the original ancestral language living 6,000 or more years ago, perhaps in the region of Asia Minor or the Black Sea, is the best known and understood. From the reconstructed vocabulary, the speakers were Neolithic agriculturalists (Dolgopolsky, 1995).

Yet earlier, around 15,000 years ago, Nostratic may have been the antecedent of Indo-European, Altaic (Turkish and Mongolian), Dravidian (southern Indian), Uralic (Finnish and Samoyed), Afro-Asiatic (Berber and Arabic), and Kartvelian (south Caucasian). Reconstructions of Nostratic have been proposed, amounting to several hundred words corresponding to common objects and concepts, such as parts of the body, sun and moon, personal pronouns, animals, and so on. The "lexicon" indicates that the speakers were hunter-gatherers, lacking agriculture but possessing domestic animals such as the dog. Indeed, the oldest domestic dog bones have been dated to that period. Nostratic would later have split into the Afro-Asiatic group of languages, whose speakers, judging by the proposed vocabulary, built fortifications, cultivated, marketed, and used the bow. Proto-Semitic may have arisen around 9,000 years ago, and provided many loan words to the Indo-Europeans, another Nostratic off-shoot, which in turn fragmented about 5,000 years ago into Indo-Iranian, Celt, Balt, Slav, Greek, Italic, and Germanic peoples, all of whom migrated to the sites of their present homelands (see e.g. Dolgopolsky, 1995; Ruhlen, 1994).

If Nostratic is a super-superfamily which includes the superfamilies Indo-European, Altaic and so on, other such super-superfamilies have also been proposed to parallel Nostratic. These include (and see Shevoroshkin, 1990) Dene-(or Sino-)Caucasian of 14,000 years ago, which is composed of Sino-Tibetan (Chinese), Yeniseian (Siberian), and Caucasian (Etruscan and Sumerian, both now extinct, and Basque). Likewise in the New World all North American languages have been classified into just three, Amerind, Na-Dene, and Eskimo-Aleut, corresponding to three migrations which occurred after 12,500 years ago (Ruhlen, 1995), and that match three distributions of gene frequencies (Cavalli-Sforza, Menozzi, & Piazza, 1994). Indeed, the recent discovery of a very early culture in the Brazilian Amazon (Roosevelt, da Costa, Machado et al., 1996), contemporary with the earliest Palaeoindians in North America, is once again throwing open the question as to when and how many were the early immigrations into the New World. Thus the accepted view on the peopling of the Americas holds that it was made from eastern Asia, via the Bering Strait along a coastal tundra that developed during the lowered sea levels of the Pleistocene glaciation. The ancestors of today's native Americans initially settled in the high plains of North America, only later filtering down to South America. These early settlers were the Clovis people, named after the type locality of their stone tools, which have been dated to just over 11,000 years ago (Meltzer, 1995a). However, a similar date now emerges for what looks like a flourishing and quite different Amazonian culture.

Even further back, Nostratic, Dene-(Sino-)Caucasian, Na-Dene, and Amerind may be paralleled with proto-Australian, Austro-Asiatic, Thai, Austronesian (Indonesian, Philippine, and Pacific Island), and Congo-Saharan (central and north African), all of which may have descended from an original tongue spoken around 35,000 years ago, and of which up to 200 words may have been reconstructed (Miller, 1981; Ruhlen, 1994, 1995).

LANGUAGE, SPEECH, AND COMMUNICATION

We should not interchangeably use the terms speech, language, communication, and vocalization (Duchin, 1990). The last may merely involve emotional expression, though such expression may be of communicatory value to conspecifics. Language involves modalities additional to speech, such as writing, sign, and maybe gesture. Speech is a form of communicatory articulation apparently unique to our species, and as one mode of realizing language it involves possibly unique peripheral and central adaptations. In addition to speech and language we retain older, nonverbal modes of communication for emotions such as fear, anger, distress, sorrow, happiness, and so on, which may be conveyed by vocalizations, expressions, or gestures. Though such communication is clearly limbic in origin, we should not discount a limbic contribution to and a subcortical (basal ganglia and thalamic) modulation of speech itself. Indeed, there are interesting comparisons between language and nonverbal, emotional communication. The former is discrete, categorical, and essentially discontinuous, whereas the latter is analogous, graded, and continuous. The former has to be learned, even though up to a certain age we are predisposed very rapidly to acquire it, whereas emotional expressions are universal and apparently "hard-wired" (Burling, 1993). There is of course an *inherited* component even to language—our capacity to acquire it—together with a *learned* component even to expressions—our ability to feign them in theatricals. Moreover, both systems involve both auditory and visual signaling. Furthermore, we add to the speech signal emotional and prosodic qualities of emphasis, stress, and intonation, qualities that, as we shall, see probably originate in different regions of the brain from where the speech signal is elaborated. Indeed, in parallel with the articulatory speech signal we also often add, with our hands, iconic gestures of size, shape, location, number, frequency, and emphasis. Language is propositional, open ended, and infinitely variable, and removed from its referent, unlike our nonverbal communication, which typically refers to the present, not to the past, future, or what is absent, and can only be feigned with some difficulty. Above all, our nonverbal channels of communication are devoid of syntax, using automatic, graded, nonpropositional, and noncategorical signals, which are well adapted for conveying subtle emotional nuances.

We shall later discuss whether there are evolutionary commonalities or possible evolutionary continua between propositional speech and nonverbal or emotional expression, but should note at this point that the gulf between our own species and the rest of the animal kingdom with respect to language, tool behavior, and even (self-) consciousness is rapidly closing. We should also note that the relationship between language and thought is unclear: Do we always think and problem-solve verbally via our first language if multilingual, or can (and do) we engage in nonverbal problem-solving when, for example, playing chess or designing complex constructions? There is no evidence that global aphasics, who have lost all power of speech, comprehensional or expressive, cannot solve problems or play board games. Be that as it may, speech is certainly our most complex skill, a unique tool for modeling reality and mentally "trying things out" in a logical manner (whether or not in the event we always *behave* logically); on the whole it is automatic, unconscious, and cognitively impenetrable—at least when we employ our "mother tongue". In fact, the very automaticity of what is nevertheless largely driven by specialized cortical areas frees us simultaneously to undertake other conscious actions, which instead are deliberate and monitored.

Language requires the ability to learn to use an arbitrary symbol to represent something not necessarily currently present, in a mutually agreed fashion, in social exchanges with others. The recipients' responses will be quite different from the fixed-action patterns elicited or released by sign stimuli in "lower" organisms, for example, a gull chick pecking at a parent's beak for food (Rumbaugh, Hopkins, Washburn, & Savage-Rumbaugh, 1991). If we had no mouths, we almost certainly would have evolved some other form of language, as evidenced by the spontaneous development of signing by congenitally deaf children who have never been exposed to spoken language. We shall shortly see that although chimpanzees may have a profound, innate capacity to acquire the meanings of hundreds of arbitrary visual symbols, they may nevertheless never fully master human language, or, above all, learn how to *speak*. In part, their incapacity may stem from problems similar to those that, until recently, have plagued designers of automatic translation systems. Thus human communicants depend deeply upon "common sense", tacit knowledge and assumptions mutually shared. Consider the sentence "Mary had a little lamb"; from context and prior experience we know whether she *owned* one, ate some at lunch, or, if a sheep herself, gave birth to one.

There are perhaps six components of human speech (Cutting, 1990). These include:

1. *Phonology*, a largely categorical left-hemisphere aspect involving the speech-related sounds (phonemes, the smallest sound differences that distinguish meaningful utterances). This aspect emphasizes the relationships between the positions adopted by the articulators, and the resulting speech sounds.
2. *Morphology*, the denotative significance of meaningful units (words, or word fragments such as morphemes, which are the smallest individually meaningful elements). Thus phonemes are combined by rule into morphemes, largely under left-hemisphere control.
3. *Syntax*, the grammatical rules to combine morphemic strings into uniquely meaningful propositions, again largely under left-hemisphere control.
4. *Semantics*, the formal meaning of a string of morphemes, to which the left hemisphere may contribute denotative meaning, and the right hemisphere may contribute some connotative or contextual meaning or associations.
5. *Prosodic or suprasegmental aspects*, involving phonological variations within categorical limits, and that do not change denotative meaning, to provide extra, interpretative, connotative meaning. Thus via changes in pitch, rhythm, stress, intonation, posture, and expression, a largely right-hemisphere contribution may be made to the broader aspects of meaning.
6. *Pragmatic aspects*, the practical use to which we may put language, as with jokes, irony, metaphor, sarcasm, or context—i.e. the point of the discourse, to which the right hemisphere largely contributes. Thus right-hemisphere damage (Siegal, Carrington, & Rodel, 1996) or prefrontal lesions (McDonald & Pearce, 1996) may lead to problems in getting the point, or to problems with sarcasm, humor, or connotative comprehension.

(HOW) DID LANGUAGE EVOLVE?

Evolutionary gradualists like Darwin favor slowly acting forces of natural selection as the predominant motor of evolution, whereas punctualists like Gould and Eldridge place more emphasis upon discrete discontinuities caused by stochastic mutations (Hauser, 1993). In the context of language evolution we see these two competing tendencies realized in, on the one hand, the Chomskian perspective, and, on the other, in the continuity viewpoint, where language is seen to have evolved from earlier forms, including primate call systems.

According to Chomsky (1980), language is the product of a specialized and unique language organ with no counterpart in earlier species, and no biological precedent. This neural structure or language organ possesses an innate mental grammar, which is responsible for the combinatorial manipulation of symbols, a finite set of which, through grammatical rules and transformations, can be recombined into an infinite variety of meaningful utterances. Consequently, despite apparently great superficial or surface differences, all languages employ a similar set of underlying grammatical rules; they have a common or universal grammar determining their deep structure. Any child can therefore readily acquire any language—though not perhaps an animal call system—despite the complexity of the rules or grammars, which usually can only be "known" at an implicit level, and cannot be overtly formulated at all easily. According to Chomsky, children are genetically preprogrammed to acquire these rules in infancy, without formal instruction, initially perhaps incorrectly overgeneralizing, e.g. "she goed" or "he holded". Chomsky is not always consistent in how he sees language appearing (Pinker, 1994), at times seeming to view it as a kind of emergent property of a sufficiently complex brain that evolved for some other reason or reasons. It should also be noted that in addition to operating via very slow, steady incremental change, evolution can also occur in a punctuated fashion, rapidly, in individuals subjected to unusual pressures or situated on the boundaries of their normal ecology. Chomsky's sudden appearance of a language organ can possibly be seen in this latter context.

Continuity theorists, on the other hand, see differences between apes and humans as merely quantitative, with respect to information-processing capacity, memory, and voluntary control of the articulators, and reject an innate linguistic organ. They see no need for an innate speech module, even though speech processing, via experience, may come to be modularized and made more or less independent of other structures or systems, which previously may have supported it during a learning or acquisition phase. Indeed, these learning or acquisition mechanisms are seen by the opponents of Chomsky's position as *general* purpose rather than specialized, though it should be pointed out that the alternative to Chomsky is not necessarily support for a behaviorist or Skinnerian interpretation. Neither, of course, need the speech mechanism necessarily be derived from a general-purpose processor; nor need language be without biological precedent if it is instead seen to result, to some extent at least, from the co-option of some pre-existing noncommunicative faculty (e.g. the frontal mediation of conditionality rules and behavior, see later) for a communicative function.

Passingham (1993) characterizes the issue of the evolution (or otherwise) of language from our primate ancestors in terms of four possible hypotheses:

1. Its neural mechanisms are essentially similar in humans and our primate ancestors.
2. The mechanisms for handling grammar evolved largely out of mechanisms we can still see in other primates.
3. These left-hemisphere mechanisms evolved out of similar structures in the human right hemisphere.
4. Our left hemispheres have acquired a unique mechanism *de novo* for generating grammar.

He notes that the first hypothesis is unlikely; the last is essentially Chomsky's position; the second is the position adopted in this book, though it is not necessarily incompatible with the third hypothesis (and see Bradshaw & Rogers, 1993). Passingham (1993) also observes that several processes are possible in the development of specialized mechanisms, including expanding the area, differentiating it into several more specialized regions, or altering its input–output connectivities and functions. Moreover, though there may have been an overall increase in the volume of our brains relative to that of other primates, structures now subserving language may merely have kept pace, not unduly expanding or altering, but the resultant *general* volumetric increase of these areas may now have, for example, permitted the handling of grammar in language, whereas they previously "merely" handled the general conditionality rules that nevertheless underlie grammar. Thus an increase in size of a structure, in pace with that of the rest of the brain, can lead to apparently *qualitative* changes of function, increased specialization and functional differentiation.

Seemingly compatible with the Chomskian viewpoint, we see an apparently innate drive to acquire language, even from a very flawed maternal or paternal model, subject to exposure before certain critical periods; in the event of, for example, congenital deafness, an alternative channel may be adopted, such as signing, with either the acquisition of a recognized signing system, or even the invention of a private language between congenitally deaf and otherwise isolated siblings.

However, theories of pattern recognition such as schema theory or of concept formation can easily accommodate the tendency of the perceiver to formulate rules from flawed or error-prone exemplars, and to improve upon what is initially given. As for critical periods (though see later), we may possibly simply be seeing the operation of progressively reduced plasticity for learning and neural reorganization with increasing age, as occurs in many other contexts. With respect to signing, we may be seeing nothing more than the drive to communicate, which in various forms is apparent in most vertebrates. Sign languages rapidly evolve true grammatical structures and forms, which are not simply "grafted on" to a host language such as English, and as with creole languages (see following, and Bickerton 1990,

1995), they can probably tell us something about the evolution of language. There are in fact strong parallels between aphasic impairments in speech and sign, both regarding lexicon and grammar, even though one is phonological and the other visuospatial. Both evidence similar anterior and posterior clinical deficits, and both channels involve the left hemisphere (Bradshaw, 1996). Sign aphasia can dissociate, like speech aphasia, from apraxia, and from loss of the ability to gesture or pantomime, even though all of these capacities may normally depend, in different ways and to different extents, upon common time-dependent, sequential functions.

Bickerton (1995) claims that language invention, in the form of syntactically organized sequences with such features as tense markers, regularly occurs in creoles, the novel languages created at ethnic interfaces by children. He contrasts creole with pidgin; a pidgin occurs when two groups of adults that do not share a common tongue first come into contact. It is essentially a collection of words that may be meaningfully juxtaposed or chained, but that do not thereby create true propositions. In that respect such utterances resemble those of a frontal or Broca's aphasic (see Chapter 6) where meaning is derived from context in the absence of syntax, e.g. "man head hit rock dead". Bickerton sees a pidgin as a protolanguage, resembling a child's first efforts at speech, or the sequences of signs produced by an ape that has been taught thus to communicate. Conversely, a creole is developed by a child exposed to a pidgin, with the formulation of an idiosyncratic, rule-governed syntax for producing novel propositions. Bickerton, like Chomsky, claims that there is no intermediate form between pidgin and creole, just as, he says, in human evolution there was a sharp discontinuity between the chained utterances of our hominid predecessors, and the syntactically formulated propositions of anatomically modern *Homo sapiens sapiens*. Though creole invention may indeed be biologically driven by the same need to communicate and by the same neural substrates that support normal language acquisition in infancy, and though syntax is certainly central to a fully developed language, it is not clear that the "utterances" of apes are necessarily entirely agrammatic, or that there is an absence of an evolutionary continuity in language and communication prior to our own anatomically modern species (Fletcher, 1996).

Nor can we invoke apparent dissociations between language and other intellectual abilities in support of a unique or modular (Fodor, 1983) language organ. Thus the absence of a drive to communicate in autism is associated with numerous other sensory, attentional, and motor deficits. Similarly, the inheritance of apparently isolated language disorders involving e.g. grammar and syntax (Vargha-Khadem, Watkins, Alcock et al., 1995) should only be invoked with caution, as invariably other deficits emerge on careful testing, such as orofacial dyspraxia and articulatory and phonological problems (see e.g. Bishop, 1992; though see also van der Lely

& Stollwerck, 1996; the latter authors report inheritance of a grammatical-specific language impairment, and note that specific language impairment is heterogeneous in presentation, though with relatively homogeneous sub-groups, such that there may or may not be co-present articulatory or phonological deficit or impaired comprehension, and subsequent improvement may or may not occur). Though in Williams syndrome there may be the apparent *preservation* of language in the face of general intellectual disability (Yamada, 1991), it should be noted that, in the "savant" syndromes and individual differences generally, such "islands" of preserved function are by no means rare.

Developmental dyslexia, which according to some estimates may affect between 5 and 20% of the population, involves a skill that has to be taught, rather than being naturally acquired, like the mother tongue; it is nevertheless informative in this context, as there is evidence both of a familial (involving perhaps chromosome 6, see Cardon, Smith, Fulker et al., 1994), and of a neuropathological component. Though there is no agreed diagnostic test, it is typically diagnosed if reading considerably lags behind other abilities during development. It may be associated with "soft" neurological signs and with subtle deficits in phonological processing such as the ability to perceive rhyme in speech. Abnormalities have been noted in activation levels in the dorsolateral prefrontal cortex (Roush, 1995), along with possible pathophysiology of the auditory thalamus (the medial geniculate nucleus), indicating an underlying *auditory* problem. An underlying *visual* problem, instead or perhaps in addition, is suggested by developmental dyslexics' problems with low-contrast, fast-moving, flickering stimuli known to be processed by the transient visual channel and the magnocellular laminae of the lateral geniculate nucleus of the visual thalamus (Walsh, 1995). (The parvocellular laminae mediate the high-contrast, stationary, or slow-moving aspects of the sustained channel.) However, just as the acquired alexias can manifest in a variety of systematic ways (see Bradshaw & Mattingley, 1995), depending on the locus and extent of lesion, so too can we fractionate developmental dyslexia into a taxonomy that may well reflect local areas of otherwise subclinical dysfunction. Thus there are probably several kinds of developmental dyslexia, each with its own aetiology.

CRITICAL PERIODS AND SPEECH PERCEPTION

As Pinker (1994) notes, the apparent effortlessness, transparency, and automaticity of language are largely illusory when seen from the viewpoint of an adult learning a second language. Why do children acquire their "mother tongue" with such apparent ease? In human society it is clearly important, selectively, for children to acquire language efficiently and early, and it may well be computationally and metabolically expensive to maintain such an acquisition system beyond when it is most needed.

Though critical developmental milestones probably largely reflect progressive (rather than discrete) changes in behavioral or neural plasticity, there is evidence for them in the development of binocular vision and in the acquisition of birdsong (Nottebohm, 1979). Moreover, children deprived of all language before puberty never acquire it properly thereafter (Fromkin, Krashen, Curtiss et al., 1974). (There are, at the time of writing, unpublished accounts of a seven- or eight-year-old boy who underwent left hemispherectomy for the relief of otherwise uncontrollable epilepsy and subsequently acquired apparently normal language, presumably via the remaining right hemisphere; however, the surgery may merely have released the right hemisphere from inhibition, which hemisphere having, perhaps due to the pre-existing epilepsy, previously acquired considerable linguistic capacity, though without expressive outlet.)

In any case, languages encountered after around eight years are likely to be spoken with a foreign accent (Locke, 1994). An earlier milestone of around six months may relate to our ability to profit from linguistic experience in perceptually discriminating between the phonemes of our (to be) native tongue (Kuhl, Williams, Lacerda et al., 1992). Thus long before an infant can utter meaningful words, hearing a particular language around it has resulted in the establishment of phonetic prototypes that enable it to organize speech sounds into categories relevant for that particular language, and ready for when it begins to acquire word meanings towards the end of the first year. At birth, all children show similar patterns of phonetic perception, irrespective of the language environment into which they were born; they can discern differences between phonetic units of many different languages that they have never experienced and never will. Later, there is a reduction in this ability to perceive differences between speech sounds that do not differentiate between words in one's own native language, a change from a language-universal pattern of phonetic perception to a language-specific phonemic one, occurring in the first six months after birth. Nevertheless, such staged changes in sensitivity to particular phonetic patterns, though demanding sophisticated processing mechanisms, do not *require* the latter to be modular, encapsulated, or totally different in kind or evolution from call systems in other species.

Infants eight months old were exposed by Saffran, Aslin, and Newport (1996; see also Bates & Elman, 1996) for only two minutes to unbroken strings of nonsense syllables, e.g. "bidakupado...". As indexed by changes in eye-fixation patterns, the infants were able to detect the difference between three-syllable sequences that appeared as a unit, and sequences that appeared in random order. This means that infants can use simple statistical information to segment word boundaries in connected speech, at a time when word recognition is beginning—a purely inductive, statistically driven learning process, which stands in contrast to the Chomskian model. Indeed, artificial neural networks can similarly induce regular patterns from imperfect but quasi-regular input to generalize to novel instances. The authors conclude that this process may be how infants induce or extract phonetic and phonological structures from raw apparently unsegmented speech, and derive word boundaries and grammatical regularities from connected speech of only a few minutes' duration. It would be interesting to know whether adults would be equally sensitive.

An insight into language-specific phoneme representations has recently been revealed by an examination of electric and magnetic brain responses (Näätänen, Lehtokoski, Lennes et al., 1997). Finnish subjects were presented with the Finnish phoneme prototype [e] as a frequently occurring stimulus, with other Finnish phoneme prototypes or a non-prototype (the Estonian prototype [ō] with its own unique, idiosyncratic pronunciation, which lies roughly between the vowels of 'sir' and 'sore') as a rare event. The brain's automatic change-detection response, reflected electrically as the mismatch negativity potential, was enhanced when the rarely occurring deviant event was a prototype (the Finnish [ö]) relative to when it was a non-prototype (the Estonian [ō]). The language-specificity of these phonemic traces was confirmed by enhancement of the mismatch negativity potential in Estonians. Moreover, the source of this native-language, phoneme-related response enhancement was located in the left auditory cortex, where presumably language-specific memory traces of such early established prototypes are elaborated and maintained.

Evidence against a dedicated system—and a critical period—for word learning in children is reported by Markson and Bloom (1997). Though children can learn (and retain) aspects of the meaning of a new word from only a few incidental exposures, a phenomenon known as "fast mapping", such a process is not limited to word learning. Thus three- and four-year-old children and adults were taught a novel name and a novel fact about an object, and were tested for retention up to one month later. The authors found that apparent fast mapping was not limited to word learning, and suggest that the capacity to learn and retain new words depends on memory abilities that are not specific to language. Moreover, there was no critical period apparent, with adults performing as well as children. Of course, such findings do not bear on a possible critical period (and/or a dedicated system) operating at the levels of phonology, morphology, and syntax.

CATEGORICAL PERCEPTION

The phenomenon of categorical perception at first sight seems to support the Chomskian position of a uniquely specialized language module. We perceive the acoustic properties underlying phonetic features in an absolute, all-or-nothing fashion; we do not hear as acoustically different the variants of the phoneme [b] in different vowel environments, e.g. ... aba..., ... ebe..., ... obo..., ... ubu.... All are heard as [b], even though on an acoustic continuum some are much closer to [p]. The relevant continuum here is the voice-onset time (VOT), the time between the sound burst caused by lips opening and the start of phonation; labial stop consonants with a VOT of between 0 and 25 msec are all uniformly heard as [b], whereas those with longer intervals are categorized as [p]. At 25 msec VOT a threshold is crossed and the listener "flips" to hearing [p], and additional acoustic variations along that continuum make no further difference to the perception of [p]. Consequently, phonetic stimuli from different categories are highly discriminable, whereas stimuli from the same phonetic category, though acoustically very different, are in fact virtually indiscriminable. The problem, however, is that other primates and even chinchillas seem to divide the human phonetic continuum exactly as we do, perceiving contrasts categorically, apparently hearing an abrupt change at precisely the same acoustic locations (Kuhl, 1988; Maurus, Barclay, & Streit, 1988). There may therefore be *no* special speech-specific mechanisms, merely certain invariant properties of the mammalian auditory system, with speech production possibly evolving to match them. Conversely, the otherwise perhaps somewhat surprising ability of other mammals to categorically distinguish between speech consonants may be a consequence of the need to localize the origin of sound sources in space, presenting often as brief discontinuous bursts. Any uniqueness of human speech may reside less at the phonetic and more at the syntactic and semantic levels—though again we shall shortly note the ability of pygmy chimpanzees to *understand* syntactically complex English statements. It is nevertheless true that the ability to discriminate between and perceive rapidly produced, sequentially complex auditory stimuli, which is left-lateralized in ourselves and many other primate and nonprimate species (Bradshaw & Rogers, 1993), is likely to have been an evolutionary precursor to language (Wilkins & Wakefield, 1995).

In a subsequent chapter we shall discuss the possibly unique adaptations of the human supralaryngeal vocal tract for the production of a wide range of our more or less unique speech sounds. It is these adaptations, acting as an acoustic filter, which generate the frequency-specific spectral cues generally thought to underlie speech recognition (Lieberman, Laitman, Reidenberg, & Gannon, 1992). Spectral energy peaks in speech (formants), for example, reflect the resonant properties of the vocal tract and provide information for the discrimination of various classes of consonant. However, recent studies of amplitude compression and spectral reduction have demonstrated that speech recognition may be far more robust than previously thought (Shannon, Zeng, Karnath et al., 1995). Thus near-perfect speech recognition may be observed even with greatly reduced spectral information, with preservation and transmission to the listener of little more than temporal envelope cues.

CATEGORIZATION IN NONHUMAN COMMUNICATION

There is recent evidence that primate (and even nonprimate) call systems can code a range of environmental events. Vervet monkeys have at least six acoustically different alarm calls for predators such as leopards, smaller cats, martial eagles, pythons, and baboons. Each call evokes an appropriately directed response (Cheney & Seyfarth, 1990). The calls of the dwarf mongoose apparently code the dangerousness of an approaching predator, its type, distance, and elevation, and an elementary form of syntax may be discerned (Beynon & Rasa, 1989). Indeed, some might argue that syntax is a more fundamental criterion than meaning (semantics) in the attribution of language. In that respect if we see a symbol as representing an idea of an event, rather than an event itself, with a generic rather than a specific meaning, with a locus displayed in time and space, rather than temporally and spatially immediate, then the behavior of vervets and mongooses may not qualify as language driven. Thus words characteristically refer in the absence of their referents, whereas vervets call either in the presence of a referent (eagle or snake), or fail to refer at all, when seeking to deceive a conspecific and gain a possible advantage thereby. Moreover, the behavior of such animals may be hard-wired or innate, rather than learned as with human language. Though learning guides birdsong acquisition, during a critical developmental period, just as with human speech, we do not know the extent to which individuals of other species also depend on learning to acquire their repertoire. (It might be noted that under certain circumstances, just as we can with some difficulty learn second languages in adulthood, so too may birds sometimes acquire new songs after the critical period, see e.g. Snowdon, 1990.) Birds, in the form of the African Grey Parrot, may share with us yet another capacity said to be fundamental to true language, the ability to categorize and abstract (Pepperberg, 1990). Indeed, one such bird "Alex" uses more than 100 English words correctly to refer to objects and actions, can refuse requests, can tell his interlocutor what to do, and can request information on color, location of an object, its nature, shape, and even number (see Barber, 1996).

LANGUAGE MEDIATION BY A DISTRIBUTED NETWORK

If language is not mediated by a unique Chomskian module, and is not simply part of a general information processor, what alternative explanation is left? Modularity of function is always likely to occur in some basic form, if trivial, and it is not clear whether degrees of modularity are possible (Fodor,

1983). Though modularity implies localization, it should be noted that there has been little success at localizing language to one or two areas at most; indeed, it is best seen as an archetypal distributed system or network interconnecting a series of relatively specialized subregions, with weak connections to other networks. Increasingly, neurons distributed through the cortex are seen as acting together in large-scale functional assemblages, leading to parallel processing of information, via functional co-activation of multiple cortical areas which are functionally inter-dependent (Bressler, 1995). Various partially overlapping networks, corresponding to different cognitive functions, will differentially share processing areas, regions, or pathways depending upon current activity. Thus where praxis and speech partially share overlapping regions in their respective networks (Kimura, 1993), there will be the potentiality for mutual interference during concurrent manual and verbal activity, as indeed is found. The networks will tend to dynamically reorganize during ongoing perceptuomotor behavior, with the more elementary cognitive functions likely to be more discretely localized, whereas more complex activities involve widespread parallel activity. The latter somehow, probably via thalamic synchronization, has to be coherently "bound" together, perhaps in the dorsolateral prefrontal cortex and/or the hippocampus. Breakdown of the system may lead to schizophrenia-like disorders, though its distributed nature will make it generally resistant to localized damage. Effects of such localized damage will tend to be generally similar throughout the network, which in consequence will tend to reorganize, though perhaps with local "flavor" or "color". One cannot therefore identify the likely function of a localized element by seeing what happens to overall functioning when its contribution is "subtracted" by injury. Such networks, and their corresponding cognitive functions, are likely to have "fuzzy" boundaries.

Under this conceptualization, language may be seen as just another complex procedural skill, underpinned by certain necessary and localized structures, realized after much practice in an effortless, automatic fashion if the individual is exposed early enough to appropriate models. The superior acquisition of musical skills when one is exposed at a very early age to great music of an appropriate kind—the Suzuki method—and the likely specialization of certain cortical structures in skilled musicians (Sergent, Zuck, Terriah, & MacDonald, 1992) all attest to the nonuniqueness of language in these respects. The fact that the pygmy chimpanzee or bonobo can *also* apparently effortlessly acquire at least the ability to *comprehend* some simple spoken English again indicates that, contrary to Chomsky, there is nothing *uniquely* human about this capacity.

The view presented above of language as part of a distributed processing system is essentially similar to that of Pinker (1994), who claims that rather than language skills being localized to specific neural structures (or circuits), instead the normal function of certain distributed regions may be necessary for the correct or normal manifestation of such skills. However, localization, at least in the context of semantic categories, and category specific deficits, has been given possible support from the positron emission tomographic (PET) neuroimaging findings of Damasio, Grabowski, Tranel et al. (1996); they note that words denoting concrete entities are retrieved via multiple regions of the left hemisphere outside the classical language areas, with separable regions processing words of different categories, such as names (temporal pole), animal words (inferior temporal lobe), and tools (temporo-occipital junction). Retrieval, however, is not the same thing as storage or mediation, and the localized PET signals may reflect accessing points or circuits.

APES AND LANGUAGE

As we shall see, chimpanzees cannot produce the range of sounds that we can achieve, owing perhaps to limitations in their vocal tract anatomy. Conversely, they employ a wide range of visual signals—manual gestures (but not, in the wild, deictic pointing, though this is readily acquired in captivity) and facial expressions (Savage-Rumbaugh & McDonald, 1988). Many are similar to our own, and we can all readily learn what they mean. Thus apes beckon, hug, beg, offer, withhold, pat, and comfort. The chimpanzee's facial anatomy is very similar to our own except for a large protruding jaw and brow ridges (Savage-Rumbaugh & McDonald, 1988); the nerves and muscles moving the various facial structures again closely resemble our own. Only recently, however, has their own *vocal* communication been studied in any detail (Boehm, 1989). They may call to mark territorial boundaries, to signal alarm on the appearance of a predator, to summon help from an ally, or to locate lost individuals. Some calls can occur in monosyllabic isolation; others may be combined multisyllabically, with changes in inflection, consisting of hoots, screams, pants, and whistles of varying intensity. Though than more than 30 discrete calls have been claimed (Goodall, 1989), it is unclear whether they merely involuntarily express the caller's emotional state, or also communicate information on the social and physical environment, or even signal deliberate *intentions*. However, they do seem to vary in pitch, tenseness, phrasing, duration, volume, formant frequencies, vowel quality, intonation patterns, and the number of repetitions. Clearly, there is the potential for a great deal of information transmission. They may possibly convey information on age, sex, identity, emotional state, size, and makeup of a hunting party, the nature and intention of agonistic situations, interest in being sociable, feeding conditions, intentions to hunt, patrol or nest, the presence of neighbours, and the direction, distance, and location of travel.

Though apparently unable voluntarily to initiate a full range of human speech sounds, chimpanzees can produce formant frequency transitions, which distinguish between classes of consonantal sounds, by rounding the lips. They can therefore produce sounds like [b] and [w], and as they can and do phonate their calls, they should be able to produce the necessary voicing distinctions between [b] and [p], and nasalized vowels approximating to our [i], [u], [æ] (Lieberman, 1995, personal communication). However, they seem unable *voluntarily* to produce speechlike vocalizations approximating words like bad, pad, bit, pit, bat, etc. Thus chimpanzees seem unable to dissociate and appropriately recombine phonemes into words.

As early as 1661 Samuel Pepys suggested the employment of manual gestures to circumvent the apparent inability, which was already recognized, of chimpanzees to make humanlike utterances. There have since been many successful programs (usefully summarized by Dingwall, 1988; Snowdon, 1990), using American Sign Language (ASL) with chimpanzees (the Gardners, Terrace, and Fouts), gorillas (Patterson), and orangutans (Miles), or using plastic symbols, or "Yerkish", with chimpanzees, by the Premacks and the Rumbaughs respectively. The relatively large size of the resultant vocabularies (between 60 and 170 words, depending on the study), the ability to generalize the referencing of individual lexical items, their spontaneous use, and so on, all suggest cognitive processing beyond the level of simple, learned conditional associations between symbol and referent.

Thus it soon became apparent that chimpanzees could use symbols to refer to objects, events or situations that were not currently present. However, debate persisted as to whether their communications were essentially concatenations, rather than the truly novel sentences we employ by rearranging meaningful components into the potentially endless number of new combinations with novel meanings that a child can produce so seemingly effortlessly. Nevertheless, it was agreed that chimpanzees spontaneously comment, announce their impressions or intentions before action, and do not simply imitate. Indeed, they can learn to ask each other for tools and for the information needed to retrieve food from locked puzzle boxes, where cooperation is needed in a task, and all the necessary resources are not available to a single animal. They sometimes assign new meanings to symbols spontaneously and creatively, correcting the experimenter and thereby indicating that there was an attached concept. According to the criteria adopted, we can surely call these actions communicative or truly linguistic, though the skeptic will always be tempted to shift the goal posts in the interests of preserving human uniqueness (Savage-Rumbaugh & Lewin, 1994), and we should in any case be wary of anthropomorphism in our use (earlier) of such terms as "comment", "refer", "announce", "ask", etc. Thus we can train pigeons to hit a ball back and forth over a net, but, despite superficial appearances to the contrary, the birds are playing to their own agenda of reinforcement, rather than an avian version of tennis.

A parallel project of language coaching using a female pygmy chimpanzee (bonobo, or *Pan paniscus*—a gracile and highly communicative species that may have separated from the other chimpanzee lineage, that of *Pan troglodytes*, only 2.5 million years ago) initially made little progress. Then it was noticed that her foster son Kanzi had been passively absorbing the signs and skills they had tried to teach his mother. He, and later another young individual, also showed much evidence of naturalistic (as opposed to trained) comprehension of spoken English, understanding many quite complex statements the first time, without the need for gestures. Often novel strings of complex multiword requests were comprehended despite being spoken by different people with different regional accents, and even where mood, stress, intonation, sex, and age information were filtered out via synthesized speech (Savage-Rumbaugh, Romski, Hopkins, & Sevcik, 1989). The meanings of more than 150 spoken English words were acquired, spontaneously, with mastery of vocabulary, semantics, and even syntactic constructions involving indirect objects, conditionals, and embedded transformations, equivalent perhaps to the ability of a two-year-old child. A smart sheepdog may learn as many words, but only after years of diligent training (Cartmill, 1995a). One is left wondering how the observing infant chimpanzee has learnt to *segment* words and speech sounds, and how it determines which words link to which referents, or even that words *have* referents. However, as Barber (1996) observes, Kanzi clearly can comprehend and appropriately use, by sign, words in the absence of their referents, and comprehend naturalistic English sentences of the sort: "From X (one of the several locations) get Y (one of dozens of objects), and chase (or tickle) A (one of several individuals) with B (various objects)." Indeed, even dolphins may be taught to comprehend commands, in the form of hand gestures or whistles, with such subtle differences as "Put the basket in the net", "Put the net on the basket", "Go over/under/through the hoop", "Touch the pipe/ball/hoop/fish/person/surfboard/basket/net/frisbee with your fluke/fin and grasp it with your mouth" (Herman, 1991).

We have already noted how protracted infancy presents greater opportunities to acquire social and communicative skills (Rumbaugh et al., 1991). The more immature the brain at birth, especially as in humans, the more flexible and adaptive the learning, which will impact upon the effective richness of the environment, which in turn will effect modifications upon neural organization, cortical growth, and dendritic branching (Diamond, 1988; Renner & Rosenzweig, 1987).

Do apes share with humans a relatively effortless capacity for language acquisition that normally takes other forms in the wild? Is there a special effect from being reared, as an infant, in a human family, over and above the linguistic environment? Does language training make young chimpanzees sensitive to other task situations? Are they unique, apart from ourselves, in having a capacity to acquire skills via direct observation of others? Thus young bonobos may briefly watch humans perform a computerized task involving moving a cursor by a joystick, and then try to take over. Is it a matter of learning the temporal and causal relationships between events, by observing the consequences of the responses of their social partners? Clearly, however, comprehension is not in their case contingent upon actual action, usage, or responding. An example of Kanzi's cognitive capacity is evidenced by what happens when he is told at which of half-a-dozen sites, in a 55-acre forest, a ball can be found; when he is then entrusted to another person who does *not* know where the ball is hidden, he will unerringly lead him or her straight to the site, even if such travel takes half an hour (Rumbaugh et al., 1991).

The demonstration, in the brains of nonhuman primates, of regions homologous to our own Broca's and Wernicke's speech areas would weigh heavily against Chomsky's (1980) nativist account of a unique species-specific language mechanism in the human brain, without prior evolutionary precedents. Such homologs have been claimed in the rhesus monkey (Deacon, 1986a,b), together with the linking arcuate fasciculus. However, these homologs may have no equivalent role in the *production* of sounds, as ablation seems to have little effect upon vocalization (Aitken, 1981; Kirzinger & Jürgens, 1982), although they may play a role in *receptive* behavior. Indeed, neurons in the superior temporal gyrus of rhesus monkeys show a selective response to species-specific monkey calls (Rauschecker, Tian, & Hauser, 1995); the lateral areas seem to be part of a hierarchical sequence in which neurons prefer increasingly complex stimuli, and may form an important stage in the preprocessing of communication sounds. Monkey vocalization may be partly controlled at a limbic level, e.g. the anterior cingulate (Rizzolatti, Fadiga, Gallese, & Fogassi, 1996; Sutton, Trachy, & Lindeman, 1981), as also, of course, is the case with humans (Laplane, Talairach, Meninger et al., 1977; Rubens, 1975).

Thus human emotional calls, like crying and laughing, may employ a similar subcortical circuitry to those mediating animal calls, with later evolution of the cortical system. Indeed, in both species the cortical and limbic circuits may comprise parallel systems for oral-vocal activity (Deacon, 1986a,b). The limbic circuit is perhaps rather less direct, being predominantly involved in the control of respiration and the laryngeal muscles, whereas the cortical system largely controls muscles of the face, jaw, and tongue. The programming of movements controlled limbically remains intact after cortical perisylvian damage. Different sectors of the monkey's homolog of Broca's area in the region of the arcuate sulcus (see Rizzolatti et al., 1996, and later) are reciprocally connected with the anterior cingulate (limbic) vocalization areas, permitting interaction between primitive vocalization systems and more complex articulatory control. Thus any apparent dichotomy between primate calls and human speech may merely reflect quantitative differences in the level of cortical involvement and the range of muscle systems to be coordinated; it may not reflect a total shift of vocal functions from limbic and midbrain areas in nonhuman primates, to neocortical centers in humans. Indeed, our own older, limbic vocalization circuits still come into play in prosodic and emotional expression, and activate our remaining species-specific calls such as laughter, crying, shrieks, sighs, groans, and sobs (Deacon, 1989). That said, however, we must not forget that whereas nonhuman communication, limbically driven or otherwise, involves a finite repertoire of calls, which may vary in intensity, human speech involves a discrete, combinatorial system, which, by the endless possibility of recombining a finite number of elements, can produce an infinite number of possible messages. As Pinker (1994) observes, there has been much fruitless debate on what qualifies as "true" language—infinity, symbols displaced in time and space from their referents, hierarchical structure, creativity, recursion. Ultimately, differences between ourselves and other primates may merely prove to be quantitative and a matter of degree, rather than qualitative and absolute.

Perhaps because of predominantly limbic mediation, we have much less conscious control over laughter than over speech; though we can say "ha-ha-ha...", we cannot easily laugh *genuinely* on cue (Provine, 1996). A laugh is characterized by a series of short (75 msec) vowel-like syllables that are regularly repeated at a rate of about 5 per second. Though various vowel sounds may serve ("ha-ha-ha..." or "ho-ho-ho...") we do not normally *alternate* between them, or greatly vary the time constants. However, laughter is not exclusive to our species; chimpanzees laugh when being tickled, pursued, or wrestled. Their laughter, though, is a breathy panting vocalization that is produced once during *each* brief expiration and inspiration, with the sound and cadence of a handsaw cutting wood, whereas the vowel-like notes of our laughter result from chopping a single expiration. Provine (1996) speculates that the close coupling of laughter to breathing in chimpanzees may have been yet another constraint on the evolution of speech and language in other primates, the inability to modulate expiratory airflow being perhaps as limiting as the structure of the vocal tract itself. Though the nature of pathological laughter further indicates a subcortical, limbic mediation, its punctuational occurrence, like pauses or fillers such as "um" at the end of phrases, suggests cortically controlled placement, with speech maintaining priority access to the single vocalization channel. Perhaps the same is true with our other species-specific, "automatic" calls such as sighs, groans, sobs, and grunts.

Grunts are laryngeally produced vocalizations that function communicatively in many species and may serve a precommunicative function in human infants (McCune, Vihman, Roug-Hellichius et al., 1996). They result when brief glottal closure is followed by abrupt vowel-like release with open or closed lips but no other supraglottal constriction. As adults, we use them to accompany effort, to mark reaction of interest or attention, and in conversation to signal continuing interest or to mark pauses. In human infants, they early accompany effort, later signify focal attention, and finally precede referential capacity via coos, syllabic babble, and true words and phrases. Though nonhuman primates may lack our fine control of the supraglottal articulators, they share with us similar laryngeal control, and, as we saw, vervet monkeys use a range of grunts in acoustically different alarm calls in response to different predators, permitting conspecifics to make effective and distinct escape responses. Thus the grunt provides a possible bridge, in the acquisition and evolution of language, between primate call systems and true language.

MacNeilage (in press) may have developed such ideas further in his proposal that speech evolved when a continual mouth open–close alternation was superimposed on the basic mammalian mode of sound generation, larynx-based phonation. Lip-smacks, which serve as a facio-visual communicative gesture and are typically accompanied by eye contact (unlike the more general calls), would have modulated such calls via articulatory control, generating the consonantal elements and syllabic form that is superimposed on the more continuous (and initially limbic?) vocalic component. Thus speech is seen as originating not in primate call systems *per se*, but in primate orofacial communicative gestures, which later became associated with sounds and, ultimately, phonemes. In this context Rizzolatti et al. (1996) notes that Area F5 of the monkey premotor cortex is active during the *observation* of hand or mouth actions by others, and may be the homolog of our Broca's area; it seems, in the monkey, to be the basis for "understanding" motor events involving meaningful activity of the face and hands in others. If so, Broca's area may derive from an ancient mechanism related to the production and understanding of orofacial communicative gestures. Gallese, Fadiga, Fogassi, and Rizzolatti (1996) develop these ideas further, noting that, according to the influential motor theory of speech perception, the objects of speech perception are not so much the sounds produced by a speaker, but rather the phonetic gestures of that speaker that would have produced those sounds, and that are represented for and recovered by the listener as invariant motor commands. Area F5, a system that Rizzolatti's group thus suggests may be important in primates for matching the observation and execution of motor actions by the hands and mouth, may therefore have evolved into our Broca's area as a system for recognizing articulatory actions and gestures.

A VIEW OF LANGUAGE EVOLUTION

In the light of the extensive homology between our own and monkey perisylvian anatomies, language functions during evolution would seem to have recruited cortical circuits that were already present, perhaps for different purposes, in our primate ancestors. In fact, our whole linguistic edifice seems to depend on a network of separate interconnected structures homologous to those of other primates, none of which may be completely indispensable, and which may be separately vulnerable to trauma, each with a characteristic syndrome. There seems to have been a gradual mosaic evolution both of such discrete anatomical structures and of cognitive-linguistic systems like phonology, the lexicon, syntax, and semantics; language is the interactive sum of each of these, each with its own, long, semi-independent evolutionary trajectory (Bradshaw, 1995). Language is *not* part of a single, general-purpose cognitive processor, on the one hand; nor, on the other hand, is it a separately evolved, quasi-independent module. Rather, its evolution, via pre-existing structures, lets us model reality, manage, and communicate abstract concepts, and reduce cognitive complexity by categorizing and labeling. Thus the hierarchical nature of concepts and ideas allows us economically to label, very simply, ever more complex concepts, which themselves are synthesized from interactions of simpler concepts (labels), and so on down to basic ideas. Mathematics, of course, works in a very similar hierarchical fashion, and computer programs, routines, subroutines, sub-subroutines, similarly. Bickerton (1995) makes an essentially similar point when he observes that language arose as a representational system, and not just as a means of communication, with the properties that distinguish human intelligence (and maybe even introspective consciousness) from that of other animals deriving from language. I would, however, observe that aphasics seem in no way to be deficient in their capacities for conscious introspection. Nor am I entirely happy with his suggestion that instead of increases in brain size and processing capacity leading to language, language acquisition led to and drove the former.

Some form of speech probably made an early appearance, with roots that were continuous with earlier primate forms or communication. With the great apes we share a capacity for manual dexterity, tool use, learning symbolic (if nonverbal) behavior, and apparent conscious self-awareness. The roots of language lie early, rather than late, and the sudden late flowering of art and culture in the Upper Palaeolithic of around 35,000 years ago was not due to the sudden saltatory appearance of language, but was a purely cultural phenomenon, perhaps consequent on the establishment of a critical mass of somewhat more sedentary individuals in locally benign environments. Indeed, a detailed analysis of art, ornamentation, burial, vocal tract (reconstructed) anatomy, brain structure, and volume (Schepartz, 1993) fails to suggest any evidence for sharply isolating anatomically modern individuals from their ancestors, either 35,000 years ago, or around 150,000 years ago on the emergence from Africa, on the basis of language or of any other major qualitative changes likely to be associated with it. Whatever impact language may have had on social systems, cooperative hunting, leadership, or strategic planning in distinguishing *Homo sapiens sapiens*, it was not the only factor in a complex, multifactorial, interactive world. In fact, language is no more the defining hallmark of humanity than is tool use, bipedalism, self-consciousness, or even warfare and politics, with increase in brain size and cortical reorganization linked to language, handedness, and tool manufacture right at the start of our trajectory, as manifested by *Homo habilis* endocasts (Schepartz, 1993). It is perhaps culture that most distinguishes us, and lets us at least partially seem to transcend the imperatives of Darwinian evolution.

The role of culture is implicit in an influential, if unifactorial, theory of language evolution (Dunbar, 1993, 1996), which has affinities with the concept of Machiavellian intelligence; there, as we saw, a major factor in the evolution of the brain and of intellect was the need to manipulate other conspecifics in society via alliances and deceit. This new theory claims that language evolved as a socially relevant form of information exchange ("gossip") for purpose of social bonding or cohesion, and to keep track of multiple social relationships in increasingly large and unwieldy social groups. Thus language enables us to interact with a number of individuals simultaneously, rather than on a purely one-to-one basis, and its use in modeling reality, logical thought, and directing activities such as hunting, etc., would only have come later. In the end, however, this is again perhaps just another *unifactorial* "just-so" story, which seeks to explain the correlations between (increased) brain size and size of home range, social grouping, foraging strategies, diet, life span, neonatal weight, interbirth interval, altriciality, delayed maturation, social learning, increased longevity, tool use, synchronization of cooperative behavior, topographic orientation, thermoregulation, and so on. Ultimately, *multifactorial* autocatalytic, pre-adaptive feedback mechanisms are to be preferred, whether in medicine, biology, ecology, or evolution (see e.g. Wind, 1989). In fact, hunting has been proposed as yet another single-factor explanation for the development of language (Noble, 1990), whereby a weaker carnivore could compete by creating efficient hunting teams via enhanced communication (compare canids and hyaenids). However, wolves and jackals seem able to operate efficiently as hunting teams without vocal signaling. Indeed, except at the planning stage of a hunt, vocal signaling would simply alert prey. Nevertheless, it cannot be denied that a reasonably sophisticated language would have been of considerable selective advantage during early human migrations, when perhaps advance scouts might have reported back on food and water availability, the terrain ahead, and possible predators.

So, to what extent would a partial, incomplete, asyntactic, or "proto-language" have been of selective or evolutionary advantage? Noble and Davidson (1996) reject the idea of gradualism in language evolution, saying protolanguages (perhaps the equivalent of modern "telegraphese", news-paper headlines, tourist attempts in foreign languages, infantile and Broca's-aphasic utterances and pidgin) are only understandable because we bring to bear our *own* fully developed language capacities. The issue could perhaps be empirically resolved if we found, for example, that two Broca's aphasics could understand each other. Noble and Davidson also argue that language depends upon symbols, which are all-or-nothing and cannot exist in partial form. Of course, almost everything in the world is capable of a connotative or symbolic meaning, and the Pavlovian associations between, say, the sound of a bell and food highlight this. In a similar vein, Bickerton (1990) argues that language proper, which depends on syntax, could not have developed incrementally, or gradually out of protolanguage, as an "incomplete syntax" is not credible. This argument, however, is no more valid than the corresponding creationist claim that partial or incomplete eyes (or wings) could not function, and so could not have evolved.

Noble and Davidson (1996) see language as appearing late in our evo-lution, coincident with the flowering of art and culture, which they regard as essentially symbolic activities, like language. Pinker (1994), however, notes that there are many forms of symbolism underlying art, religion, tool behavior, and language, and holds that language is not dependent on art, or coevolved with art. It is of course the viewpoint in this book that language—and art—both had long and more or less independent traditions.

GESTURE AND LANGUAGE

Gesture is often invoked as a precursory stage in the appearance of true speech (Armstrong, Stokoe, & Wilcox, 1995; Corballis, 1991), with a general scenario of an upright posture, freeing up of the hands, and leading to tool use, gesture, and then language (Hewes, 1976; Kimura, 1976). We readily fall back on gesture, retardates may rely on it, and we can teach a chim-panzee a gestural channel of communication with us. Among primates, only humans and orangutans possess palms that are unpigmented and clearly visible (although the significance of this observation is reduced when we note a similar lack of pigment on the soles of the feet). Gesture may be superior to speech in showing how to do things and there may be syntactic commonalities between gesture and language (Kimura, 1982) with gestures closely following speech patterns. However, gesture really only comes into its own in the contexts of pointing, alerting others, attracting attention, paralinguistic emphasis, and demonstrating how to do things. Moreover, gesture does not fit well in any such proposed evolutionary sequence leading on to spoken language, because, as we saw, chimpanzees use many gestures similar to our own (Harré & Reynolds, 1984), even though they are not *habitual* users of tools. The ancestor common to apes and humans presumably also employed these gestures, though Tomasello (1990) questions the extent to which such gestures are species specific, directly imitated, or shaped in a social environment. He opts for a form of conventionalized learning, as occurs when a child raises its arms, initially to facilitate being picked up, and later to request it. Facial expressions may involve an even more ancient ancestry; thus, like us, monkeys pout, smile, frown, employ eyebrow flashes, and threat grimaces, and exhibit immediately and mutually (with us) intelligible expressions of mirth, fear, surprise, nausea, and disgust.

A further argument against a gestural stage in language evolution is the probability that increasing tool behavior would have hampered gesture and so have tended to favor speech, as indeed would also the requirements of communication in poor light, among vegetation, or over a distance (Hewes, 1977)—though on the other hand one can of course argue that gestures might have held back the development of tool behaviors until after language switched to the oral/acoustic mode. Conversely, speech, compared with gesture, does have the disadvantage of alerting prey or predators, and interferes with swallowing and breathing. We have, however, already seen that *orofacial* gesture (via lip-smacking, which may have modulated and "chopped" vocalic calls) may have played a role in a transition from (largely limbic) primate call systems to human cortically controlled speech (Rizzolatti et al., 1996).

SUMMARY AND CONCLUSIONS

The geographical distribution of spoken languages closely overlaps that of different human populations as defined by genetics. Moreover, language "inheritance" obeys principles similar to those operating in the molecular realm, in both cases permitting backwards extrapolation to common ancestors. Though Indo-European is currently the most thoroughly reconstructed protolanguage, dated to maybe 6,000 years ago, progress has been made on the likely vocabularies of certain very common words for super-superfamilies such as Nostratic at twice that age. However, communication is more than language, and the more automatic, unconscious, emotional, and prosodic aspects of speech must not be forgotten, especially as they show a clearer continuity with the calls of our primate ancestors. Nevertheless, despite claims to the contrary, there is little to support the view that language is the product of a specialized and unique language organ or module with no counterpart in earlier species and no biological precedent.

Nor is it simply the product of a general processor or problem-solver, though it may have taken over regions previously employed in other functions such as conditionality rules.

It is certainly true that we have a drive to acquire a mother tongue, that this is best achieved within certain critical periods, that in the event of e.g. deafness alternative (e.g. signing) channels may be developed with their own grammar, that language impairment (or abnormal facilitation) may occur in isolation from generally high (or low) intellectual functioning, and that speech sounds may be categorically perceived. None of these observations, however, is necessarily incompatible with an evolutionary continuity with earlier primate systems of communication. Other species evince categorical perception and critical periods, and can meaningfully communicate a range of environmental events. Language is best seen as part of a distributed processing system, which, though not a general problem-solver or processor can nevertheless participate to some extent in a range of other functions. Much of the system is homologous with and derives from similar structures in other primates, whose living members such as the bonobo differ most from us in lacking an articulatory capacity.

Nevertheless, debate continues about how much chimpanzees really can comprehend or produce novel grammatical sequences, and about the likely evolutionary pressures to true language. Theories are often of a unifactorial "just-so story" type, and there is really little evidence that during evolution manual gesture preceded language. However, Machiavellian manipulative or social intelligence may feature strongly in a multifactorial, autocatalytic feedback model, which involves a number of interacting elements. Moreover, several converging lines of evidence (work in humans and chimpanzees on laughter and grunts) highlights our unique ability to "chop" (consonantally, into syllables) semi-continuous and frequency-modulatable vocalic "calls" of the sort that other primates can also achieve; indeed, a homolog of our Broca's area in the monkey premotor cortex has been identified, which may mediate orofacial gestures and so perhaps led on to articulatory control of the level that we can achieve.

FURTHER READINGS

Bickerton, D. (1995). *Language and human behavior.* Washington, DC: University of Washington Press.

Burling, R. (1993). Primate calls, human language and nonverbal communication. *Current Anthropology, 34,* 25–53.

Cavalli-Sforza, L.L., Minch, E., & Mountain, J.L. (1992). Coevolution of genes and languages revisited. *Proceedings of the National Academy of Sciences, 89,* 5620–5624.

Dunbar, R.I.M. (1993). Coevolution of neocortical size, group size and language in humans. *Behavioral and Brain Sciences, 16,* 681–735.

Dunbar, R.I.M. (1996). *Grooming, gossip and the evolution of language.* London: Faber & Faber.

Hauser, M.D. (1996). *The evolution of communication.* Cambridge, MA: MIT Press.

Pinker, S. (1994). *The language instinct.* New York: William Morrow.

Renfrew, C. (1994). World linguistic diversity. *Scientific American, January,* 104–110.

Ruhlen, M. (1994). *On the origin of languages.* New York: Wiley.

Savage-Rumbaugh, E. S., & Lewin, R. (1994). *Kanzi: The ape at the brink of the human mind.* New York: Wiley.

Schepartz, L.A. (1993). Language and modern human origins. *Yearbook of Physical Anthropology, 36,* 91–126.

Tomasello, M., & Call, J. (1994). Social cognition in monkeys and apes. *Yearbook of Physical Anthropology, 37,* 273–305.

CHAPTER SIX

The central and peripheral realization of speech

Speech requires central and peripheral adaptations for its successful achievement, adaptations that quantitatively if not qualitatively may appear unique to our species. In this chapter we review the central mechanisms, as determined by clinical aphasia and modern neuroimaging techniques, for the production and reception of language-related behaviors, and the peripheral adaptations to the supralaryngeal vocal tract that have occurred at some point in our evolution. We ask whether palaeoneurological evidence indicates whether *Homo habilis* may have possessed the necessary speech centers in the brain, what limits articulation, peripherally, in the chimpanzee, and whether *Homo erectus* and the Neanderthals could generate as full a range of speech sounds as we can.

SPEECH AND ARTICULATION

Human speech is dualistic (MacNeilage, 1987), being simultaneously ordered at two syntactic levels—sound and meaning. Each level operates in a frame-content mode: Consonants and vowels insert into *syllabic* frames, whereas at the morphological level lexical items (words) insert into frames consisting of *syntactic morphemes*. Thus an open-ended system allows the generation of an infinite number of possible sequences from a finite set of elements like molecules from atoms, and organisms from genes (Studdert-Kennedy, 1990).

Other primate call systems are certainly far less complex, reflecting the absence in such species of whatever special needs have driven the evolution of our speech. Even the sounds of speech are special (Lieberman, 1985), permitting data transmission perhaps 10 times faster than any other auditory system of signaling could achieve. We can of course *visually* process *nonphonological* ideographic symbols like Japanese *Kanji* (and even phonological *Kana*) at an even faster rate: Thus it might initially seem that our ultra-fast *speech* mode of processing and our modern vocal-tract morphology have evolved parasitically on a *general purpose* information processor. In a general sense, of course, speech production, like all motor skills, involves rapid goal-directed gestures by the articulators towards target loci.

Our vocal apparatus consists of a sound-producing organ (larynx, with its vocal folds or cords), the throat (pharynx), the nasal cavity (nasopharynx), tongue, and lips. Speech is generated by the supralaryngeal vocal tract (SVT) acting as an acoustic filter on noise sources generated by turbulent airflow, and by quasi-periodic phonation generated by laryngeal activity (Lieberman et al., 1992). The formant frequencies, the major determinants of phonetic quality, are the frequencies at which relative energy maxima will pass through the SVT filter. Neither the individual articulatory gestures of, for example, the tongue, nor their acoustic consequences can be identified in terms of specific oral or pharyngeal components. Moreover, the acoustic cues specifying individual vowels and consonants are fused together or encoded in syllable-sized units, rather than strung out like letters in a written word. During speech, air is forced from the lungs, which act as elastic bellows, requiring regulation of the normal respiratory cycle to fit current linguistic or sentential constraints; a long sentence is "planned for" and accommodated by a larger prior inspiration of air.

There are therefore two fundamentally different sources of acoustic energy in speech (Lieberman et al., 1992): periodic phonation, stemming from laryngeal activity, and aperiodic turbulent noise. The former involves partial closure of the vocal folds or cords shortly before (around 60msec) the onset of phonation. According to the preset tensions imposed on the vocal folds, and the alveolar air pressure, the vocal folds will rapidly and cyclically oscillate in and out, at rates from around 60Hz for some adult males to around 1500Hz for young children—generating the fundamental voice frequency or pitch that identifies the speaker's person, sex, and emotional state. The only other energy present comes from the harmonics or integral multiples of the fundamental frequency.

The second source of acoustic energy, the aperiodic turbulent noise, is generated by turbulence at constrictions along the airway. Such constrictions at the lips, or between the tongue tip and the teeth, generate the heard consonant sounds, whose rate of onset can be adjusted. This segmenting of the much more continuous, though still variable, vocalic stream by periodic closures, partial or complete, produces the various consonants, which enable us to segment or parse words and syllables. Chimpanzees have a much more tight coupling between breathing and vocalization, producing only one phonation per exhalation or inhalation, whereas we can rapidly "chop" in various ways each exhalation, in part owing to a much finer control of the diaphragm (Provine & Bard, cited by Aldhous, 1996). Chimpanzees' problems in articulation may therefore have forced them to rely upon a graded vocal system utilizing pitch, intensity and duration for transmitting affective information (Savage-Rumbaugh & Lewin, 1994). Thus the SVT acts as an acoustic filter, impeding or attenuating the transmission of acoustic energy generated at the vocal folds. The minimal level of attenuation at certain frequencies corresponds to the speech signal's formant frequencies, which help determine phonetic quality. Thus vowels and consonants differ in terms of their characteristic formant frequencies whose rapid change permits our rapid rate of speech transmission.

THE SUPRALARYNGEAL VOCAL TRACT IN APES AND HUMANS

Our SVT, with its lowered larynx, appears quantitatively if not qualitatively unique to our species (Lieberman et al., 1992) (see Fig. 6.1), as indeed is the case with the driving neural mechanisms. Other mammals possess a high larynx, which can be locked into the nasopharynx, the air space near the nasal cavity, so that all breathing is restricted to the nasal route, as the oral cavity is closed, by the overlapping of soft palate and epiglottis. In this way the danger of choking from the inhalation of food particles is minimized.

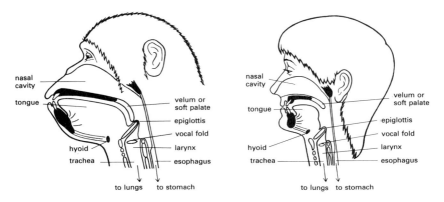

FIG. 6.1. Supralaryngeal tracts of chimpanzee and adult human. In the chimpanzee the epiglottis and velum can seal, whereas in the adult human the lower position of the larynx makes it impossible to lock into the nose. From Bradshaw, J.L., and Rogers, L.J., *The evolution of lateral asymmetries, language, tool use and intellect*, Academic Press, 1993, with permission.

Indeed, for this very reason the larynx does not "descend" until after infancy, when some measure of voluntary control is possible. In consequence therefore of our upright bipedal posture, with the head in a balanced erect position over the center of the spine, and the tongue partially lowered down the throat to form the back of the oropharynx (Savage-Rumbaugh & Lewin, 1994), we can now modulate the oropharyngeal cavity to form a wide range of speech sounds.

While the chimpanzee SVT should be able to generate many of our speech sounds, in a nasalized fashion, certain "quantal" vowels like [i], [u], and [a], as in "mee", "moo", and "ma", and velar consonants like [g] and [k], may be unique to ourselves. (The question here, of course, is what we mean by ourselves—*Homo sapiens sapiens* alone? Neanderthals? *Homo erectus*? The debate continues and is at times acrimonious.) If we lower the larynx and lengthen the SVT we can generate low-frequency [u], whereas a raised larynx with a shorter SVT permits production of high-frequency [i]. Our uniquely positioned and fashioned hyoid bone permits these laryngeal maneuvers, as it can be raised or lowered, along with the larynx, by muscles linking it to the skull, mandible, tongue, and sternum. However, the evolutionary modifications that make these maneuvers possible come at a price, in terms of increased danger of choking, suggesting the very high selective pressure of and for speech. They are a developmental feature, present only in adults and individuals beyond infancy, as infants' SVT, which is not descended, otherwise resembles that of other primates. The adult form coincides with the appearance of articulate speech.

The phonemes of a stop consonant preceding a vowel are altered by the following vowel, as the SVT already starts forming for the vowel while still making the consonant; thus the formant frequency transitions differ for the [d] in [di] and in [du], even though *listeners* always *hear* the [d] as qualitatively similar in both cases, automatically correcting what is heard in the vowel context. Moreover, the listener must estimate the length of the speaker's SVT so as to assign a formant frequency pattern to a particular speech sound; for this operation, the "supervowels" [i] and [u] are particularly suited, as they differ qualitatively between the sexes and between young and old.

Listeners, of course, have little conscious awareness of speech processing, which is "cognitively impenetrable", with phonology typically transparent to semantics; we perceive the meaning directly, rather than hearing the individual component speech sounds. Moreover, whereas objects of nonspeech auditory perception generally correspond fairly closely to acoustic structure, in the acoustic *speech* signal, dimensions of the percept may correspond, as we saw, a lot less closely, corresponding in fact more to the patterns of vocal tract activity that might have *produced* the signal. Furthermore, according to the phenomenon of categorical perception, we perceive the acoustic properties underlying phonetic features in an absolute, all-or-nothing fashion; we do not hear the different variants of [b] in different vowel environments. All are heard as [b] even though on an acoustic continuum some are much closer to [p]. However, as we saw earlier, we now know that categorical perception is not unique to our own species, or even to the auditory modality; it may be a universal feature of nervous systems to categorize inputs.

THE SUPRALARYNGEAL TRACT IN APES AND NEANDERTHALS

Though the tongue and suprahyoid muscles, which, as we saw, help determine the character of speech sounds, may have generally similar configurations and identical innervations in chimpanzees and humans, in chimpanzees the muscles have different angles of insertion from their homologs in humans (Duchin, 1990), thereby restricting the chimpanzees' articulatory potential. There has been spirited debate as to what might be the case with fossil hominids such as *Homo erectus* and the Neanderthals. It is not of course easy to reconstruct soft-tissue vocal tracts from hard fossilized material, though an indication can be gained from the flexion of the basicranium, the direction of the styloid process, the distance between the basion and the palate, and the positioning of the palate and mandible (Duchin, 1990; Houghton, 1993). (Note, however, that according to Ross & Henneberg, 1995, the flexion of the basicranium may not have differed between *Australopithecus africanus, Homo erectus* and modern *Homo sapiens*, even though these taxa clearly differed in cranial capacity; consequently, basicranial flexion, said variously to provide a better balance of the head on the vertebral column, to accommodate increased brain size, and to create a larynx suitable for generating vowel sounds for speech, may in fact be irrelevant for the last.)

One view (Duchin, 1990) is that though chimpanzees are clearly different, the Neanderthal SVT lies statistically within modern range, with no evidence of inability to produce certain phoneme distinctions, whatever the uniqueness of Neanderthal craniofacial morphology. Indeed, there have been many criticisms of alternative reconstructions (Lieberman, 1989, 1991); one can argue that human partial laryngectomies, and parrots, can all efficiently produce quite comprehensive and comprehensible speech sounds, despite gross differences in their vocal tracts. The discovery (see Fig. 6.2) of a Neanderthal fossil hyoid bone at Kebara (Arensburg, Tillier, Vandermeersch et al., 1989), identical to modern forms, also seems to indicate that this taxon *could* have spoken, irrespective of whether or not *it did*.

However, Lieberman (1994) argues that the shape of the hyoid is not relevant to whether that taxon could speak as, he says, the *pig* hyoid

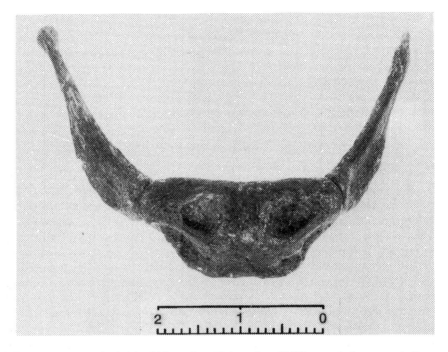

FIG. 6.2   The Neanderthal hyoid bone from Kebara 2, *c.* 60,000 years before present. Reprinted with permission from Arensburg, B., Tillier, A.M., Vandermeersch, B., Duday, H., Schepartz, L.A., & Rak, Y., A Middle Palaeolithic human hyoid bone, *Nature*, 1989, *338*, 758–760. Copyright © (1989) Macmillan Magazines Limited.

resembles ours in shape; more important is the position (height) of the hyoid in the neck. Height cannot be judged from shape, as the latter does not change, even though height does, during the normal ontogenetic descent of the larynx. He also criticizes Arensburg et al. (1989) for their metrical analyses of the shape of the Kebara hyoid so as to reconstruct that fossil's supralaryngeal tract, arguing that we *cannot* thereby conclude that Neanderthals were capable of speech. In a personal communication (1995) he observes that the "speech" of parrots is very impoverished, and that the human listener generates expectancies and by top-down processing "fills in" the missing information. He concludes that the modern (in *Homo sapiens sapiens*) vocal tract improves on our ancestor's relatively poor existing speech capacities, with better formant frequency encoding. It is nevertheless clear that except in noisy (in acoustic and informational senses) environments, the human speech signal is so redundant that it can survive greatly reduced spectral information and still remain near-perfectly intelligible (Shannon, Zeng, Karnath et al., 1995).

DID *HOMO HABILIS* POSSESS SPEECH-RELATED AREAS IN THE BRAIN?

If the evidence for speech in Neanderthals and *Homo erectus* from vocal tract anatomy is equivocal, what conclusions can be drawn from the other side of the coin, the central nervous system? It has been apparent for some time that the skull of *Homo habilis* has gyral and sulcal impressions similar to our own, and distinct from the pongids (Tobias, 1987). There is a prominent Broca's area in the posterior part of the inferior frontal convolution, and a well-developed inferior parietal lobule, especially in the region of Wernicke's area and the supramarginal and angular gyri—all major speech-related regions involved in speech production and perception (see later). Lieberman (1995, personal communication) comments that the apparent presence of such cortical structures may not bear on the issue of speech, as subcortical structures, such as basal ganglia and thalamus, would also have to be in place, and clearly we can tell little from skull impressions in that regard. Though this is of course true, it is nevertheless anatomically unlikely that (surface) cortical features would appear without the concomitant evolution of the associated subcortical forebrain structures that transmit and modulate ascending and descending information (Passingham, 1993). Similarly, one can ask what, if *Homo habilis* had the brain structures for language but not the vocal tract, was the function of those brain structures (Wilkins & Wakefield, 1995)? Is it likely that either system would have evolved out of step with the other? It seems clear from both sets of evidence, and from what we have already discussed, that though the pygmy chimpanzee is capable of a level of comprehension of spoken speech somewhere between that of a two or three year old, *Homo habilis*, whether or not on our direct evolutionary trajectory, was likely to have been somewhat further in advance. Comprehension of the level of a six year old, but still without articulate speech of any kind? Somehow, the latter seems unlikely.

SPEECH-RELATED AREAS AND APHASIA IN *HOMO SAPIENS SAPIENS*

The view adopted in this book is that just as the peripheral adaptations for articulatory speech in the human supralaryngeal vocal tract have a long evolutionary history in the primates, so too the central specializations in the nervous system are ultimately derived from structures and networks involved in earlier primate modes of communication. Even that, as once thought, curiously human idiosyncrasy, handedness (in praxis), and cerebral asymmetry for limb control and processing species-specific calls, is now known to be pervasive throughout the mammalia and even beyond (Bradshaw & Rogers, 1993). That said, there are nevertheless degrees of specialization, inter- and intrahemispherically, in humans that far transcend those found in even such closely related species as the chimpanzee. This is hardly surprising, given the complexity and sophistication of human speech, certainly the most complex skill we are ever, any of us, likely to acquire. (It could be argued that the term "skill" should be reserved for procedures acquired largely or entirely via learning and practice. Clearly, learning and practice play a major role in the acquisition of the local mother tongue, along with hard-wired and maturational factors. The same, however, can be said of any "true" skill, and throughout biology the borderline between the genetically determined and the environmentally influenced is hard to identify in complex systems where both contributions closely interact and mutually modify each other.)

Every voluntary speech act initiates an interlocking pattern of neuromuscular activity (Goodglass, 1993), some of which (e.g. in the lips and tongue) we may be consciously aware of, as movements are rapidly made to target positions; we are not, however, normally aware of the uvula as it opens or blocks nasal passages to create distinctions between nasal and oral phonemes. Given the degree of precision and timing required, it is surprising how robust the system can be in the face of damage.

It is an old truism in the neurosciences that if we want to understand how a system works, we study its breakdown in the face of local injury. Though lesions can be strategically placed in nonhuman species, for that option in humans we clearly have to await the "experiments of nature", where tumors, road accidents, or military misadventure place for the neuroscientist a lesion in the locus of interest. However, equally clearly we must be wary of assuming that change of behavior, *after* such a lesion, reflects in a simple way the subtraction of the contribution of that site from the system as a whole. Neural network research is revealing the extent to which complex systems can reorganize in the face of local—or diffuse—damage, and conclusions relating to localization of function must be made with caution.

Many speech difficulties acquired after local injury that do not involve disorders of planning (the true aphasias) come under the rubric of disorders of programming (speech apraxias) and of execution (dysarthrias). With oral or buccofacial dyspraxia, there are problems with purposeful movements involving the facial muscles in response to such commands as "Pretend to blow out a candle!", or "Purse your lips!", though the patient may still be able spontaneously to do these things in an appropriate context such as at a party. With speech apraxia the patient may not be able to produce an orderly sequence of phonemes, even though individual phonemes may be correctly achieved, and overlearnt speech automatisms ("Bloody hell!"), or formulaic utterances ("How are you?") may be preserved in an appropriate context such as pain or encountering a friend. Conversely, with dysarthria the patient may be unable to generate clearly *individual* phonemes or speech sounds. With speech apraxia there may be damage in the vicinity of Broca's motor speech area, though other regions have also been implicated including the supplementary motor area; with dysarthria there tends to be damage to the motor-speech pathways themselves, including the primary motor-sensory cortex, pyramidal, extrapyramidal and spinal nerve tracts, cerebellum, and basal ganglia. We are already seeing, here, the extensive nature of the neural networks that subserve human speech, involving various cortical and subcortical regions.

In a recent study, Dronkers (1996) succeeded in localizing the region involved in coordinating speech movements, from a study of patients with articulatory planning and coordination deficits indicative of speech apraxia, to a discrete region of the left precentral gyrus of the insula. This general region is a limbic cortical area beneath the frontal and temporal lobes, and does not include any traditionally known language area. The insula is considered part of the paralimbic cortex, and has otherwise been implicated in visceral sensory functions, motor functions of respiration and gastro-intestinal activity, and as a supplementary motor area affecting gross body movements and movements of the lips, larynx, and face. It may also function as a second somatosensory area. The precentral gyrus of the insula is directly anterior to the central sulcus.

The borderlines between speech apraxia and dysarthria, on the one side, and true disorders of planning (the aphasias) on the other are often blurred, though in both instances the left hemisphere is largely involved. Though the distributed nature of the network must be emphasized, there are nevertheless local regions that seem to contribute aspects of functional specialization to the overall working of the whole system. Indeed, the description that follows was formally adumbrated over 120 years ago by Wernicke in Germany and subjected to the first connectionist taxonomy by Lichtheim (1885) (see Fig. 6.3). As an early diagram maker, effectively mapping the topography of hypothetical language functions on the brain, Wernicke anticipated many of the conclusions of modern connectionists and localizationists such as Geschwind (1965). Nevertheless, we must be wary of trying to localize a particular symptom to damage to a single structure. In any case, brain damage rarely respects gyral, sulcal, cytoarchitectonic, or anatomical boundaries; its effects may be transient, and its severity can depend upon lesion size, when and how abruptly it occurred, and even the sex, handedness, and educational level of the patient.

Aphasia, a disturbance in formulating or comprehending language, involves a breakdown in the two-way process mediating between thought and language. It may relate to auditory, vocal, written, or signed (as in the case of the congenitally deaf) material at the levels of morphology (phoneme sequence), lexicality (meaning), or syntax (grammar).

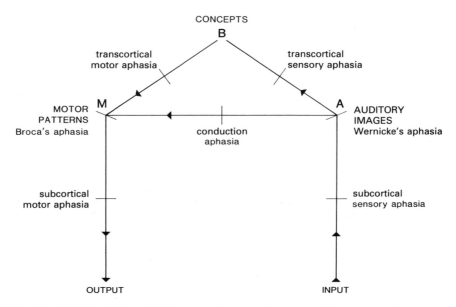

FIG. 6.3. Lichtheim's "house". The pioneering neurologist over 100 years ago thus conceptualized the relationships between the various types of observed aphasia (lower case) in terms of breaks (slashes) in information flow between or within processing regions (upper case). Variations upon this connectionist approach are still proposed. From Bradshaw, J.L., and Mattingley, J.B., *Clinical neuropsychology: Behavioural and brain sciences*, Academic Press, 1995, with permission.

An irreducible core for spoken language consists of two closely adjacent and interconnected structures straddling the Sylvian fissure in the left hemisphere, Wernicke's and Broca's areas (Mesulam, 1990), though their exact boundaries are still a matter of dispute. Wernicke's area, a posterior sensory system, is centered on the posterior part of the superior temporal gyrus adjacent to the primary auditory area, and extends into the planum temporale, a horizontal continuation of the superior temporal gyrus within the Sylvian fissure. Damage to other adjacent regions, the middle temporal gyrus, the inferior parietal cortex and the supramarginal and angular gyri adds to the clinical picture (see Fig. 6.4). Broca's "motor" speech area is centered on the posterior portion of the third frontal convolution (the inferior frontal gyrus) next to the motor face area. It is essentially a premotor region and therefore involved in speech organization and initiation.

Wernicke's area occupies the semantic-lexical extremity of a language network, whereas Broca's area lies at the syntactic-articulatory end (Mesulam, 1990) (see Fig. 6.5). It accesses the lexicon, a distributed, multidimensional network of sound–word–meaning associations, and acts as a

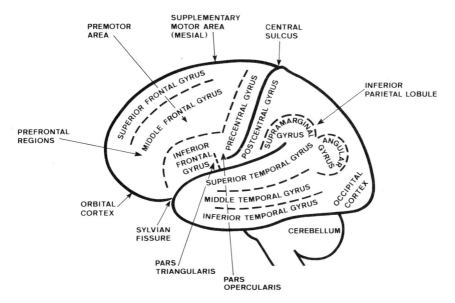

FIG. 6.4. Major surface landmarks of the left-hemisphere convexity schematically shown. From Bradshaw, J.L., and Mattingley, J.B., *Clinical neuropsychology: Behavioral and brain sciences*, Academic Press, 1995, with permission.

bidirectional interface between speech on the one hand, and meaning and thought on the other (Bradshaw & Mattingley, 1995). A series of simultaneous approximations (initial sound, number of syllables, vowels, consonants) may serve to generate a word's initial representation. Benign failure of the system in daily life may manifest in the tip-of-the-tongue state, when we temporarily cannot come up with a word or name. Such anomia is common in Wernicke's aphasia.

Though Wernicke's aphasia primarily involves a deficit in comprehension, without necessarily any loss of ability to conceptualize, in practice production of speech is also normally affected. Thus, despite the common representation of Wernicke's area as an auditory comprehension center, comprehension also involves acoustic, phonological, syntactic, and lexical processing, largely in parallel via a distributed network of cortical and subcortical processors. Wernicke's area instead processes speech sounds so as to map conceptual meanings on to words and vice versa, with full auditory comprehension occurring later via the operation of the entire system (Mesulam, 1990). Speech in Wernicke's aphasia is typically fluent, well-articulated, and syntactically and prosodically correct, though word-finding problems (anomia) abound, and the speech is curiously devoid of meaning or substance.

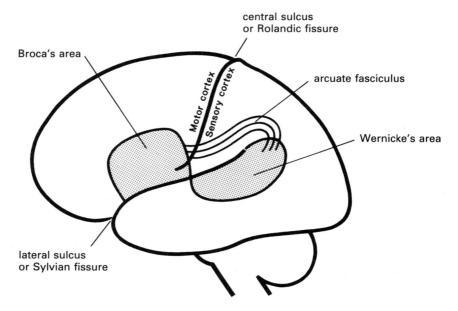

FIG. 6.5.   Broca's and Wernicke's areas. Their exact boundaries are subject to debate. From Bradshaw, J.L., and Mattingley, J.B., *Clinical neuropsychology: Behavioral and brain sciences*, Academic Press, 1995, with permission.

Broca's area occupies the syntactic-articulatory pole of the language network; neural word representations, originating perhaps in Wernicke's area, are transformed into the corresponding articulations, via sequenced phonemes, morphemes, and syntactically arranged words (Mesulam, 1990). In conversation, both regions electrophysiologically are simultaneously active; word selection occurs in parallel with the anticipatory programming of syntax and articulation, whereas grammatical structure influences word choice, which constrains syntax. During speech, Wernicke's area monitors the phonology, semantics, and syntax of the intended output, prior to its release by the basal ganglia and thalamus for articulation by Broca's area. During conversation we simultaneously decode our partner's speech, generate our own, monitor it phonologically, semantically, and syntactically, and release it, via Broca's and Wernicke's areas, via their interconnecting white-matter tracts, such as the arcuate fasciculus, and via the basal ganglia and thalamus.

Damage to Broca's classic area in the posterior portion of the third frontal convolution leads, we now know, at most to a mild or transient speech disturbance. For true motor aphasia to manifest, damage to other adjacent premotor and motor areas is required, together perhaps with the underlying white matter, insula, and basal ganglia. True Broca's aphasia ranges from near-complete muteness to slowed deliberate speech constructed with great economy from very simple grammatical forms. It is nonfluent, effortful, dysarthic, telegraphic, and agrammatic, with abnormal prosodic stress or intonation. In many ways, therefore, it is the converse of the fluent empty speech of the Wernicke's aphasic, as meaning is now largely preserved, though at the cost of great apparent speech effort. PET studies (Stromswold, Caplan, Alpert, & Rauch, 1996) indicate that Broca's area is involved in the mediation of syntactic processing, though clearly adjacent regions and probably other more distant structures in the network may also play an important role.

Over 120 years ago Wernicke predicted that damage to white-matter tracts interconnecting Broca's and Wernicke's areas, such as the arcuate fasciculus, thereby disconnecting them, should result in conduction aphasia; the patient should have particular difficulty in repeating words spoken by the examiner, with relatively unimpaired ability to comprehend such speech, and to produce one's own independent material. Recently, however, findings have emerged (Shuren, Schefft, Yeh et al., 1995) indicating that conduction aphasia may result from lesions sparing the arcuate fasciculus, which may not therefore be necessary for speech repetition. Conduction aphasia after supratemporal damage that spares the arcuate fasciculus indicates the importance of a second white-matter pathway extending from the superior temporal gyrus to Broca's area.

CATEGORY SPECIFICITY AND SEMANTIC REPRESENTATION

A maplike topographic organization of cortical representations has been found extensively in the animal and human cortex, sensory and motor; adjacent cortical areas represent adjacent points on the retina or skin surface, or adjacent muscle systems. These maps are not static, but are subject to experience-driven reorganization. Neuropsychological studies have shown that brain-damaged patients may exhibit selective impairments regarding specific semantic categories (Bradshaw & Mattingley, 1995), such as living things versus inanimate objects, fruits and vegetables, animals, body parts, indoor objects such as furniture, small manipulable objects like tools or kitchen utensils, and artefactual objects generally. Spitzer, Kwong, Kennedy et al. (1995) asked whether this phenomenon indicates the possible existence of semantic maps, with localized cortical representation of semantic information. They used a picture-naming task involving four different semantic categories with normal healthy individuals under functional magnetic resonance imaging. Small left-lateralized fronto-temporal cortical sites of category-specific activation were found, suggesting the existence of multiple maps that code high-level representations of objects. Thus meaningful distinctions may govern the distribution of semantic storage and representation in the cortex. Another study (Perani, Cappa, Bettinardi et al., 1995) found that animal recognition was associated with activation of inferior temporo-occipital areas bilaterally, whereas artefact recognition predominantly engaged the dorsolateral frontal cortex on the left. Similarly, Damasio, Grabowski, Tranel et al. (1996) reported that PET activation was evident in the left temporal pole during retrieval of names, in the left inferior temporal lobe with animal words, and in the left temporo-occipital junction with tools. We have previously discussed what such findings may mean for localization and network theories in the context of processing, storage, or retrieval.

NEUROIMAGING AND SPEECH LOCALIZATION

The use of new neuroimaging technology, such as positron emission tomography and the less-invasive functional magnetic resonance imaging, with normal healthy individuals avoids the problem, alluded to earlier, of whether we can "subtract" the functional contribution of a damaged area from that of the normal brain, and thereby determine its role. Other problems, however manifest now, such as the meaning and significance of greater cortical activation during a particular cognitive task; does such activation necessarily reflect *specialization* by such areas? Be that as it may, a wealth of new information at least complementary to lesion and accident studies is now emerging, which is relevant to issues raised in this chapter. Thus we can now ask what happens when fluent bilinguals speak in their second-acquired language. It turns out (Klein & Milner, cited by Barinaga, 1995) that the putamen, an important input structure for motor functions to the basal ganglia, becomes active, perhaps reflecting increased linguistic processing load.

Another intriguing application of neuroimaging techniques to language comes in the context of synaesthesia, the phenomenon experienced by a possibly very small percentage of the population whereby hearing a particular sound or word can elicit the simultaneous experience of a particular color. Thus, for example, the number six, or the day Wednesday, may evoke blue, while three, or Thursday, may be associated with green. There is no evidence of commonality of associations between different synaesthetes. Paulesu, Harrison, Baron-Cohen et al. (1995) found that in both synaesthetes and control subjects, word stimulation compared with tone stimulation activated the classical language areas of the perisylvian regions. However, in synaesthetes a number of additional visual association areas were also activated, including the posterior inferior temporal cortex and the parieto-occipital junction. The former has been implicated in the integration of color with shape, and in the verbal tasks, which require attention to visual features of objects to which words refer. Synaesthetes also showed activation of the right prefrontal cortex, insula, and superior temporal gyrus, but not of the primary visual cortex.

There is already a proliferating neuroimaging literature in the context of reading, but the latter, though an aspect of language, involves an acquired skill, lately invented, and present only in literate societies. Findings do not therefore relate directly to language as currently addressed in this book, and will not be discussed further, though see Bradshaw and Mattingley (1995), Posner and McCandliss (1993), and Price, Wise, Watson et al. (1994).

It is clear, therefore, that very many brain regions are active during thought and language - and indeed the two often cannot easily be separated. We certainly cannot seek, or invoke, a unique language *"organ"* (Chomsky, 1980), unless it is very widely distributed indeed throughout the brain. Though much of what we do while engaging in language-related activities does depend upon certain essential structures in the vicinity of Broca's and Wernicke's areas, they certainly do not tell the whole story. It may be that much of what we call language is an emergent property of an enlarged brain, whose enlargement may have been selected for by a number of other evolutionary pressures additional to communication *per se*. Though that does not mean that language may necessarily have employed much of the pre-existing circuitry for primate call systems, it does mean that the full sophistication of modern language far transcends those pre-existing mechanisms, irrespective of whether or not they employed homologs of Broca's and Wernicke's areas. It also means that though the existence, if indeed it can be unambiguously demonstrated, of these areas in fossil hominids is *compatible* with their possession of some form of language, it may well have been vastly impoverished compared with our own. That said, there is still no reason to suppose a sudden transition, say in the Upper Palaeolithic, in central nervous system functioning so as to support advanced speech, thought, and action. There is absolutely no reason to doubt, at least in *Homo sapiens sapiens*, the existence of a fully developed system. Numbers, critical mass, the nature, and composition of society may have been the trigger for cultural change; at least until very recently there were still societies whose lifestyles left very little traces, partly because of the perishability of their artefacts. Discussion of these issues will be resumed and extended in the context of praxis in a later chapter.

SUMMARY AND CONCLUSIONS

Speech involves complex hierarchical sequencing at several levels simultaneously, though temporal limitations are imposed more at the level of peripheral realization, despite parallel control of the articulators, than from the central nervous system itself. Both chimpanzees and humans share largely similar vocal tracts and central nervous systems, though in apes the information-processing capacity of the latter is clearly reduced, and the configuration of the former is suboptimal for producing fine phonemic discriminations. Moreover, chimpanzees possess a tighter coupling between breathing and vocalization, producing only one phonation per exhalation or inhalation, forcing them to rely upon a graded vocal system for transmitting affect. At what point in our evolutionary trajectory did we obtain "modern" central-nervous-system representation of speech, and the ability to produce a sequence of rapidly modulated and clearly differentiated phonemes? Could Neanderthals speak like us, or did some articulatory or central deficiency lead to their competitive demise? On this issue the fossil record is ambiguous, though modern speech is clearly highly redundant. Though as early as *Homo habilis* there is some evidence of enlargement in structures known to be speech related in anatomically modern humans, such enlargement may merely have been pre-adaptive for the later evolution of speech, and may at the time actually have participated in other roles. However, the evidence reviewed in this chapter is at least consistent with the thesis that speech has evolved largely from earlier primate systems of communication.

Aphasiology, capitalizing on the accidents of nature, helps us to understand the normal workings of the brain in speech control, though it must be remembered that cerebral reorganization after localized damage can qualify any conclusions based on a "subtractive" approach. Nevertheless, an irreducible core for spoken language consists of the perisylvian cortex on the left, the inferior-parietal lobule, and the inferior frontal gyrus. Between them and their cortical and subcortical interconnections they constitute a parallel distributed network of control at the phonological, lexical, semantic, and pragmatic levels simultaneously. Injury anywhere in the system is clearly disruptive, though anterior damage is associated more with the syntactic and expressive side, whereas posterior damage tends more to affect semantic and receptive aspects. Debate continues as to the extent of localization of representation (or maybe of access) of different semantic categories of knowledge. Neuroimaging in the normal brain provides information complementary to the clinical picture, but other problems of interpretation must now be addressed. Nevertheless, it is clear that many brain regions are active in the two-way interface between thought and language, and that we should not seek, or invoke, a modular or encapsulated language organ unique to humans and without biological precedent.

FURTHER READINGS

Benson, D.F. (1993). Aphasia. In K.M. Heilman & E. Valenstein (Eds.), *Clinical neuropsychology* (3rd Edn, pp. 17–36). Oxford: Oxford University Press.

Benson, D.F., & Ardila, A. (1996). *Aphasia: A clinical perspective.* Oxford: Oxford University Press.

Goodglass, H. (1993). *Understanding aphasia.* San Diego, CA: Academic Press.

Houghton, P. (1993). Neandertal supralaryngeal vocal tract. *American Journal of Physical Anthropology, 90,* 139–146.

Kimura, D. (1993). *Neuromotor mechanisms in human communication.* Oxford: Oxford University Press.

Kirshner, A.S. (Ed.). (1995). *Handbook of neurological speech and language disorders.* New York: Marcel Dekker.

Lieberman, P. (1991). *Uniquely human: The evolution of speech, thought and selfless behavior.* Cambridge, MA: Harvard University Press.

Lieberman, P. (1994). Functional tongues and Neanderthal vocal tract reconstruction: A reply to Dr Houghton (1993). *American Journal of Physical Anthropology, 95,* 443–452.

Lieberman, P., Laitman, J.T., Reidenberg, J.G., & Gannon, P.J. (1992). The anatomy, physiology, acoustics and perception of speech: Essential elements in analysis of the evolution of human speech. *Journal of Human Evolution, 23,* 447–467.

Wilkins, W.K., & Wakefield, J. (1995). Brain evolution and neurolinguistic preconditions. *Behavioral and Brain Sciences, 18,* 161–226.

CHAPTER SEVEN

Tool use and praxis

Praxic manipulation and the ability to make and use tools—often thereby to make other tools—is a mark of our species no less than the possession of language and a sense of aesthetics. Indeed, just as symbolism may underlie both art and language, rapid sequential control of multiple, fine muscle systems to discretely defined targets may be common to both language and praxis. In this chapter we examine the evolution of the hand, tool use in nonhuman species, hominid tool use and possible commonalities with chimpanzee behavior, the brain circuits that control praxic manipulative skills, clinical evidence from apraxia, and whether we can accommodate, in evolutionary terms, a possible synthesis between praxis, tool use, and language.

HANDS AND TOOLS

The archetypal terrestrial tetrapod is traditionally viewed as possessing four limbs each with five digits. However, very early species *Ichthyostega* and *Acanthostega* of the Devonian period (390–340 million years ago) possess, respectively, seven hindlimb digits and eight forelimb digits (Coates & Clack, 1990). Five fingers, perhaps an optimal number for human manipulation, may in fact be a happenstance, not a necessity, for tetrapods (Gould, 1991). Thus, though digital amputees will attest to the inconvenience of loss of even a single finger, there is no evidence for any substantial advantage (except possibly in playing a custom-built wind instrument) for those occasional individuals or families born with six digits.

Grasping, of course, is not limited to primates or even mammals, though it is certainly a mark of the order, and the ability of a limb extremity to surround an object is made possible by the evolution of the prehensile hands. Grasping was probably an early adaptation for arboreal locomotion among prosimians, which are restricted to a whole-hand power grip. More than 35 million years ago higher primates evolved the ability to control individual digits on the hand, and some even developed an opposable thumb (MacNeilage, Studdert-Kennedy, & Lindblom,1993). Baboons can learn to open complicated puzzle boxes via a variety of latches, hasps and doors, at up to seven or eight acts per second, and crab-eating macaques can use a precision grip in holding objects between thumb and forefinger.

Though the precision grip is of course essential for efficient tool manipulation, it is likely that processing fruits, seeds, and nuts (cracking, peeling, shelling, etc.) via a range of techniques served as an essential preadaptation for tool behavior and further cognitive development (Mac-Neilage, 1990). Much of our insight into the capacity of nonhuman primates for complex bimanual skilled activity comes from naturalistic observation and experimental study of the chimpanzee (see e.g. Savage-Rumbaugh & Lewin, 1994); however, gorillas naturally engage in very complex, lengthy, bimanual preparation of leaves and vegetation before consumption (Byrne, 1995a). Thus they employ sequences of finely coordinated movements, delicately controlled and organizationally complex, to remove stings, spines, etc. The two hands are carefully coordinated in their different roles; some action patterns are repeated and used as subroutines in other techniques or contexts. These behaviors are not innate but learned by observation of and coaching by the mother, who often deliberately removes inedible plants from the infant's hand or mouth, indicating successful anticipation of the possible consequences of the offspring's actions. Rote learning seems not to be involved, as each individual has its own preferred set of variants for each stage of a process; the actions are adaptive in that only the generalities of the mother's behavior are initiated, with precise details of action sequences, subroutines, and hand coordinations fleshed out by individual experience, much as an apprentice learns a craft. As with a human apprentice or craftsman, clearly a working memory, thought to reside in the most evolutionarily "advanced" region of the human brain, the prefrontal cortex (Goldman-Rakic, 1992), must be involved.

Though classical archaeologists are notorious for creating an entire inscription from a few, fragmentary, surviving letters, and palaeontologists for reconstructing a whole animal from a single bone or tooth, it is nevertheless noteworthy that the broad head of the first metacarpal of the human thumb is absent in apes and *Australopithecus afarensis,* which went to extinction at least half a million years before the first stone tools appeared (Aiello, 1994; Susman, 1994); there are no thumb metacarpals yet for *Homo habilis*, but this *tool-using* adaptation is certainly present in *Homo erectus* and probably in *Australopithecus africanus* and *Australopithecus (Paranthropus) robustus*. The last-mentioned small-brained hominid was contemporaneous with *Homo habilis* at 1.8 million years ago. Indeed, the human hand is specifically adapted with a powerful thumb for tool use, with three unique muscles lacking in African apes: the flexor pollicis longus for flexing the thumb, the flexor pollicis brevis for forcibly opposing the thumb towards the other fingers, and the palmar interosseous muscle of Henle, which stabilizes the thumb across its knuckle. Of course, apes and capuchins without stout thumbs *can* still deploy tools, though with less dexterity. There is evidence, however, that the hand of *Australopithecus afarensis* went part way toward the human hand in adaptations such as a long thumb in relation to other fingers, and the ability to spread and oppose thumb and fingers as for cupping and gripping objects such as stones (Aiello, 1994; Susman, 1994).

Marzke (1997) provides a recent, comprehensive review on the question of power (strong squeezing) and precision grips, hand morphology, and tool use in hominid evolution. He finds that *precision* (but not *power*) grips are essential for habitual effective stone-tool manipulation, where objects must be precisely maneuvered as well as firmly held, and identifies three such modes wherein we outperform chimpanzees:

- Pad-to-side, between thumb (pad) and side of index finger, as when we hold a car key. A modern variant involves the pads of forefinger and thumb, as in holding a thread to the eye of a needle.
- Three-jaw-chuck or pinch grip (the baseball grip), as when holding a baseball.
- Cradle or precision pinch-grip by the thumb and the four fingers.

Marzke concludes that morphological studies reveal a number of features distinctive of modern humans that facilitate use of these grips, including muscle adaptations for stabilizing the proximal thumb joint; several of these features occur in *Australopithecus afarensis*, but limited thumb mobility-would have compromised aspects of tool making by that taxon. *Australopithecus afarensis* would nevertheless still have used tools more effectively than chimpanzees.

NONHUMAN TOOL USE

A tool may be defined as something detached and separate from the user's or operator's own anatomy, which is not attached to any substrate, and which is used to change the state of another object, either directly or at a distance as by aimed throwing (Parker & Gibson, 1977). Tool use connects means to goals and causes to effects, adaptively to task requirements (Limongelli, Boysen, & Visalberghi, 1995).

Parrots may use nut shells, bottle tops, or teaspoons to obtain water for drinking from otherwise inaccessible locations (Pepperberg, 1989), whereas bluejays may shred paper for sponges to mop up wet food the easier to eat. Egyptian vultures use stones to break open eggs, and monkeys may use objects as drinking vessels, or make sponges out of seed pods to soak up and extract nutritional plant exudate (Hauser, 1988). Monkeys may also separate grain (which floats) from sand (which sinks) by dropping the contaminated mixture into water (Kawai, 1965). Macaques may hammer open oyster shells with stones, and use stones for crushing scorpions and for grooming (Falk, 1989). In the New World the capuchin (*Cebus capucinus imitator*), after 40 million years of evolutionary independence from Old World primates, closely resembles Old World apes in biology and behavior. Its cerebral cortex is similar to the Old World macaque's in sulcal patterns (Falk, 1989), its brain ranks fourth after ours after allometric scaling, and it is renowned for its precision grip, manipulative skill, and repertoire of tool-using behavior as complex and diverse as that of the chimpanzee (Chevalier-Skolnikoff, 1990). Its behaviors seem flexible, adaptive, and nonstereotyped, and include use of stones to crack nuts, "sponges" to transport liquids, sticks to lever, probe, rake in objects, to extract syrup from narrow openings, and to threaten with. The behaviors all appear deliberate and insightful, though this has been disputed. Thus their success may in fact stem more from enormous persistence and trial-and-error behavior, whereas chimpanzees may succeed in far fewer trials through prior planning, modeling, and abstraction, with apparently clear concepts of cause and effect, and of a final goal (Visalberghi, 1993). Thus we must distinguish between trial-and-error learning, imitative learning, and innovative insight. The latter can only be inferred if an individual is *naïve*—something that often cannot easily be ascertained. Repeated trial-and-error attempts may substitute for insight, if persisted with, though an analysis of resultant errors may permit the observer to infer the absence of insight and clear mental representations. On the other hand trial-and-error learning in certain circumstances may be better than imitation in acquiring a new skill. Conversely, demonstration of imitation also needs more than mere repetition of a behavior previously performed by another individual, as that behavior may be innate in both individuals (Visalberghi, 1989); to label repetition of a behavior as imitation one must be sure that the observer of the model is naïve, and that the behavior is otherwise improbable for the observer.

Boesch (1996) commenting upon Hunt's (1996) report of tool-making and tool-using behavior by crows (see later), observes that *standardization* in tool manufacture can stem from at least three possible mechanisms. Progressive trial-and-error modification until the object becomes a tool that happens eventually to fit a particular, restricted role is distinct from where the maker possesses a preconceived idea, concept, or mental model beforehand; the latter can be demonstrated when all modifications are made ahead of actual tool use. Finally, standardization may stem from social norms, and may be demonstrable where more than one equivalent and equally satisfactory device will suffice, with all the members of one social group adopting the same pattern, which differs from that of other social groups. Chimpanzees achieve standardization at all three levels, and, as we shall see, produce task-specific tools varying in length, hardness, weight, and so on, with evidence of some anticipation of future use.

Captive capuchins have been observed manufacturing stone flakes as cutting tools and chisels, even striking the latter with a stone hammer so as to open objects (Westergaard & Suomi, 1994). Their use of stones to modify bone fragment tools, similar to that observed in a pygmy chimpanzee, is reminiscent of what was thought to be the uniquely human capacity of tool use to *make* tools. However, all our supposedly unique human attainments of language, tool use, bipedalism, and self-consciousness seem to be falling.

In the wild, chimpanzees strip twigs to fashion probes for termite "fishing", first sweeping off the leaves, holding the stick with one hand, probing, and then wiping off the insects with the other hand. They chew leaves to make sponges so as to soak up and transport water (Goodall, 1968), and may extract sap from oil palms with a "pestle" and drink it with a fibre "sponge" (Sugiyama, 1994). They use sticks as weapons, rakes, and ladders. Even within one type of tool use, such as nut cracking, geographically separated chimpanzee communities vary, depending on the materials used for hammer and anvil (McGrew, 1992). Captive animals may learn how to strike sharp flakes off a cobble held in one hand with a hammer stone wielded by the other, using the flakes to cut string around a box containing food. Wild chimpanzees may bring several tools to bear on a task, applying them in a precise sequence like a toolkit, to get access to a honey source (Brewer & McGrew, 1990). Thus a large branch with a sharp end may serve as a chisel to pierce the wax coating, followed by a shorter, thinner stick to enlarge the hole, with next a long, thin, trimmed branch to puncture the seal; finally, a vine may be used to extract the dripping honey. Wild chimpanzee mothers may even actively *coach* their offspring, or at least perhaps arrange matters so that the offspring optimally acquire new procedures (Boesch, 1991). Thus they are said to leave nuts and a "hammer" near an appropriate "anvil", intervening when the young animal encounters problems, by repositioning the nut and appropriately holding the hammer. All this seems to suggest that the mother understands what her pupil does *not* know, recognizing the extent to which its performance is suboptimal. However, some of these conclusions should perhaps be treated with some caution.

Intelligent tool use presumably reflects an understanding of the causal relationships between the tool, the environment, and the actions required to attain a goal, which can often only be achieved through behavioral flexibility. There is solid evidence that when nuts are not yet in view, chimpanzees seek, select, and transport appropriately sized and shaped hammers of wood or stone according to the hardness of the nuts they intend to crack; there is also experimental evidence with manipulative puzzle tasks that chimpanzees understand the causal relationship between tool use and its outcome (Limongelli et al., 1995). Indeed, though both capuchin monkeys and chimpanzees may use sticks to obtain food from within a clear tube, only chimpanzees may demonstrate evidence, from modifying previously unsuitable sticks, of comprehension of the causal relationships necessary to avoid errors (Visalbeghi, Fragaszy, & Savage-Rumbaugh, 1995).

Similar considerations apply to recent reports (Hunt, 1996) that crows in New Caledonia can make tools out of leaves and twigs for extracting invertebrates from holes. Two main types of tool may be used, hooked twigs held angleways in the bill, and leaves cut to create a probe and held longways. Several minutes typically would be spent removing unwanted material; the birds then used rapid back-and-forth movements when the insects were partially hidden and slow, careful movements when the prey became visible. As Boesch (cited by Spinney, 1996) observes, and as is discussed earlier, it is unclear whether the birds have a mental image of what they are trying to achieve in making and using the tools, and whether they are indeed engaging in mental planning, though Hunt (1996) does observe that the crows securely positioned their tools for subsequent use between foraging expeditions.

Clearly, many species successfully employ tools in a more or less stereotyped fashion. Perhaps only the higher primates can use the same tool for more than one end (e.g. a stick as a probe, and as a rake). Perhaps only apes and humans can use different tools for the same end (e.g. a "toolkit" of different sequentially chosen sticks of various thicknesses, lengths, and sharpness in obtaining honey from a wild bee's nest), or can combine more than one tool together (hammer and anvil), or can coach their offspring (Savage-Rumbaugh & Lewin, 1994). Perhaps only humans—and New Caledonian crows!—systematically put tools aside for future use, thereby evidencing forward planning and advanced typically prefrontal behaviors, or use tools to make other tools. Otherwise, there is a progression rather than a sharp transition between the repertoire of the apes and the behavior, as inferred from the fossil record, of our hominid ancestors.

The apparent Oldowan behavior of 2.5 million years ago would at first sight seem to fall within the range of the apes' adaptive grade, with nothing exclusively humanlike in the oldest known archaeological evidence (Wynn & McGrew, 1989). Thus there is debate as to whether Oldowan tools exhibit evidence, as nowadays, of shared knowledge of (perhaps arbitrary) design, or of sophisticated mental processes (Lewin, 1995c). In fact, it is not easy to make on demand a sharp flake; the core should possess an acutely angled edge, and must be hit with a properly positioned and directed glancing blow to produce a long, sharp flake of the kind not infrequently observed in Oldowan assemblages. One can of course instead ask whether apes could make *Oldowan* tools; they are certainly known in the wild to be selective in choosing stones of the correct hardness for hammering open different kinds of nuts—granite for panda nuts, quartzite for cola nuts—and carry the materials hundreds of meters from source to nut-cracking sites. They can also certainly be *taught* to knock cobbles together, and to use resulting, randomly produced flakes for cutting string so as to gain access to food. Indeed, when chimpanzees select, trim, and make twig-tools for "fishing" for termites, they go through a complex sequence of spatial operations, maybe as complex as those required for Oldowan production.

Recent observations of a pygmy chimpanzee, Kanzi, bred and reared in captivity, at all times in close proximity to human caretakers and researchers, indicate that he learnt by observation (not coaching) and by trial and error to become ever more skilled and practiced at producing good, sharp flakes for cutting; this included a range of techniques and postures, such as flaking and directed throwing. He exhibited insight in problem-solving in his placement of materials, hard substrate, etc. However, he never apparently achieved an Oldowan level of skill, possibly owing to biomechanical factors (in particular, the anatomy of the thumb and its muscles, see earlier) rather than to any cognitive inadequacy. Of course, we do not know the level that might have been attained, given enough time and more experimental subjects. Nevertheless, though for us and maybe our hominid ancestors such tool making may be a natural part of our repertoire, the chimpanzee may require human contact, otherwise failing to discover or invent it naturalistically.

HOMINID TOOL USE

Clear evidence of the presence of worked stone tools at a site tells us of the presence of *Homo* at a time that may be dated via a variety of methods. A frequent problem, however, at ambiguous sites is whether the objects are the product of natural lithic phenomena (shattering from falling, etc.) or are genuine human artefacts. Possible criteria include the average number of flakes removed across items in a sample, the acuteness of edge angles, and the logical sequence, if any, of flake removal. It is clearly not enough to prove that a specimen *could* be an artefact—one must also prove it could not be a *geofact*. This is not easy, as there are many ways that nature can mimic humankind (Meltzer, 1995b). However, unlike naturally occurring fractures, and even the deliberate flaking of Kanzi, Oldowan stone flakes tend to be clearly fractured from appropriately shaped rocks with appropriately angled blows; according to Toth (cited in Savage-Rumbaugh & Lewin, 1994), and contrary to Wynn and McGrew (1989), the Oldowan tool-makers had mastered the principles of conchoidal fracture, unlike Kanzi. However, it may not have been until Acheulian times and *Homo erectus* that tools become more standardized and symmetrical, with the makers apparently clearly possessing a sense of intention and aesthetics.

The earliest reliably dated artefacts, as we saw, go back to around 2.5 million years ago—the Oldowan industry of the east African Rift Valley localities—and were contemporaneous with early *Homo habilis* and the robust australopithecines *Australopithecus* (*Paranthropus*) *robustus* (Toth & Schick, 1993). This industry lasted to around 1.5 million years ago in Ethiopia (Omo) and Kenya (Koobi Fora), when a technological shift occurred to the handaxes, cleavers, picks, or bifaces of the Acheulian, coincident with the emergence of *Homo erectus*. The technologically simple Oldowan tools, unlike the much more advanced Acheulian, may have needed comparatively little in the way of a mental template or spatial intelligence to fabricate, consisting mostly of cores and flakes and being determined largely by the size, shape, and nature of the available raw material. However, the manufacturers clearly could recognize acute angles on cores to serve as striking platforms from which to detach flakes, and had good hand–eye coordination in striking the core appropriately with the hammer stone, and a good precision grip. Individuals also clearly transported raw materials to preferred sites, and to judge from an analysis of the observed sequence of detached flakes, were preferentially right-handed, like ourselves (Toth, 1985). (Westergaard & Suomi, 1996, report that in the laboratory capuchins—*Cebus apella*—are preferentially right-handed for striking stones against a hard surface when making "knives" and for cutting open food packages, suggesting that anthropoid handedness for the production and use of stone tools predated handedness in the earliest hominids.) With the advent of the Acheulian culture, standardization and symmetry indicated that the artisan had a clear sense of what was being aimed at, together perhaps with an aesthetic sense (Wynn, 1989). Toward the end of the Acheulian, the Levallois technique for making flakes arose around 200,000 years ago; there was much more intensive core preparation, and complete flakes were struck off at a single blow. Around 150,000 years ago there arose the Middle Palaeolithic Mousterian culture, with an apparent sense of stylistic order coincident with the Neanderthal populations; however, available technology and materials, and the need for resharpening, were constraints that necessarily imposed shape and form, and the end product was always partly the consequence of such forces. This tradition, with its increasing use of bone, antler, and ivory lasted until around 35,000 years ago, with the advent of the Upper Palaeolithic revolution of the Aurignacian culture and the anatomically modern Cro-Magnon peoples who rapidly replaced the archaic forms of *Homo sapiens* in Eurasia. Of course, if earlier cultures had extensively used such perishable materials as wood, bone, antler, and ivory, little or no trace would have survived, and we may be underestimating their actual or potential capacities.

Wynn, Tierson, and Palmer (1996) provide an ambitious analysis of the conceptual requirements necessary to achieve the various levels of sophistication apparent in the evolution of hominid tool manufacture, as reviewed earlier. They ask whether the spatial concepts involved in such activities relate in any way to the sex differences in cognitive ability, which may be apparent in modern populations. They rightly note that such differences—a male superiority in spatial thinking and a female advantage in verbal skills—are very slight, and usually apparent only with sophisticated and artificial laboratory tests rather than in daily life. At a spatial level, a male superiority may occur in the ability to identify the horizontal or vertical within a distracting frame, to view a complex figure and select from possible choices the one that is a rotated view of the original, to identify simple target figures embedded in a complex background, and to predict the time of arrival of a moving object at a designated point. They ask whether any of these differences relate to possible tool manufacture (or use) or hunting (i.e. weapon) behavior, where (at least in modern societies) such activities tend to be a male prerogative. However, they note that when examining the evolutionary basis of a trait, one must realize that the trait's mere existence does not mean that it was necessarily favored by natural selection; it may simply be the product of genetic drift or pleiotropic genes, or the by-product or side effect of other adaptations. In any case, male spatial superiorities are apparent even in nonprimates (Bradshaw & Rogers, 1993), and it is unclear whether such differences, small as they are, relate in some way to equally small sex differences (in many species) in behavioral and brain asymmetries.

In the Langda village in the central mountains of Irian Jaya (western New Guinea) perhaps the last stone axe (strictly, adze) makers were first encountered in 1984 (Toth, Clark, & Ligabue, 1992). These four-and-a-half-foot tall male horticulturalists had a high local status in manufacturing adzes hafted with the working edge at right angles to the handles. There were many stages of operations performed in different places—quarrying, rough flaking, fine flaking, grinding, hafting—and, after use, regrinding. It is unclear how closely we can view this surviving culture as a model of ancient tool making; nor should we confuse similarity of performance with identity of mind—clearly, the artisans nowadays could easily learn to survive in a modern high-tech society, while the same probably would not be true of *Homo erectus*. However, it is certainly true that the level of technological sophistication observed in an earlier culture can only reliably indicate a minimum level of intellectual attainment, as clearly individuals might always be capable of much more if circumstances permit, or demand. Despite the huge range in sophistication of contemporary artefacts, there is no evidence of significant genetic or biological differences between extant peoples. Conversely, the anatomically modern skeletons of *Homo sapiens sapiens* 40,000 years ago do not *necessarily* mean that individuals were fully modern, behaviorally or cognitively; we can only make that judgment, if at all, from an examination of the remaining technological artefacts. Indeed, we may well ask why anatomically modern *Homo sapiens sapiens* apparently took so long to *behave* in a "modern" way, why and when this occurred, and whether such a *behavioral* change caused the competitive extinction of previously coexisting Neanderthals in the Levant, see e.g. Tattersall (1995).

Though the evolution of the brain necessarily proceeds along Darwinian lines, with genetic changes having phenotypic consequences that are advantageous, neutral, or deleterious, depending on the environment, the evolution of technology and culture proceeds along much more Lamarckian lines, with acquired traits inherited via learning (Toth & Schick, 1993); thus ultra-rapid technological change can occur via the invention or diffusion of radical new inventions. Of course, these cultural catalysts may themselves feed back in an autocatalytic fashion on brain evolution and cognitive development.

We have already disposed of the idea that humans are unique in using tools, though few other species may use tools to make new tools; nor, probably, are we unique in hierarchically organizing and embedding sequences of operations within larger sequences, despite the appealing apparent parallelism in this regard between language and tool behavior. Thus language is seen as involving a dualistic and serial structure (Mac-Neilage, Studdert-Kennedy, & Lindblom, 1984); at a phonological level, consonant and vowel elements are inserted into syllabic frames, whereas at a morphological level, words are inserted into syntactic frames. Many would argue that the syntax of language has its counterpart in the syntax of manual praxis, owing to (or causing?) the close mutual adjacency in the left hemisphere of regions responsible for the control of manual praxis, and of the articulators (Kimura, 1982, 1993). Indeed, Greenfield (1991) claims a commonality of hierarchical organization between the two forms of activity both ontogenetically (i.e. at the level of development) and in terms of homologous (rather than analogous) prefrontal structures on the left - Broca's area. However, frontal aphasia can dissociate, despite the close adjacency of face and hand regions in their representations in many parts of the motor system. We also know that, in the event of damage, adjacent areas, perhaps subserving quite different functions, can be "co-opted" to take over the damaged region's responsibilities; thus we cannot assume homology between regions subserving praxis and speech. Nor does the foregoing use of the terms "areas" or "regions" mean that functions are in fact necessarily localized discretely.

Areas and regions are nowadays seen more as participating within much wider circuit or network activity, and thereby as contributing their own functional specializations to the overall behavior of the network. Broca's speech area has close temporoparietal connectivities, whereas other parietal regions connect to the frontal areas involved in praxis. Indeed, the syntax of language involves a hierarchical organization and embedding of sub-sequences within larger sequences, whereas the praxis of tool manufacture, and to a lesser extent of tool use, instead requires a more linear chain of rote sequences learnt by repetition and practice (Wynn, 1991), or at most a simple linking-together of subroutines. Tool behaviors really possess little of the organizational complexity characteristic of everyday adult language. Thus language has enormous spontaneous productive power, and speakers can almost instantaneously generate new sentences without any prior practice, quite unlike what we see in tool behavior. Indeed, the (perhaps deceptive) simplicity of tool-using behavior suggests that it antedates language, and that the prior existence of language was not essential for the emergence of hominid tool behavior, which in fact is much closer to chimpanzee tool behavior than it is to human language. In any case, we do not teach new tool-using techniques by language or verbal instruction so much as by actual demonstration.

Finally, we must not forget that though tool behaviors involve physical, inanimate objects—and seem not to have played a major role in the selective increase in brain volume and processing capacity—language involves interaction with conspecifics. We shall later discuss the role that such interactions, in the context of Machiavellian intelligence, may have played in selection for increase in brain size and intellect. For a full discussion of the various models relating the evolution of language to that of praxis, see Ingold (1994).

MOVEMENT, THE FRONTAL-BASAL GANGLIA CIRCUITS, AND PRAXIS

Object recognition, of course, is of little use if we cannot in consequence adaptively respond in some way. Most animals have a more or less complex repertoire of responses, none perhaps more than *Homo sapiens*. Broadly and imprecisely, we can distinguish four such classes:

1. Reflex, like coughing or snatching the hand away from a hot surface.
2. Automatic, like walking and chewing, where the responses, once

initiated, are largely stereotyped, repetitive, automatic sequences. Only the initiation and termination may be thought of as voluntary.

3. Semivoluntary, like the need to stretch or to yawn, and certain "compulsive" behaviors as in Tourette's syndrome and obsessive compulsive disorder.

4. Voluntary, which are fully intentional, planned, purposeful, and goal-directed. It is such activities that of course characterize *Homo sapiens* par excellence. It is to the last category that we shall now turn.

"Primitive" vertebrates like the lamprey have few needs other than propulsion, feeding, and reproduction, for which a brain stem and cord mediate a few basic rhythmic responses that are sustained by oscillatory program generators (Steg & Johnels, 1993). Terrestrial quadrupeds require more highly developed control of posture, locomotion, and skilled paw manipulation. Simple programs for postural and locomotor control continue to be maintained in the brain stem and cord, whereas the newly evolved cortex coordinates different motor programs into purposive behavior. To these abilities humans have added the unique ability to predict and plan, to initiate appropriate and suppress inappropriate emotional responses. Much of this advanced supervisory control and "executive" functioning resides in our enormously evolved prefrontal cortex, which subserves our capacity to think, model, and plan (Benson, 1993). These regions are larger than those found in any other species relative to the rest of the brain (Deacon, 1989), and when allometrically corrected for body weight (Jerison, 1986).[1] Indeed, they constitute about one-third of our neocortex (Kimberg & Farah, 1993), yet their function has until recently remained largely mysterious. They have no simple sensory or motor function, and are not the seat of intelligence as measured conventionally. However, their major executive and supervisory role may lie in the selection of voluntary actions and the useful *deployment* of intelligent behavior, otherwise and elsewhere mediated, via set, flexibility, and an overall grasp of the current situation (Damasio & Anderson, 1993). In many ways, the region is where our individual essential personality resides. Though its exact functions are yet to be fully understood and localized, and are not easily subsumed under a single principle, it manages behaviors sequentially in space and time, organizing goals, intentionality, and anticipatory set, which it maintains or changes as appropriate. It plans, prepares, formulates, and organizes.

---

[1] Footnote: The "traditional view" of a relatively disproportionate prefontal expansion in humans has recently been questioned. Damasio (1996) found that the frontal lobe is around 30% of the telencephalon in macaques, 35% in the gibbon, orangutan and gorilla, and between 35 and 40% in the chimpanzee and human. Only the white matter core in regions anterior to the basal ganglia was larger in humans.

The frontal lobe may be divided into six regions: motor cortex, oculo-motor cortex (frontal eyefields), lateral premotor cortex, supplementary motor area and mesial premotor cortex, ventral (orbitofrontal) cortex, and the dorsolateral prefrontal cortex (Passingham, 1993).

The *motor cortex* is specialized for the voluntary control of discrete movements of the limbs, extremities, and face, especially where fine manipulation or targeting (as in control of the articulators) is important. It is not essential for nonlearned movements like automatic reaching, walking, or (axial) movements of neck or trunk.

The *lateral premotor cortex*, just anterior to the motor cortex, mediates the selection of movements that are currently appropriate, in spatio-temporal contextuality for execution. Projecting to the motor cortex, it receives input from the parietal cortex (where the spatial aspects of behavior are elaborated), and from the cerebellum (for the coordination of muscle groups). It is particularly active when movement is in response to external events, and has to be selected rather than merely repeated.

The *mesial premotor cortex* including the *supplementary motor area* is the mesial continuation, between the hemispheres, of the lateral premotor cortex. The main difference in function from that of the latter is that it is particularly responsive to *internally* generated volitional (willed) activity, rather than where action is externally cued or triggered. It receives input from the basal ganglia via the thalamus for the sequencing of behavior. Damage leads to problems in sustained action or attention unless the circumstances are novel, stimulating, or intensely gratifying. Major damage can result in profound apathy or indifference; interests and ideas may be relatively intact, but are not translated into the least demanding action.

The *frontal eyefields* lie just anterior to the lateral premotor cortex, of which they are an anatomical and functional extension, for the control of exploratory eye movements and fixations. Though a mesial extension is more responsive to internally generated targets, the lateral region responds typically to external targets in the real world. By contrast, the lateral premotor cortex may be more responsive to nonvisual external information.

The *dorsolateral prefrontal cortex* occupies a yet more anterior position, and enjoys a more general, less specific role than the premotor cortex in the selection and generation of responses, especially in the absence of specific external cueing, and when working memory is involved. Thus it is impli-cated when a response has to be delayed, or where an arbitrary decision, often of a strategic nature, must be made after weighing up the evidence. It integrates multimodal sensory information, and is involved in the generation of hypotheses, planning, goal direction, the deployment of strategies, and maintaining or changing set. Damage is associated with distractibility, interference from irrelevant information, difficulty with nonautomatic behaviors, especially under load or where responses must be delayed, withheld or alternated, reductions in fluency or creativity or the flow of ideas—i.e. the organizational or executive side of behavior (Shallice & Burgess, 1991). It outputs to the lateral and mesial premotor cortices and basal ganglia.

The *ventral (orbitofrontal) cortex* lies at the base of the frontal lobes and receives major inputs from the temporal lobe limbic regions, hippocampus, and amygdala. It outputs to the autonomic nervous system via the amygdala and hypothalamus and is important in drives, rewards and learned behaviors, novelty seeking, and exploration. Via the nucleus accumbens in the basal ganglia, and the dopaminergic reward system, it plays a major role in regulating and "gating" appropriate or inappropriate behaviors, acting as a sort of filter (Early, 1993; Saint-Cyr, Taylor, & Nicholson, 1995). Damage can result in marked personality changes, apparent lack of insight, social disinhibition and inappropriate behavior, poor impulse control, tactlessness, and so on; the patient, however, can usually still describe accurately what should and should not be done (Damasio & Anderson, 1993). Less severe malfunction may occur with Tourette's syndrome and obsessive compulsive disorder.

Each of these cortical regions receive afferent input from a specific pathway through the basal ganglia (Cummings, 1993), a structure that generally behaves like a filter in selecting appropriate information from various cortical regions for transmission to the appropriate frontal or prefrontal destination (Brooks, 1995).

After the elaboration of goals, the selection of appropriate strategies, and the direction of attention, via prefrontal mechanisms, information for movement is typically directed to the premotor and supplementary motor areas. The supplementary motor area receives information, via the thalamus, from the basal ganglia, and outputs to the primary motor cortex, cerebellum, and the basal ganglia, thereby effectively closing the cortex—basal ganglia—cortex loop. This loop appears to mediate the serial release of components of learned sequences of skilled movements—whereas the cerebellum handles the automatized coordination of individual muscles, especially under visual guidance. (Note that according to a recent reformulation by Gao, Parsons, Bower et al., 1996, the cerebellum may instead play a major role in fine sensory discriminations during motor performance, rather than motor control *per se*, thus explaining its apparent involvement in perceptual and cognitive processes; however, its special role in controlling timing and fine temporal coordination in motor learning seems well established, see e.g. Raymond, Lisberger, & Mauk, 1996.) Thus the supplementary motor area is very important in the controlled release and temporal sequencing of previously learned and internally cued movement sequences (Tanji & Mushiake, 1996), whereas the adjacent premotor area plays a major role in the control of more novel, externally cued movement sequences.

Along with the insula and anterior cingulate, these cortical structures manage the conscious level of the skilled motor performances at which *Homo sapiens* excels, whereas the cerebellum controls the timing and precision of voluntary bursts of muscle activity, and phasically implements muscle force; the basal ganglia scale the size of the initial burst of agonist muscle activity, while inhibiting inappropriate or antagonist activity, and generally monitor and optimize muscle activity for maximum efficiency (Berardelli, Hallett, Rothwell, & Marsden, 1996; Brooks, 1995). The descending corticospinal tract helps determine the spatial and temporal recruitment of individual motor units, whereas, posteriorly, the parietal cortex maintains the map of extracorporeal space wherein behavior is elaborated, responses are initiated, and exploration directed (Bradshaw & Mattingley, 1995). Unilateral damage to these parietal regions leads to loss of the will to explore manually space on the opposite side of the body, or even to respond to objects or events therein. Conversely, unilateral mesial frontal damage can disinhibit parietal and cingulate exploratory centers and result in contralateral utilization behavior—the hand may exhibit forced exploration or grasping, utilizing objects, or imitating the actions of the examiner in a manner quite contrary to the patient's own expressed will (Stuss, Eskes, & Foster, 1994). In this "alien hand" or "*main étrangère*" syndrome, the limb feels foreign and typically engages in complex unintended autonomous activities that are perceived as involuntary, but are usually well executed and apparently goal directed, but are nonetheless distressing to the patient. Each supplementary motor area normally controls the execution, as we saw, of the motor programs in the contralateral limb (i.e. on the other side of the body), inhibiting via the corpus callosum (the massive fiber tract interconnecting the two halves, or cerebral hemispheres, of the brain), the simultaneous action of the *other* supplementary motor area on the *same* (ipsilateral) limb; thus cooperative activity of the two hands in continuous reciprocal control can occur, as, for example, in knitting. Damage to the corpus callosum and to one supplementary motor area can therefore lead to a premotor-area-driven imbalance with excessive *externally* driven involuntary activity and no callosal inhibition from the *other* supplementary motor area (Della Sala, Marchetti, & Spinnler, 1994); the (intact) parietal and cingulate cortices respectively provide the necessary spatial information and drive for the action to appear well formed and intentional. Indeed, purposeful action that is contextually appropriate and correctly targeted must be deeply integrated with visuospatial, tactuospatial and kinaesthetic-spatial perception, which is mediated by parietal and parieto-frontal circuits.

On the other hand, generalized damage to the basal ganglia, which, as we saw, act as a filter for the successive release of intended or inhibition of unintended movements, can lead to different kinds of movement disorder.

Parkinson's disease results in the hypokinetic inability to release wanted movements (akinesia) or slowness in their execution (bradykinesia); with Huntington's disease, Tourette's syndrome, or obsessive compulsive disorder, unwanted movement patterns may be released in the form of hyperkinetic chorea, tics, or complex behaviors, respectively (Bradshaw & Mattingley, 1995; Comings, 1995; Como, 1995; McGuire, 1995). Indeed, just as we have two *visual* systems, a parietal system for telling us *where* action or events are taking place or objects are occurring, and a temporo-occipital system for their *identification* (Mishkin, Ungerleider, & Macko, 1983), so too may we have two *motor* systems: The intentional *"when"* system involving the basal ganglia and supplementary motor area, when damaged, is associated with hypo- or hyperkinesia, whereas the praxic *"how"* system, involving the parieto-frontal axis, when damaged, is associated with apraxia.

APRAXIA: THE LOSS OF THE ABILITY TO USE TOOLS

Movement disorders associated with damage to circuits within the basal ganglia are characterized by disturbances to the more automatic aspects of movement control, and the initiation or maintenance of appropriate (or inhibition of inappropriate) sequences. Deliberate voluntary action, parti-cularly by the hands, as in tool use or construction, involves cortical centers distributed between the parietal and the (pre)frontal cortices. Whereas the patient with basal ganglia disease typically still knows what should be done, the apraxic patient with disorders of skilled voluntary action may now seem to suffer from amnesia for the action itself.

Apraxia is a disorder of learned or skilled movement, which is not just due to weakness, incoordination, sensory loss, or an inability to compre-hend task requirements—though these problems may well also co-occur (Harrington & Haaland, 1992). Apraxics, often unaware of their disability or even strongly denying it, rarely present with the disorder as the chief complaint; usually it is noticed later in the context of acquired speech dif-ficulties (aphasia). Indeed, many aphasics are also apraxic, though not all apraxics are also aphasic; in fact, any association with aphasia is likely to stem from anatomical contiguity between the centers responsible for the two conditions, rather than from a common underlying mechanism.

For over 100 years a distinction has been made between ideomotor and ideational apraxia. Not everyone accepts this distinction, and the definitions themselves are blurred and often disputed. To an approximation, ideomotor apraxia, after anterior damage, may affect the intentionality to move, with preservation of the actual memory engrams themselves, stored elsewhere, probably in the inferior parietal lobule (supramarginal or angular gyri, see e.g. Ochipa, Rothi, & Heilman, 1994). With ideational apraxia there may instead be loss of the actual memory engrams themselves, and amnesia for the action. Thus the ideomotor apraxic may be unable to pantomime or imitate an object's use, though still be able more or less correctly to handle real objects within a natural context, but perhaps making some production errors; on the other hand, the ideational apraxic, though perhaps being able to imitate usage, and able to perform individual movements in isolation, will typically be unable correctly to sequence movements or to manipulate or operate even real tools within a natural real-life context, making content errors. Skilled tool use and praxis therefore involve a cortical axis encompassing the inferior parietal lobule, where visuo-kinesthetic spatio-temporal engrams for movement control may be stored, and the supplementary motor and premotor areas, where chains of responses are instantiated in response respectively to internal or external (sensory) cues. Thus with anterior lesions the otherwise intact engrams are now disconnected from motor areas; the patient still knows what is correct but cannot produce an appropriate response, unlike the posterior patient, who now no longer even remembers or knows what is a correct response sequence. The left hemisphere (even in New World monkeys, see e.g. Westergaard & Suomi, 1996) seems to be particularly important, just as in speech, for praxic activities, perhaps mediating the ballistic, open-loop aspects of response timing, whereas the right is more concerned with the more rapid, online, closed-loop aspects under visual control (Winstein & Pohl, 1995). Conversely, the consciously controlled aspects of praxis may rely heavily upon the (right) premotor area (with its responsivity to external information), the right dorsolateral prefrontal cortex (where working memory is elaborated), and the parieto-occipital cortex; more unconscious automatic aspects, however, of praxis may instead depend on the supplementary motor area and basal ganglia, with their mediation of internal cueing (Grafton, Hazeltine, & Ivry, 1995). When we grasp an object, prior to manipulation, whereas the (right) inferior parietal lobule may pragmatically analyze the object's shape for (unconscious) control of grasping, the (left) inferior temporal lobe may mediate its conscious identification, taxonomic relationships, and usage (Jeannerod, Arbib, Rizzolatti, & Sakata, 1995). Even minor damage in these areas may reveal, to sophisticated kinematic analysis, subtle deficits in joint coordination and synchronization, and in optimal joint angles and phase relationships between different joints (Poizner, Clark, Merians et al., 1995).

At a general level the foregoing neuro-anatomical account of praxis and apraxia applies equally to nonhuman primates, subject to their limitations in repertoire. Just as with language, an elaboration of pre-existing circuits seems likely in the evolution of tool-using behaviors, rather than the sudden appearance, *ab initio*, of a Chomskian organ of language—or praxis. A tool can of course be viewed as an extension of the hand in both a physical and a perceptual sense, and tool and hand may be assimilated into a composite schema. Iriki, Tanaka, and Iwamura (1996) trained macaques to retrieve distant objects with a rake, while recording neuronal activity in the caudal postcentral gyrus of the parietal lobe where somatosensory and visual signals converge. They found numerous bimodal neurons, apparently coding the hand schema; during tool use, their visual receptive fields were altered to include the entire length of the rake, or to cover the expanded accessible space. The authors suggest that these findings may represent the neural correlates of the modified schema of the hand in which the tool was incorporated.

PRAXIS, TOOL USE, AND LANGUAGE EVOLUTION: IS A SYNTHESIS POSSIBLE?

Despite the appealing commonalities of central representation and of function between tool-related praxis and language, it is unlikely that the latter evolved from the former, though they may well have acted to some extent synergistically during their two evolutionary trajectories. Both involve sequential behaviors, though recursivity is far more pronounced in language and both involve parieto-temporo-frontal structures (and see Rizzolatti, Fadiga, Gallese, & Fogassi, 1996). In both the human and the monkey there is a system devoted to the recognition of hand actions and gesture by others. The cortical areas constituting this network are located in the superior temporal sulcus of the left hemisphere, and the caudal part of the left inferior frontal gyrus—i.e. in the region of Broca's area (Rizzolatti, Fodiga, Matelli et al., 1996). The fact that some processing space is common to speech and praxis is also evident from the degree of mutual interference during concurrent activities, but such interference is far less than would occur with true commonality, and it is simplistic to infer that language evolved from manual gesture. Language, moreover, is clearly not a pre-requisite for acquiring tool behaviors, which are better acquired by imitative and observational apprenticeship. Tool use and praxis on their own probably were not solely responsible for driving the evolution of a bigger brain, as apes, monkeys, and even nonprimates are highly dextrous; conversely, *advanced* tool behavior only appeared very late in our trajectory, and large-brained cetacea are among the least manipulative of all higher mammals. Language may be thought of as a spin-off from increased brain size, but at least some specially evolved regions seem to be necessary—which may even have been present in small-brained *Homo habilis*—and microcephalic dwarves may have reasonably good linguistic (and praxic) skills. This, however, may merely reflect the enormous functional spare capacity in the human brain, especially when immature and capable of plastic reorganization. Though tool use, praxis, language, intellect, problem-solving, conscious self-awareness, and culture doubtless all interacted and co-evolved to their mutual evolutionary benefit, it may be the increasing importance of social or Machiavellian intelligence, to be discussed further later, which really drove language evolution. The latter was, however, almost certainly founded in the communicatory systems of our primate ancestors, with utilization and further evolutionary development of existing and previously little-used cortical pathways; this is evidenced by the anatomical common-alities, cortical and subcortical, between the central articulatory mechanisms of ourselves and other primates.

Language thus depends anatomically upon various, interconnected anatomical structures, many but not all of which are also represented—or possibly duplicated—in a parallel system for praxis, none of which is individually completely indispensable, at least some of which are homo-logous with structures involved in other primate systems of communication, and all of which are separately vulnerable to trauma, each with a char-acteristic aphasic (or apraxic) syndrome. With a gradual evolution both of the anatomical substrates and of the resulting cognitive systems, language (and, separately, praxis) are to be seen as the interactive sum of the above structures; each has a long and possibly semi-independent evolutionary trajectory, as seen by existence of various *developmental* (as opposed to *acquired*) aphasias and apraxias. Neither language nor praxis are merely part of a single, general-purpose cognitive processor, nor are they separately "evolved" quasi-independent Fodorian modules. Nor did language evolve, possibly from praxis, via an intermediate (*manual*) gestural stage, despite, again, superficially beguiling generative commonalities (Corballis, 1991) between language, gesture, and praxis. Gesture would always have suffered from too many clear sensory limitations, and would have interfered with ongoing praxic and other activities. *Orofacial* gestures, however, may well have modulated primate call systems and provided the evolutionary bridge to human speech (Rizzolatti, Fadiga, Matelli et al., 1996).

Armstrong, Stokoe, and Wilcox (1995) seem to move between two positions, that gesture *preceded* speech, and that manual and vocal com-munication developed *in parallel*, with language emerging through visible bodily action. (Primates do, of course, maintain close eye contact, and are very sensitive to *orofacial* gestures of the sort already described.) They note that sign languages in the deaf are fully developed human languages more or less independent of the spoken languages of a given region's linguistic communities. Though deaf sign languages certainly have all the hallmarks of a natural language (see Bradshaw, 1996), thus providing an excellent argument for a gestural origin of language, we should note that they in fact only provide a minority *alternative* to true speech, and one which is there-fore in certain ways necessarily less efficient, rich, or flexible. Indeed, much of the complexity of spoken language lies in the very fine temporal dis-criminations that convey, for example, important information on place of articulation and that may have no equivalent counterpart in signing. Such temporal discriminations may also be important in nonhuman species-specific discrimination of calls, discrimination that seems to be left-lateralized well "below" the mammalia (Bradshaw & Rogers, 1993). There is much less evidence of such "early" left-lateralization of gesture and praxis, further supporting the continuity, maybe via *orofacial* gestures, of human speech with primate call systems.

The relationship between gesture and speech has been explored in detail by Goldin-Meadow, McNeill, and Singleton (1996). Language, of course, is independent of modality (speech, or manual sign in the congenitally deaf), but hearing speakers also supplement what they say with expressive gesture, though in this case the latter is typically devoid of grammatical properties. Instead, the manual modality is iconic, mimetic, imagistic, and global in accompanying speech, and is not characterized by the segmentation and hierarchical organization characteristic of grammar, speech, and deaf signing. Gesture becomes grammatical only when it assumes the full burden of communication as in the deaf, or, exceptionally, if a hearing person is forced for some time to communicate by sign. Then, primitive sequential segmentation may occur, with simultaneous variation of both handshape and motion. Why, then, did we evolve speech rather than sign in evolution? Much, as we saw, has been written on keeping the hands free for praxis, communication in the dark or at a distance, but as Goldin-Meadow et al. (1996) note, it is easier to have a segmented, *oral* system coexisting with a mimetic, iconic *manual* channel, than where these relationships are reversed. Speech may be the predominant medium not because it is well suited to the linear sequentiality of symbolic human communication (the manual system is equally good), but rather because it is inferior to the hands at capturing the imagistic aspects. Such considerations clearly count against a gestural stage in language evolution, and are compatible with continuity with earlier primate systems of communication; they also suggest that segmentation and combination are not necessarily properties of thought *per se*, but may arise from the constraints of communication.

SUMMARY AND CONCLUSIONS

Five fingers, perhaps optimal for manipulation, may be an evolutionary happenstance in tetrapod evolution, where a range of species are more or less adept at such manipulatory activities. Though the precision grip is essential for efficient tool use and dexterity, the processing of vegetable foods may have served as an essential preadaptation. Indeed, coaching and observational learning in these activities is a mark of the higher primates. Tool use, of course, is not limited to primates or even mammals as a whole, though it may not have been until *Homo habilis* that it became established as a major behavior pattern. Nevertheless, chimpanzees even in the wild show evidence of complex, adaptive, sequential tool-using behavior, and coach their offspring in appropriate actions; indeed, the earliest Oldowan toolkit is not markedly different from what chimpanzees might be expected to achieve under optimal circumstances. Moreover, the earliest hominid tools of 2.5 million years ago are often not easily distinguishable from naturally occurring geofacts. Indeed, it may not have been until Acheulian times and *Homo erectus* that tools became standardized and symmetrical, with the makers apparently possessing a clear sense of intention and aesthetics. Around 150,000 years ago, in the Middle Palaeolithic, the Mousterian culture of the Neanderthals apparently introduced further technical advances, which persisted until the Upper Palaeolithic revolution of the Aurignacian culture in Europe, associated with the arrival there of anatomically modern *Homo sapiens sapiens*. The latter taxon had certainly appeared elsewhere before that date, but without apparently major technological advances, suggesting that social factors may have played an important role in further advances. Nor is it clear to what extent language and tool manufacture mutually interacted and developed; language and praxis both involve closely adjacent brain areas, and it is possible that anatomically and behaviorally there was synergistic evolution, though the parallels between the two forms of behavior have in the past been somewhat overemphasized or exaggerated.

Tool manufacture and use, par excellence, involve skilled sequential, voluntary behaviors under conscious control, and under the direction of a goal or master plan that may be hierarchically achieved. Prefrontal structures, lateral and mesial, and under the filtering and sequencing guidance of the basal ganglia, are needed to achieve such behaviors, and are maximally evolved in our species; spatial organization is under the control of interconnected parietal structures. Though ethological studies of primate behavior in the wild, and experimental studies with humans, can tell us much about fine, praxic, manipulative limb control, individuals apraxic after localized (typically, left-hemisphere) lesions provide us with additional information about the actual neural structures involved. Aphasia and apraxia commonly co-occur, but they can and do dissociate. Both behaviors, language and tool use, are perhaps best seen as involving networks of interconnected and overlapping structures that are more or less homologous with those of other primates. Neither are separately evolved, quasi-independent Fodorian modules.

FURTHER READINGS

Benson, D.F. (1993). Aphasia. In K.M. Heilman & E. Valenstein (Eds.), *Clinical Neuropsychology* (3rd Edn, pp. 17–36). Oxford: Oxford University Press.

Benson, D.F. (1993). Prefrontal abilities. *Behavioural Neurology, 6,* 75–81.

Berardelli, A., Hallett, M., Rothwell, J. C., & Marsden, C.D. (1996). Single joint rapid arm movements in normal subjects and in patients with motor disorders. *Brain, 119,* 661–674.

Berthelet, A. & Chavaillon, J. (1993). *Use of tools by human and nonhuman primates.* Oxford: Clarendon Press.

Brooks, D.J. (1995). The role of the basal ganglia in motor control: Contributions from PET. *Journal of the Neurological Sciences,* 128, 1–13.

Cummings, J.L. (1993). Frontal-subcortical circuits and human behavior. *Archives of Neurology, 50,* 873–879.

Damasio, A.R. (1994). *Descartes' error: Emotion, reason and the human brain.* New York: Putnam.

Damasio, A.R., & Anderson, S.W. (1993). The frontal lobes. In K.M. Heilman & E. Valenstein (Eds.), *Clinical neuropsychology* (3rd Ed, pp. 409–460). Oxford: Oxford University Press.

Dubois, B., Verin, M., Teixeira-Ferreira, C, Sirigu, A., & Pillon, B. (1994). How to study frontal lobe functions in humans. In A.-M. Thierry, J. Glowinski, P. S. Goldman-Rakic, & Y. Christen (Eds.), *Motor and cognitive functions of the prefrontal cortex* (pp. 1–16). New York: Springer.

Gibson, R.K., & Ingold, T. (Eds.) (1993). *Tools, language and cognition in human evolution.* Cambridge: Cambridge University Press.

Goldman-Rakic, P.S. (1992). Working memory and the mind. *Scientific American, 3,* 72–79.

Heilman, K.M., & Rothi, L.J.G. (1993). Apraxia. In K.M. Heilman & E. Valenstein (Eds.), *Clinical neuropsychology* (3rd Edn, pp. 141–164). Oxford: Oxford University Press.

Jeannerod, M., Arbib, M.A., Rizzolatti, G., & Sakata, H. (1995). Grasping objects: The cortical mechanisms of visuomotor transformation. *Trends in Neurosciences, 18,* 314–320.

Kimberg, D.Y., & Farah, M.J. (1993). A unified account of cognitive impairments following frontal lobe damage: The role of working memory in complex, organized behavior. *Journal of Experimental Psychology: General, 122,* 411–428.

Kimura, M., & Graybiel, A.M. (1995). *Functions of the cortico-basal ganglia loop.* New York: Springer.

Levin, H.S., Eisenberg, H.M., & Benton, A.L. (Eds.) (1991). *Frontal lobe function and dysfunction.* Oxford: Oxford University Press.

MacKenzie, C.L., & Iberall, T. (1994). *The grasping hand: Advances in psychology, Vol. 104.* New York: Elsevier.

Marzke, M.W. (1997). Precision grips, hand morphology, and tools. *American Journal of Physical Anthropology, 102,* 91–110.

Milner, A.P., & Goodale, M.A. (1995). *The visual brain in action.* Oxford: Oxford University Press.

Passingham, R.E. (1993). *The frontal lobes and voluntary action.* Oxford: Oxford University Press.

Porter, R., & Lemon, R. (1995). *Corticospinal function and voluntary movement.* Oxford: Oxford University Press.

Rizzolatti, G., Fadiga, L., Gallese, V., & Fogassi, L. (1996). Premotor cortex and the recognition of motor actions. *Cognitive Brain Research, 3,* 131–141.

Rothwell, J. (1994). *Control of human voluntary movement.* London: Chapman & Hall.

Toth, N., & Schick, K.D. (1993). *Making silent stones speak: Human evolution and the dawn of technology.* New York: Simon & Schuster.

Watson, R.T., Rothi, L.J.G., & Heilman, K.M. (1992). Apraxia: A disorder of motor programming. In A.B. Joseph & R.R. Young (Eds.), *Movement disorders in neurology and neuropsychiatry* (pp. 681–690). Oxford: Blackwell Scientific.

Wing, A., Haggard, M. & Flanagan, J.R. (Eds.) (1996). *Neurophysiology and psychology of hand movements.* San Diego, CA: Academic Press.

CHAPTER EIGHT

Encephalization and the growth of the brain

Art, language, praxis, and tool behavior all require considerable computational space, and the brain is metabolically an expensive organ. Though a large body requires a large brain to run it, remaining capacity may be subject to further adaptive pressures, qualitatively and quantitatively, to mediate cognitive function. In this chapter we review the growth of encephalization in the fossil record, the organization of the cortex to permit general perceptuo-motor processing, neurogenesis, and the two-way control of brain and body growth during ontogenetic development, the extent to which reorganization can occur to neural networks and mediating regions beyond the developmental period, and the vexed issue in our species of a possible relationship between brain size and intellectual capacity.

THE ALLOMETRIC RATIO

Evolution is no inevitable ladder of directed progress, tending for ever "upwards" towards ever-increasing complexity (Gould, 1991). Nevertheless, within the hominoids there has indeed been a progressive increase in cranial capacity, and by inference, brain size and probable processing power, both in absolute terms and relative to body mass. Indeed, according to the principle of allometry (see e.g. Harvey, 1986), brain size (BR) increases with body size (BO), but not in a 1:1 ratio. A power function best describes the relationship, with a straight line when logarithms are used on both the BR and the BO axes (Jerison, 1986):

$$BR = aBO^b$$
$$\text{or } \log BR = \log a + b \log BO$$

An exponent (b) of around 0.75 is typically found (Aboitiz, 1996), with brains increasing in mass (volume) roughly three-quarters as fast as bodies. Encephalization, the residual remaining capacity after meeting the basic allometric requirements of a large/small brain to drive a large/small body, represents the additional processing capacity beyond that required for routine control of body functions, and clearly relates to whatever we may mean by "intelligence". Thus the encephalization quotient (EQ) is the ratio between the real and the expected brain weight for the animal's body size.

THE GROWTH OF ENCEPHALIZATION IN THE FOSSIL RECORD

An examination of the allometric ratio in the fossil record indicates that reptiles were small brained 300 million years ago, and are no different now; nor were the dinosaurs particularly small brained, so we cannot conclude with popular belief that that was the reason for their demise (Lewin, 1992). With the appearance of archaic mammals around 200 million years ago we see an allometric increase in capacity, especially perhaps in the neocortex; with the appearance of modern mammals near the end of the Cretaceous, 65 million years ago, corresponding perhaps to a move from nocturnal to diurnal habits, encephalization starts to take off, increasing dramatically 30 million years ago with the evolution of ungulates, carnivores, and especially primates, the last of which quickly evolved a fully modern encephalization ratio. (Prosimians appear in the geological record around 55 million years ago in the Paleocene; New World monkeys branch off from Old World stock around 35 million years ago in the Oligocene, and the split between Old World monkeys and apes may be dated to 25 million years ago in the Miocene, see Milton, 1993.) Thus monkeys average two to three times the value for other modern mammals; we reach six times that value, much of the "excess" being represented in "association" areas, where processing from the different senses is cross-integrated for the production of mental maps. (The fact that the degree of encephalization of *Australopithecus afarensis* equalled that of the chimpanzee suggests that being bipedal places no further demands on encephalization.) Such developments in turn permitted exploitation of a wider range of environments and the attainment, generally, of a larger body size and a reduced reproductive rate. Introspective self-consciousness may have been a consequence of the ability to generate ever better cognitive maps and internal representations or models of reality.

LAMINAR AND COLUMNAR ORGANIZATION IN THE CORTEX

Quality, of course, is no less important then *quantity*. The mammalian (and therefore the primate and human) cortex is unique in its laminar and columnar organization, compared with the telencephalic organization in birds in terms of discrete nuclei. Thus the mammalian system, together with its format of repeating modules, is highly flexible, permitting the multiplexing of input and output functions (see e.g. Karten, 1991). The columns of the cerebral cortex are the elementary functional units and building blocks, the *quantitative* aspect of evolution being achieved by expansion of the number of columns. *Qualitative* changes, which have been harder to document, are achievable by altering patterns of connectivity between different cortical regions, and by altered functional activity in these regions.

NEUROGENESIS AND BRAIN–BODY GROWTH AND DEVELOPMENT

In a very real sense, during ontogeny the brain, via the pituitary and hormonal regulation, determines bodily growth. Thus embryological neurogenetic processes ultimately determine both target brain size of the adult (directly) and ultimate body size (indirectly) (Deacon, 1990). The human brain grows exactly as if it were in a giant ape's body; however, partly because of decoupled growth in different brain regions (enormous prefrontal enlargement, with considerable reductions, relative to our overall greatly expanded cortical mantle, in size of visual areas and primary motor cortex), it ultimately regulates body growth as though it were the size of a chimpanzee brain. Thus our large brains may effectively stem from slowing bodily compared with brain development. However, other developmental factors may also play a role (Deacon, 1990). Thus metabolic rate scales to the 0.75 power of body size in mammals, thereby influencing if not determining the correlations between adult and fetal brain size, fetal litter size, adult metabolic capacity, and altriciality (degree to which the infant is nest bound) or precocity (degree of early independence or mobility) at birth. Though only 2% of body weight, our brains demand 20% of our resting metabolic or energetic budget. (The figure is 9% in chimpanzees and 2% in typical marsupials, see e.g. Smith & Tompkins, 1995.) As body size increases, so too does the basic metabolic rate, and brains may ultimately only become as big as the body can support further increases in metabolic rate. Moreover, large brains also have a lower tolerance for extremes of temperature and pose obstetric problems as well as compromising locomotion. They are thus conceivable as an investment that only pays off in a life-long time scale via a quantum increase in complexity of behavior, itself the combined product of a large brain, slow development, extended parental care, and enhanced learning. Indeed, our strategy in this respect (when to be born, when to be weaned, to stop growing, to reproduce, to die) is one of a long gestation, a relatively (to adult body weight) large neonate size, few young, an extended period of dependency (i.e. altriciality), slow growth, delayed reproduction, and long life span—factors, as we saw earlier, all probably relating to the evolution of a home base, food sharing, a division of labour by sex, the development of the family, and the evolution of language and culture (Smith & Tompkins, 1995). However, it is far from clear when in our evolution these patterns emerged, or whether they all emerged at the same time, though our altriciality contrasts with the generally precocial pattern of the other primates. Thus it takes the human neonate about a year to reach the stage of motor development equivalent to that of a newborn chimpanzee; moreover, whereas our brains are about one-quarter that of the adult at birth, in *Pan* the figure is one-half, and two-thirds in *Macaca*. Rosenberg and Trevathan (1996) observe that we resemble precocial mammals, with small litters, long gestations, and large brains, but are altricial in giving birth to very undeveloped young. In this we are perhaps best charaterized as secondary altricial.

While mammalian brain–body size trends are usually reported in terms of *adult* values, it may well be instructive to view them as endpoints of ontogenetic brain–body growth trajectories. In most mammalian species these brain–body growth trajectories are *bimodal* when expressed in log coordinates, with two roughly linear trends following sequentially in development—a steeper *embryological* function and a shallower subsequent *postnatal* function. Typically, we see a slope (exponent) of about 1.0 for the initial embryological phase of neurogenesis (see Fig. 8.1), and postnatally a much smaller exponent of 0.1 to 0.2, relating mostly to growth in cell size and myelination. In some species somatic growth may continue well past reproductive maturity and cessation of brain growth, whereas humans seem to get their large brains (12 billion neurons, 10 trillion synapses) through a prolonged *period* of brain growth, without any unusual growth *rate*. Thus whereas primates generally grow their brains at the same rate as other mammals, but increase body size more slowly, we continue brain growth for up to 1 year after birth, leading to an effective gestation of 21 months, and a brain three times the size of a human-sized ape. This postnatal growth period may have only been possible with full bipedal terrestriality, the latter itself resulting from climatic change and loss of trees (Stanley, 1992). The final endpoints in the allometric ratio of log brain to log body weight in different species tend approximately to align along a single linear function— the adult interspecific allometric trend—even though *individually* their pre- and post-natal functions may be quite different. The size that a particular functional brain area ultimately attains in adulthood is not purely determined by early neurogenesis or neural growth, but rather by a subsequent

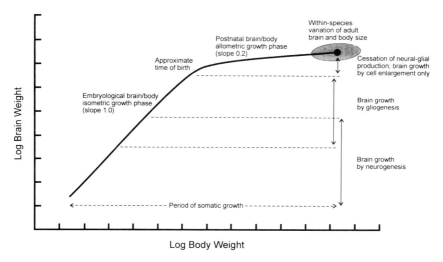

FIG. 8.1. Diagrammatic representation of an idealized mammalian ontogenetic brain–body growth curve in log–log coordinates. There is a slope of about 1.0 for the initial embryological phase of neurogenesis, and postnatally a much smaller exponent. Reprinted with permission from Deacon, T.W., Problems of ontogeny and phylogeny in brain-size evolution, *International Journal of Primatology*, 1990, *11(3)*, 237–282.

competition of neurons and axons for synaptic space. In this context prefrontal cortex, containing a major speech area, Broca's area, is heavily over-represented compared with that of the apes. There is little evidence of entirely new structures or novel neuronal connections evolving; instead, the human brain has slowly recruited and modified areas and circuits, perhaps once important for somewhat different functions, for newly evolving cognitive operations. Thus our prefrontal cortex probably inherited space and circuitry once more important for a range of other functions (Deacon, cited by Gibbons, 1993b).

Ultimately, of course, brain size and the size of constituent structures is determined by the rate and duration of cell division during neurogenesis. The number of neurons can be increased by increasing the rate of production of neuronal precursors, or by increasing the length of time for producing the latter, or by reducing the rate of neuronal death. During early brain development in mammals, neuronal precursor cells, mostly located on the ventricle surface of the neural tube, undergo symmetric division, each cell producing two daughters, which themselves may continue so dividing. Neurons appear when a precursor cell divides asymmetrically, the resulting daughter neuroblast exiting the precursor pool and differentiating as a neuron (Finlay & Darlington, 1995).

Almost half of our 10^5 genes contribute to building the brain (Sedvall & Farde, 1995). In the adult, the brain contains around 10^{10} neurons. Each of these directly contacts, via synaptic connections, tens of thousands of other neurons especially in the cerebral cortex, and their function is determined by thousands of continuous chemical events. Information transfer within this neuronal network is mediated by chemical neurotransmitters that each interact with one or several specific subtypes of receptors located on the "receiving" neuron. More than 100 such transmitters, gaseous messengers, and growth factors have already been identified, along with 300 or so receptor subtypes (Sedvall & Farde, 1995), though so far only a few have been mapped with regard to their anatomical distribution, and our knowledge of how they operate is very sketchy. Nonetheless, were the possible number of resultant brain states to be calculated, it would rival or exceed the number of molecules in the Universe (Gazzaniga, 1992). Indeed, any major increase in processing capacity, were evolution to select for such an increase, might be difficult to achieve because of the balance that must be maintained between the size and number of neurons and the blood vessels that nourish them. Any increase in connectivity would demand longer and thicker axon trunks, which in turn would require thicker myelin insulation, and better blood supply—all competing for physical space with the processing elements themselves. We may already be near the physical limits of evolutionary growth, without perhaps some radically new solution in design.

Equally impressive, and little understood, is how the developing brain is put together, and how the neurons migrate—navigate their axonic extensions—to their final target destinations (Roush, 1996). Their pathfinding seems to involve an array of proteins that guide, attract, and repel. It is perhaps surprising that things go wrong so comparatively infrequently, with neurodevelopmental disorders such as childhood autism, and schizophrenia, which, though typically manifesting clinically in the early adult years, nevertheless have their origins during pregnancy (Bradshaw & Mattingley, 1995). Barinaga (1996) reviews recent studies of genetic mutations associated with anomalous cortical structure. Young cortical neurons normally travel from regions deep within the brain along roadways formed by support cells known as radial glia; the latter lead to a layer of cells (the preplate) near the outer surface of the developing brain. The migrating neurons enter the preplate, which eventually forms a series of neat layers of cortical cells, with subsequent generations of young neurons continuing to enter from below. They pass though the layers already in place to form fresh, overlying layers, until there are eventually six. Clearly, there are many opportunities, genetic or environmental, for the process to go awry.

At a macro level, the brain comprises a diverse collection of neural structures, cortically and subcortically, each with a distinctive, characteristic shape and intricate internal architecture. Van Essen (1997) proposes that,

during development, mechanical tension, working against internally generated hydrostatic pressure, is a major driving force for many aspects of
morphogenesis. The human cerebral cortex attains a surface area of about
1600cm^2, nearly three times what it would in the absence of convolutions,
whereas in other, smaller-brained species the cortical sheet remains smooth
or lissencephalic. This may result from differences in the duration of neurogenesis, which increases steeply with brain size for the cerebral cortex and
less steeply for subcortical structures. Thus convolutions increase with brain
size primarily because the expansion of the cortical sheet outpaces the
minimal area needed to envelop the underlying cerebral volume. For a given
species, the convolutions maintain a consistent position in relation to
identified cortical areas in some regions, whereas elsewhere there may be
considerable individual variability. Van Essen suggests that tension-based
morphogenesis can account for both the variability and the consistency, in
terms of underlying patterns of connectivity, between cortical areas. He
notes that many structures have pronounced anisotropies in axonic,
dendritic, and glial orientation, and proposes that if such processes are
under tension, their springiness will make the tissue differentially elastic in
different directions. During cerebral growth, tension along axons acting
together should pull interconnected regions towards one another, resulting
in shorter axonic connections and more compact neural circuitry.

PLASTIC REORGANIZATION IN THE ADULT BRAIN

If we understood how the brain initially organizes, and reorganizes after
injury and during learning, we might be able to assist in repair. However,
recent evidence (Hallett, 1995) indicates that reorganization and reworking
of synapses is not, as was generally thought, limited to critical developmental periods before and shortly after birth, but may extend, though
perhaps less dramatically, throughout the life span. Thus the "wiring" and
connectivity of the adult brain is far from fixed; the brain is a dynamically
changing structure in response to limb amputation, after injury or stroke, or
even merely after extensive training. After loss of a finger, sensorimotor
areas previously responsible for that finger now become additionally
available for and extend the dexterity and sensitivity of adjacent fingers
(Merzenich, 1987). After hemispherectomy, removal of all cortical tissue on
one side of the brain for the control of otherwise intractable epilepsy,
neuroimaging studies show that recovery of lost motor function on the
affected contralateral side of the body is mediated by the other residual,
unaffected motor cortex; similarly, the size of the motor cortex devoted to
muscles moving the operating fingers increases in blind Braille readers,
piano players, and individuals learning complex motor sequences (Hallett,
1995). Even more dramatically, blind (but not sighted) subjects show PET

activation of primary and secondary *visual* cortex during meaningful (but not meaningless) tactile Braille tasks (Sadato, Pascual-Leone, Grafman et al., 1996), indicating that loss of sight does not lead just to increased (tactile) activation in the somatosensory cortex, but also in the visual areas.

All this may be achieved by a variety of mechanisms, which include changes in synaptic strength, increases in synaptic density, axonal sprouting, which permits new synaptic connections to be formed, and changes in the balance of excitation and inhibition. Indeed, individual neurons normally have potential access to much larger regions of anatomical connectivity within the cortex than is apparent from their usual functional territory. Such additional areas are normally kept in check by tonic inhibition, which, if removed by accident or injury, allows a rapid increase in influence. Though the "final" shape of the developing brain in childhood may reflect a "sculpting" process, or the "pruning" of excess cells or connections (Katz & Shatz, 1996), that is not necessarily the end of the matter, with further change, though less dramatic or extensive, being possible throughout the life span. Of course, with pathology such as Alzheimer's disease, runaway cell loss can be devastating, and we can even speculate on whether plastic reorganization always acts in an adaptive fashion, to the benefit of the individual in a particular environmental context. Thus early pathological loss of left-hemisphere language circuits in the developing child may result in relatively unimpaired language processes; these seem to "parasitize" upon corresponding right-hemisphere structures that would normally subserve spatial functions, to the latter's detriment. In this respect there may be limits to processing space, which is competed for by various functions, of which language seems to dominate. Whether this domination is predetermined or a consequence of social interactions is uncertain.

WHOLE-OBJECT RECOGNITION AND "BINDING"

We generate an internal perceptual representation of the outside world in the posterior parts of the brain—the occipital and inferior temporal lobes (visual object recognition), superior temporal cortex (hearing, speech, recognition of sounds), and anterior parietal cortex (the identification of objects by touch). Somehow we achieve cross-modality matching, i.e. recognition of an object such as a coin by *either* sight *or* sound *or* feel, by *binding* together its various qualities, perhaps by means of temporarily correlated neuronal activity (Friedman-Hill, Robertson, & Treisman, 1995); such synchronization may be achieved by the thalamus (Bressler, Coppola, & Nakamura, 1993; Singer, 1994), a collection of cell groups or nuclei located deep in the forebrain and managing the transfer of information to and from the cerebral cortex. Coherent or synchronous activity may therefore be the means whereby we group, segregate, or selectively attend to certain objects, and "bind together" the relevant perceptual qualities. The thalamus and cortex of course co-evolved with the mammals, reaching their maximum development with the primates and ourselves. Steriade and Amzica (1996) report that fast (30–40Hz) coherent electrical field oscillations appear during brain activation among closely located cortical foci and through reciprocal cortico-thalamic networks.

BRAIN SIZE AND INTELLECTUAL CAPACITY

Our increased level of encephalization clearly relates somehow to our supposedly superior intellectual capacities, which include language and tool use. However, a small brain (of around 300cm^3, i.e. in the chimpanzee range) is not incompatible in microcephalic dwarves with some level of articulate speech (Jensen-Jazbutis, cited in Jerison, 1982) and reasonable sensorimotor abilities. Microcephaly is typically defined in terms of a head circumference of more than two (or three, according to some authorities) standard deviations (SDs) below the age mean. While some studies claim that most microcephalics are mentally retarded (see e.g. Dorman, 1991, for review), at two or more SDs below the mean for age there may be many school children who are indistinguishable from their normocephalic peers in intelligence. Indeed, there may be no straightforward relationship between (diminished) head size and (reduced) intelligence (though see Holden, 1991; Lynn, 1993). It may be that normal intelligence in what is technically a microcephalic reflects an enormous level of spare processing capacity in the average human brain. This, indeed, is evident from clinical cases where in infancy very large areas of cortex ("hemidecortication") may be surgically removed to control otherwise intractable epilepsy; thus in such cases near-normal intelligence may be reported on testing at adulthood (Goodman & Whitaker, 1985). Presumably, with such developmentally early surgery, plastic reorganization can occur, allowing remaining structures to assume affected functions. In any case, even at a regional level the correlation between area size and resultant functional capacity may be relatively weak, as indeed Gall (cited by Marshall, 1980) observed in 1835 in the context of the now out-dated "science" of phrenology; it is all too tempting to try to explain away exceptions as the consequence of an ever-increasing list of exceptional circumstances or limiting factors—including experience or the environment.

It is also possible that an internal mosaic reorganization of the brain, consequent upon selection for such functions as speech and manipulative skills, may be a more fundamental determinant of intellectual capacity, with an *overall* brain enlargement occurring as a secondary consequence of selective reorganization and enlargement of just a *few* such structures (Deacon, 1986a,b). Indeed, a cascade of such consequent changes may occur even in remote regions, owing to embryonic coupling rather than via direct selection for such remote regions. Such changes may in turn increase the potential for new abilities, which in turn will perhaps select for further reorganization and/or encephalization (Kien, 1991). Increases in encephalization could in this way occur via a series of plateaux, rather than a steady growth, as an inspection of cranial capacities in the fossil record would indeed indicate.

A concrete example of selective pressures on a specific region (occipital cortex) from a specific ecological demand (vision), with enlarging visual structures driving an overall increase in brain size was recently reported (Barton, Purvis, & Harvey, 1995). High visual acuity and analysis of form and color are computationally expensive, requiring large neural networks and considerable brain tissue. This may best be achieved by changing the gross rate of neurogenesis for the whole brain. Bigger brains, even if driven via a single function (such as vision) and locus (occipital cortex) may lead to the rapid evolution of many new capabilities. Similarly, a structure previously subserving conditional responding may have grown in step with the rest of the brain during our recent evolution, and that structure's increased capacity now might permit it to mediate *grammar*—a highly developed specialization of a more general application of conditionality rules (Passingham, 1993). Thus increased capacity can lead to increased specialization and an apparently qualitative differentiation of function. It was in fact recently reported (Finlay & Darlington, 1995) that the sizes of most brain structures correlated closely with absolute brain size, the only exceptions being the olfactory structures and, perhaps, the prefrontal cortex. It is the latter region that subserves our essential human-ness, personality, and social behavior and social or Machiavellian intelligence. We shall turn to the latter issue in the next chapter.

SUMMARY AND CONCLUSIONS

In accordance with allometric principles, brain size generally increases somewhat more slowly than body size, according to a power function with an exponent of around 0.75. Encephalization, which represents the additional processing capacity beyond that required for routine control of body functions, accelerated with the evolution of the primates, reflecting their visuomotor adaptations. Further increases in encephalization occurred with the advent of the hominids, presumably reflecting the growth of cognitive maps. The *quantitative* aspects of brain growth seem to be achieved by increasing the number of cortical columns rather than by changing neuronal density; *qualitative* evolutionary changes in brain function may be achievable by altered patterns of area connectivity and of function.

Target adult brain (and body) size is largely determined during embryogenesis, with, in humans, the brain growing as if it were in a giant ape's body, and with bodily development slowed compared with that of the brain; an ultimately limiting factor is probably adult metabolic capacity. Nevertheless, we are unusual in the prolonged duration of brain growth for up to a year after birth, perhaps as a consequence of full bipedal terrestriality. Though our prefrontal cortex is particularly evolved, there is little evidence of entirely new structures or novel neuronal connections. Instead, the human brain has slowly recruited and modified areas and circuits previously subserving somewhat different functions, for newly evolving cognitive operations. The prefrontal cortex previously seems to have been more important for vision and smell.

During embryogenesis, the architecture of the brain is under the control of a host of poorly understood neurochemical factors, and it is then that neurodevelopmental disorders as ultimately devastating as autism and schizophrenia may first strike. However, the wiring and connectivity of the brain, contrary to what was believed until very recently, is far from fixed and is subject to change and adaptation as a result of learning, experience, or injury. Moreover, it is also becoming increasingly apparent that widely distributed areas of the brain can become simultaneously or synchronously active in response to complex stimulation via the coordinated activity of dynamically shifting functional networks. The thalamus, also highly evolved in humans, may play a central coordinating role. Though it is hard not to believe that our advanced cognitive function is largely a consequence of our increased encephalization, there nevertheless seems to be much spare brain capacity. There is only a loose correlation between intelligence and brain size, and hemidecortication may, if performed in infancy, result in relatively little apparent deficit. Nevertheless, bigger brains, even if driven via selection for a single function, may lead to the rapid evolution of many new capabilities, with, consequently, new selective pressures for yet further changes.

FURTHER READINGS

Aboitiz, F. (1996). Does bigger mean better? Evolutionary determinants of brain size and structure. *Brain, Behaviour and Evolution, 47*, 225–245.

Changeux, J.-P., & Chavaillon, J. (Eds.) (1995). *Origins of the human brain.* Oxford: Clarendon Press.

Deacon, T.W. (1990). Problems of ontogeny and phylogeny in brain-size evolution. *International Journal of Primatology, 11*, 237–282.

Finlay, B.L., & Darlington, R.B. (1995). Linked regularities in the development and evolution of mammalian brains. *Science, 268*, 1578–1583.

Friedman-Hill, S.R., Robertson, L.C., & Treisman, A. (1995). Parietal contributions to visual feature binding: Evidence from a patient with bilateral lesions. *Science, 269*, 853–857.

Gazzaniga, M.S. (1992). *Nature's mind: The biological roots of thinking, emotions, sexuality, language and intelligence.* New York: Basic Books.

Jerison, H.J., & Jerison, I. (Eds.) (1986). *Intelligence and evolutionary biology.* New York: Springer.

Ross, C., & Henneberg, M. (1995). Basicranial flexion, relative brain size and facial kyphosis in *Homo sapiens* and some fossil hominids. *American Journal of Physical Anthropology, 98,* 575–593.

Rushton, J. P. (1996). *Race, evolution and behavior.* New Brunswick, NJ: Transaction Publishers.

Rushton, J.P., & Ankney, E. (1996). Brain size and cognitive ability: Correlations with age, sex, social class and race. *Psychonomic Bulletin and Review, 3,* 21–36.

CHAPTER NINE

Intelligence, social intelligence, consciousness, and self-awareness

Intellectual capacity is traditionally measured by intelligence tests, though there is much disagreement about the nature of intelligence, how (and whether) it should be measured, whether there are multiple intelligences, and where in the brain may reside the anatomical correlates of such processes. In terms of general problem-solving capacity, one region, the prefrontal cortex, seems to be particularly important and is highly evolved in our species. In this chapter we also explore the probable role of social or Machiavellian intelligence in primate (and human) evolution, and the place of possible positive (altruism, empathy, reciprocity) as well as "negative" (exploitation, deceit, retaliation, manipulation, and plot) aspects in the evolution of social behaviors, social consciousness, and a "theory of mind"—aspects that may be singularly deficient in human autism. The need to be able to see things from another's point of view may have been crucial in the evolution of consciousness and of self-awareness, as may perhaps be indexed by an individual's responses to its own mirror reflection. Consciousness, however, like praxis, tool use, language, and intellect cannot be localized to a single structure or circuit, though certain networks undoubtedly play particularly important roles.

THE EVOLUTION OF INTELLIGENCE

Behaviors do not fossilize, though we can infer changes in behavior from their likely skeletal effects. Thus changes in the thickness and cross-sectional morphology of the human humerus around 20,000 years ago may be associated with a change from spear-thrusting to spear-throwing coincidental with the appearance, in the archaeological record, of new kinds of (throwing) spear (Fischman, 1995b). We tend to view intelligence as the ability to solve novel problems (e.g. a wild vervet monkey discovers how to extract nutritive sap with dry pods, see Hauser, 1988), and to juggle, wield, or manipulate several disparate ideas simultaneously (Calvin, 1994). Alternatively, we may define it as an ability to deal adaptively with the ever-changing demands of the environment, to proceed efficiently to appropriately set goals, and to identify commonalities across varying situations or experiences—aspects, perhaps of prefrontal executive function. There is in fact no single definition of intelligence (Neisser, Boodoo, Bouchard et al., 1996); a given person's intellectual performance may well vary on different occasions, in different domains, as judged by different criteria, and many are concerned that a hypothetical abstract, or even various sets of disparate performance scores, have been "reified" into a single entity devoid of independent existence. This is not the place to consider possible population and gender differences, environmental and cultural contributions, problems of standardization, reliability, validity, and utility in daily life (Rushton & Ankney, 1996), whether the various systems of abilities ("intelligences") can be captured by standard psychometric tests, and what such tests should be used for, such as selection, diagnosis, or evaluation (Neisser et al., 1996). Suffice it to say that studies of monozygotic twins reared apart indicate that a very substantial proportion of the observed variation in intelligence can be attributed to genetic variation (see Turner, 1996, for review), and that genes on the X chromosome may code for aspects of intelligence. The female, of course, is a mosaic of two X chromosomes, one of which is methylated and inactivated randomly early in embryogenesis. Consequently, the male with his single X chromosome is more likely to be affected either by advantageous genes or disadvantageous mutations—and, indeed, though the distribution of intelligence-quotient (IQ) scores (whatever they measure) is bell shaped, with both sexes having the same mean, there is considerably wider variability (i.e. a bigger range) in the male. This is quite separate from a probable male superiority in mathematical and musical abilities, and a female verbal superiority (Bradshaw, 1989, Chapter 9).

Though, until recently it has been attractive to contrast verbal and spatial processes in the context of sex differences in cognitive style—and there is some support from brain-imaging studies for the idea that females may possess additional brain regions devoted to language, see e.g. Shaywitz, Shaywitz, Pugh et al. (1995)—it may be overly simplistic to invoke an overall male superiority in the spatial domain. It is certainly the case that in most human cultures and in various infrahuman species the male tends to play a more exploratory role, perhaps reflecting a dimorphism in competition for territory and dispersal. For this reason, the idea of male hunting and female food gathering in hominid evolution and the sharing of labor has also long found favor. The problem is that spatial abilities, maybe of a different kind, are surely just as important in foraging and gathering, such as remembering the location of food sources, identifying them as "signals" from a background of visual "noise", and so on. Conventional intelligence tests typically ask participants to match patterns, to assemble shapes into higher-order configurations, and, in the verbal domain, to make judgments about the semantic similarity or relatedness of various words or concepts—all of a somewhat abstract and artificial flavor.

Silverman and Eals (1992) examined possible sex differences within the spatial domain with a variety of novel tasks, at least some of which, though also involving a memory component, were also rather more naturalistic in approach. Thus they presented displays consisting of various everyday objects randomly scattered; after a period of inspection and a further retention interval with the display removed, participants were tested with new arrays where some of the items had been removed, or transposed, or where additional items had been added. Females outperformed males on these tests of object and learning memory—a finding certainly compatible with the idea of female foraging, of visually disembedding food objects from within a background, and of having to remember the location of key items and whether their disposition had in any way altered during the passage of time. Males, on the other hand, may outperform females on the more traditional tests of mental rotation, map reading, maze learning, and spatial relations. Tests of mental rotation require participants to designate which of several alternatives represents a target object presented in various orientations; space relations tests require, for example, decisions about which three-dimensional objects could or could not be constructed from given two-dimensional or unfolded patterns. A male bias for hunting could probably benefit from a general ability to orient oneself in relation to objects and places, as assessed by tests of mental rotation, map reading and maze learning; however, it must be stressed that sex differences in all these tasks are typically small, and the exact adaptive significance, in terms of hunting, gathering (and, in the case of language abilities) nurturing, is not always clear. Nor is it clear which might have come first, the underlying capacity or the overt behavior.

Conventionally, overall intelligence-test scores are converted to a scale with a mean of 100 and a standard deviation of 15, such that 95% of the population scores within two standard deviations of the mean, i.e. between 70 and 130. However, individuals rarely perform equally well on all the different test items, with one person perhaps performing somewhat better on verbal and another on spatial items. Nevertheless, subtests measuring different abilities do tend to correlate positively, with people scoring high (or low) on one such subtest being likely to be above (or below) average on others. Though these complex correlations can be clarified by factor analysis, it is unclear whether there is a single, common, underlying ability or general factor, g, representing what all the tests have in common. One view envisages a hierarchy of factors with g at the apex, though there is no agreement on what g may mean—a mere statistical regularity, a kind of mental energy, a generalized abstract reasoning ability, or an index of central processing speed (see e.g. Neisser et al., 1996).

One approach is to relate g to "fluid" problem-solving ability in dealing with novel situations, compared with the application of "crystallized" intelligence in employing existing skills and knowledge. It may be useful to distinguish between analytic problem-solving skills and synthetic creativity in strategically and creatively developing novel solutions (Sternberg, 1985), with a possible third factor, practical daily-life "intelligence" in an overall triarchic account. Analytic problems, of the type suitable for test construction, tend to have been formulated by others, to be clearly defined, to come with all necessary information for solution, to have only a single right answer reachable by a single method, to be divorced from daily life and to have little practical relevance. Conversely, practical problems are poorly defined, requiring recognition and formulation of the problem, to have various possible solutions, to relate to practical experience and daily life, and to require personal involvement.

We may even need to invoke a multiplicity of unrelated forms of intelligence, including language abilities, logical and mathematical reasoning, spatial reasoning, body-movement skills, and social sensitivity (Gardner, 1983), though some of these forms of intelligence may perhaps more appropriately be described as special talents. Support for this approach comes from the idea that the architecture of the mind consists of a number of discrete, independent, and "encapsulated" modules (Fodor, 1983), all operating in a quasi-autonomous fashion. Clinical neurology has long demonstrated the discrete effects of lesions in generating such *deficits* as aphasia, agnosia, apraxia, and so on, and, conversely, in the idiot-savant syndrome and sometimes in autism, preserved *abilities* (mathematical, calendrical calculation, drawing) in the face of overwhelming general deficits; nevertheless, nowadays, we are increasingly moving toward a view of the mind that invokes distributed processing and massively parallel interactive networks, and a concept of the brain in terms of highly interconnected circuits rather than discrete, relatively isolated processing centers. We can further contrast anterior and posterior modes of information processing, in that the more traditional ideas of specialist processors or "expert systems", perhaps subserving aspects of "crystallized" intelligence, may apply more in regions posterior to the sulcus centralis. Conversely, prefrontal structures, known to subserve important aspects of working memory (Goldman-Rakic, 1992), may be where "fluid" intelligence, problem solving, and strategic aspects may operate.

Apparently intelligent behavior in nonhuman primates (see Fig. 9.1) may not necessarily reflect individual problem-solving behavior so much as proficient imitation or social learning (Visalberghi & Fragaszy, 1990). Imitation of a successful conspecific is of course a good way of learning, especially when trial-and-error learning would be slow or costly, and there are many instances in the primate literature of other members of a troop rapidly "catching on" to a successful innovation by a troop member, for example, washing food items or separating grain from sand by "flotation". Imitation itself, of course, requires some considerable cognitive capacity. Nor is it always clear whether an individual is imitating another, or has independently *rediscovered* the process, perhaps as a consequence of attending to the relevant circumstances and/or putting himself/herself into the appropriate contextual situation (Tomasello & Call, 1994). Successful monkeys in fact seem not to copy potential models exactly, appearing to do better with directed trial-and-error learning; apes seem particularly skilled at imitative learning in complex situations such as "fishing" for termites, dipping for ants, cracking nuts and using leaves as sponges to extract nutritive liquids. Thus we can perhaps distinguish between three types of social learning (Visalberghi & Fragaszy, 1990):

FIG. 9.1.   Example of a chimpanzee engaged in problem-solving behavior. Materials kindly supplied by Daniel Povinelli; photograph by Donna T. Bierscwhale, University of Southwestern Louisiana/New Iberia Research Center.

1. *Social facilitation*, where the probability is incremented of performing a behavior pattern *already* in the animal's repertoire, in the presence of another conspecific already performing it.
2. *Stimulus enhancement*, where an individual's attention is drawn to the locus of a behaving conspecific, or to whatever it is interested in, so that again it performs something already within its repertoire.
3. *Imitation*, where the behavior is truly novel and not within the individual's repertoire, but results from observing another; the behavior then very closely resembles that of the model.

We should therefore distinguish between copying a motor act by rote, and finding a guiding rule. This is the difference between so-called bottom-up and top-down processing. Tool use is in fact uncommon among monkeys (but not apes) in the wild, and involves learning rules relating action, object, and outcome from the behavior of an effective model. Learning rules (by trial and error) may be easier for apes than straight imitative copying, whereas monkeys may not be particularly good at either (Visalberghi & Fragaszy, 1990). Thus capuchin monkeys, though very successful tool users in captivity, are not good at modifying tools in advance of their use.

The sudden appearance of Oldowan tool use in the hominid archaeological record may suggest not so much trial-and-error solutions independently achieved by many different individuals, but rather imitation, rule-mastering, and even apprenticeship, as nowadays. Humans are pre-eminent in the adaptive acquisition of new behaviors, and the co-evolution of tool behavior and increase in imitative capacity may have been mutually facilitatory, leading to the rapid dissemination of new behaviors. Such a conceptualization leads to the linking of technical and social (Machiavellian) intelligence in a mutually interdependent fashion.

Monkeys lack the empathy and levels of understanding of which chimpanzees and our own species are capable. Thus macaques may be trained to perform complementary roles in a single task (Povinelli, Parks, and Novack, 1992), whereby an animal works with a human partner for a food reward visible only to one member who cannot retrieve it, whereas the other member of the pair can perform the necessary retrieval operations but cannot see the correct location of the target. Chimpanzees, but not monkeys, can successfully swap roles with their human partners; though the apes could learn by watching others, the monkeys seem to have understood little about the nature of their partner's duties or actions. As we shall see, apes, but not monkeys, seem to have a concept of themselves as individuals, distinct from others, to be able to recognize themselves in a mirror, to be aware of their own capabilities and those of other individuals, and to be able to put themselves into another's position, imagining what it does and what it knows.

THE THEORY OF MACHIAVELLIAN INTELLIGENCE

The interests of individuals within groups are rarely identical, despite the fact that group membership may lead to greater access to resources and reduced susceptibility to predation for the member. Indeed, group membership involves the constant need to reassess one's standing in a changing social network of peers. Social skills allow us to form alliances and switch tactics when necessary or advantageous. We therefore spend much time gathering information on social relationships and trying to ascertain the intentions of others and their attentional states. Intense social competition, where our conspecifics may even be our worst enemies, will result in manipulation and deception, the balancing of competitive and cooperative options, reciprocity and deceit, tactics, plot, counterplot, and gamesmanship to permit the weak to beat the strong. Human infants from birth are extremely sensitive to social stimuli, responding to the sounds of speech and the pictures of faces in quite a different way than to other forms of stimulation.

Social or Machiavellian intelligence (Humphrey, 1976; Whiten, 1991), a characteristic of the higher primates, may therefore be seen as the ability to outwit peers and competitors by predicting their likely responses to our own changes in behavior, relationships, or alliances (Dunbar, 1993), and by interpreting their behavior in terms of inferences about such intrinsically unobservable states as desires, intentions, and beliefs (Povinelli & Preuss, 1995). A possible criterion for the achievement of such a "theory of mind", said to be present by the age of five years in most children, is an understanding that another individual could have a false belief about a given physical or social situation (Povinelli & Preuss, 1995); thus one must be able simultaneously to keep track of the state of the real world and the possibly discrepant beliefs of another individual. The ability, therefore, deliberately to deceive others, i.e. to give them a false belief about the world, is held by some to demonstrate possession of a theory of mind and the application of Machiavellian intelligence. Clearly, the term "deliberately" is important here, as lies otherwise are notorious in the animal kingdom (Savage-Rumbaugh & Lewin, 1994); for example, we see the employment by the plover parent of an apparently broken wing in misleading and leading potential predators away from the nest. (Indeed, Ristau, 1991, notes that such feigning of injury may depend on the intruder's actually *looking toward* the nest, as if the bird really imputed intentionality to the intruder.)

The problem is that much of the evidence for animals' creativity, intentionality or deliberate deception tends inevitably to be anecdotal, though if we reject it we run the risk of losing a major potential source of scientific information (Cartmill, 1995b). Premack (1988) describes how a chimpanzee, needing human assistance to get to food elsewhere, would pull the human across, while first trying to remove a blindfold placed over that person's eyes—but not over the nose or mouth. Whiten (1991) reports that a chimpanzee could differentiate between guessing and knowing in a pair of observers, consistently seeking the help of the one who it knew "knew" what was necessary. In this context chimpanzees are reported (Savage-Rumbaugh & Lewin, 1994) to pretend to eat imaginary food, or to pull an imaginary toy with an imaginary string, "permitting" it to get stuck in an imaginary crack in the floor. Again, however, there are numerous anecdotal reports of elephants, bears, and even ravens sliding in play (Brown, 1994)—must we again include "intentionality" in our criteria, and how do we define or assess it? Savage-Rumbaugh (cited by Anderson, Holmes, & Else, 1996) describes an instance of a bonobo demonstrating possession of a "theory of mind", when Panbanisha watched a human secretly substitute a bug for some sweets in a box; when a second human tried to open the box, the first human asked the bonobo "what is she looking for?" Panbanisha signed in reply that the human was looking for sweets, and that the first human was "bad" to play such a trick.

Relative to apes, we certainly have improved capacities not just in problem-solving, motor skills, praxis, and communication, but also in social-event perception, shared attention, imitation, pantomime, cooperation, deception, and reciprocal communication of intentions. Byrne (1995b) notes that platyrrhine and catarrhine monkeys, and presumably their common ancestors likewise, can deceive and cooperate, but perhaps not understand why their actions have certain effects on objects and other animals; this insight perhaps only emerged about 16 million years ago with orangutan-human ancestors, and is maybe confined, among today's primates, to the great apes and ourselves (Heyes, 1995). In Byrne's view, this second watershed in the origin of human intelligence includes the capacity to mindread or attribute mental states to others, and, allowing for forward planning, tool making, imitation, and teaching, it is a necessary precursor for the ultimate evolution of language. This viewpoint is indeed the one currently espoused in the present book, and is supported by the above-mentioned demonstration (Povinelli, Parks, & Novack, 1992) that pairs of rhesus monkeys, unlike chimpanzees and ourselves, were unable to reverse roles after being trained to perform complementary parts of a single task, in which one member could see where food was hidden but could not retrieve it, whereas the other could not see the food but was in a position to retrieve it. However, a Japanese macaque is reported (Tokida, Tanaka, Takefushi, & Hagiwara, 1994) to have discovered how to retrieve an apple from the middle of a transparent tube by throwing a stone at the former down the latter—and to have adjusted the force of her throw in the presence of rival conspecifics, implying both a theory of mind and an appreciation of the laws of physics. She eventually even brought her (*own*) infants to the tube, pushed them in, and got them to fetch her the apple!

Apes recognize kinship relationships in grooming and food-sharing, and form alliances in resource acquisition, against aggressors, in gaining access to females (such that an accomplice may even distract the attention of a dominant male), and in seeking revenge for past transgressions (Tomasello & Call, 1994). Thus they may manipulate the behavior of others, and learn how to predict their behavior in certain circumstances. They can judge when individuals are not merely *doing* something, but when they are *trying* to do it. There are, as we saw, apocryphal tales of captive chimpanzees leading blindfolded human collaborators by the hand to a food source, even trying to remove the blindfold so as to facilitate matters, and being able to differentiate between "guessing" and "knowing" in a human accomplice. A hand-reared gorilla is reported looking back and forth between a target and a human bystander's eyes, as if to establish both attention and intentionality, and as if it understood that an agent's behavior may depend on what it is looking at and attending to (Gomez, 1991). Indeed, human-raised and language-trained animals seem particularly sensitive to such social nuances, perhaps because the human environment may focus attention on others' intentions, or because symbol use presupposes an understanding of others as intentional agents. (It is, however, noteworthy that though a chimpanzee may deliberately employ a variety of deceptive signals to gain an advantage, there is as yet no evidence that they use their own conspecific patterns of vocalization actively to mislead or deceive, suggesting that their call system may be less under voluntary neocortical control than our own.)

Povinelli and Eddy (1996) are rather more cautious in ascribing to chimpanzees an awareness of the underlying state of attention behind another's gaze, even though they may be able to track the gaze of others, and by two and a half years of age human infants appear to understand the specific role played by the eyes in deploying attention in others. The investigators systematically explored how the presence of eyes, direct eye contact, and head orientation and movement affected young chimpanzees' choice of two experimenters from whom to request food. They found that the animals could be selectively attracted to other creatures making direct eye contact with them, or that they even exhibited postures or movements that indicated directed attention, though perhaps not necessarily appreciating the underlying mentalistic significance of these behaviors.

Machiavellianism of course emphasizes the negative aspects of expediency, manipulation, and selfish advancement, and human society reflects the tension between those aspects and the traditional virtues of trust, honor, decency, altruism, cooperation, morality, and ethics—the balance between exploitative and cooperative behaviors (Wilson, Near, & Miller, 1996). Though Niccolo Machiavelli (1469–1527), the Florentine diplomat, characterized (in every sense) the dark side of humanity, such behavior does have costs—e.g. retaliation and avoidance by others. Sociobiology examines the possible role of strategy optimization in such circumstances, and evidence is now emerging, along with questions of conscious self-awareness, of empathy, sympathy, reciprocal obligations, and maintenance of group harmony among chimpanzees; animals may take account not only of how their conspecifics *do* behave, but how they *ought* to. De Waal (1996) addresses the paradox that genetic self-advancement (evolution's motor) has given rise to remarkable capacities for apparent sympathy, care, reconciliation, reciprocity, and so on among animals with tightly knit social groups, such as wolves, elephants, and chimps. In this context it is interesting to note that behavioral scientists are happy to characterize negative behaviors or emotions in primates in anthropomorphic terms—enemies, cheating, selfishness, aggression, violence, and spite—but are less easy with the more positive aspects—friends, honesty, altruism, etc.—where often other euphemisms are sought. Why are we so reluctant to accept the possibility of benign motives and emotions in animals, and why do we seek so hard to unearth possible selfish motives for seemingly self-sacrificing acts?

In the context of apparent altruism, debate continues on whether evolution occurs at the level of an individual's reproductive interests (the classical Darwinian viewpoint), at the lower level of the gene (the "selfish gene" hypothesis, Dawkins, 1996), or at the other extreme, in certain cases, at the level of the group ("group selection", as espoused e.g. by D.S. Wilson, see Lewin, 1996). In the last instance, individuals within a group may appear to behave altruistically, sacrificing their individual reproductive future if, in consequence, related members of the group benefit and their own genetic interests are indirectly favored via their relatives' differential survival or reproduction. Though apparently altruistic behavior is not uncommon even among nonhuman species (surrogate care of infants, even suckling by other members of the group who may be more or less closely related to the infant), it is of course always open to exploitation by "cheats" bent on boosting their own reproductive success at the expense of others who hold back for the sake of the group. Group selection, however, may only operate when groups, rather than individuals, are in competition with each other, or when in some context the level of competition between clearly defined groups exceeds that between individuals within a group. Viewed this way, one can speculate that competition may occur at the genetic level within the individual (the "selfish gene" in clear view) in the case of malignant metastasizing tumors. Ultimately, it may be all a matter of how or at what level we define the individual. Be that as it may, Ridley (1996) notes that we were forced by natural selection, having evolved in small groups in which reciprocal trading was important, with trust between participants of crucial significance. Thus it is important to be able to distinguish between the many individuals likely to be involved, to remember their reputations, and to earn their trust. Indeed, we have an amazing capacity to distinguish faces and to detect deceit, and an almost irrational—in the face of possible freeloading by cheats—inclination to cooperate.

Pointing with the index finger is universal to all human cultures, and its emergence in infancy has traditionally been linked with the early development of perspective taking, intersubjectivity, and empathy. Chimpanzees do not, however, readily develop a pointing gesture with the index finger, and without tuition rarely point by gesturing with hands or arms. The "fault" may in fact lie with differences in the resting morphology of the index finger in humans and chimpanzees (Povinelli & Davis, 1994). However, as we have seen, gestural communication is important for the great apes in maintaining close-range social interaction with conspecifics; although distal pointing may not be a characteristic of apes in their natural habitat, many animals that have had extensive contact with humans do learn to use referential pointing to direct the attention of humans to distal entities and locations. This includes such species as chimpanzees, bonobos, gorillas, and orangutans (Call & Tomasello, 1994). Training in some kind of communication, or general acculturation, seems to facilitate both production of pointing responses and comprehension of their significance by others. Leavens, Hopkins, and Bard (1996) reported on the spontaneous index finger and other referential pointing in three laboratory chimpanzees who had *not* received language training. The behavior generally occurred in the presence of a human, referred to objects in the environment, and appeared intentionally communicative. The authors conclude that referential pointing with the index finger is therefore not necessarily species-unique to humans, or dependent on linguistic competence or explicit training.

While pointing may or may not be a natural part of ape repertoire, aimed throwing of feces, spitting and direction of urine may be (Butovskaya & Kozintsev, 1996), and is often accompanied, when directed at human caregivers, by an expression of *Schadenfreude*, a mixture of malice, slyness, curiosity, and playfulness. Such quasi-aggression may occur only with certain human targets, and in certain contexts, and, though again implying possession of a "theory of mind", it may even partake of certain aspects of primitive humor.

The ability to teach conspecifics, as manifested by, for example, evidence reviewed earlier of mother chimpanzees coaching their offspring in how to crack nuts, seems to imply the insight that another is ignorant and must acquire knowledge. It is noteworthy that the mother in such situations typically behaves abnormally slowly, and carefully (re)positions objects. One must, of course, distinguish teaching from other forms of social learning where there is no active participation by instructions (Caro & Hauser, 1992). We should perhaps distinguish between where offspring are given opportunities to practice skills (opportunistic learning), and where the behavior of young is actively modified by adults (coaching). Only in the latter instance can we impute the ability of an instructor to attribute mental states to others; even then, in the face of anecdotal evidence of mother cats modifying their usual smooth sequence of predatory behavior in their young's presence, carrying live prey directly to them and letting them play with it, recapturing it if it escapes, we may always be unwilling to avoid such an imputation.

Baron-Cohen (1995; see also Baron-Cohen, Campbell, Karmiloff-Smith et al., 1995) applies these considerations to human development, discussing the ontogeny of mindreading (which, surely incorrectly, he thinks exists only in humans), and what happens if the process is blocked. He suggests that the process normally has four steps or mechanisms: the detection of intentionality, the detection of gaze direction, a mechanism for shared attention, and a mechanism for the theory of mind (see also Heyes, 1995). Autism, Baron-Cohen says, is the result of a developmental arrest between the second and third stages, with the autistic suffering from mindblindness, being largely unaware of beliefs and intentionality in others. It is certainly true that autistic children lack some or all of these social abilities, and though still well able to judge physical causality (and to appreciate the laws of physics), they may be notably deficient at understanding the behavior of others and at being able to predict their actions or even understand their intentions (Frith, 1989; Leslie, 1990, 1991); they are therefore said to lack an adequate theory of mind, or to be unable to put themselves in another's position. A typical experimental demonstration with children involves two dolls, Sally and Anne; in Sally's basket there is a marble, but nothing in Anne's. Sally leaves the room (and her basket) and so cannot see Anne move the marble to her own basket. When Sally returns, the children are asked where Sally will look for the marble. Normal and Down's syndrome children claim that Sally will look for it where it was before she left the room, whereas autistic children say that she will look for it where it currently is. With adults, and with experiments on theory of mind, essentially similar scenarios, appropriately adapted, are employed.

The capacity to pretend, play games of pretence, understand pretence in others, know when others are wrong, and impute beliefs, knowledge, expectancies, or intentions in others all seem deficient in autistic children, where a neurodevelopmental disorder of the prefrontal cortex, along with temporal and cerebellar regions, may be involved (Bauman, 1992; Ciaranello & Ciaranello, 1995). (Because of the often profound language impairment in autism, it is traditional to emphasize left-hemisphere damage; however, Ozonoff and Miller, 1996, note that the autistic deficit in *pragmatic* language functions—literal or inappropriately concrete interpretations, misjudged intentions, problems with figurative speech, jokes, sarcasm, and double meanings by high-functioning autistics—suggest a *right*-hemisphere involvement as well, or instead.)

We have already discussed the disproportionately enlarged prefrontal cortex in humans, the major site of brain enlargement in human evolution, occupying nearly a quarter of our total cortical area compared with about one-seventh in the great apes (Blinkov & Glezer, 1968, though see Damasio,

1996). As we saw earlier, the dorsolateral prefrontal cortex plays major social, supervisory, and executive roles, and it and adjacent areas are probably the substrate whereby mental representations of the state of the world, including our conspecifics, influence attention, memory, and action; it may be the locus of our peculiarly human, insightful, self-reflective thought. Neuroimaging studies show that it is active during the performance of complex sequential problem-solving tasks that place demands on working memory (Baker, Rogers, Owen et al., 1996), and during the performance of theory-of-mind tasks (Baron-Cohen, 1995; Goel, Grafman, Sadato, & Hallett, 1995), whereas orbito-frontal damage can result in a dissociation between knowledge and action in the realms of morality and ethics (Damasio & Anderson, 1993). Such damage is also, not surprisingly, associated with problems with the pragmatics of language, such as realizing the sarcasm in a statement such as "You *are* a fine fellow" (McDonald & Pearce, 1996). In a PET study of patients with Asperger syndrome, a mild variant of autism with normal intellectual functioning, Happé, Ehlers, Fletcher et al. (1996) found that during a theory-of-mind task, no task-related metabolic activity occurred in the left medial prefrontal cortex, as with normal volunteers, but only in certain adjacent regions. Is the left medial prefrontal cortex the actual locus of our insight into the minds of others? Damage in this vicinity, in the ventromedial prefrontal cortex to be precise, may also impair our ability to follow our "gut feelings" or intuition in making apparently rational or logical decisions (Bechara, Damasio, Tranel, & Damasio, 1997; see also Vogel, 1997). It may be part of a system that stores information about past rewards and punishments, and triggers the nonconscious emotional responses that we normally register as intuition or a "hunch". Patients with damage here seem unable to make good decisions, in life or in experimental situations, even though able otherwise to describe what should be done, and typically show little emotion when choosing badly.

The prefrontal cortex is part of the heteromodal association cortex, which also includes parts of the superior temporal and inferior parietal cortices. These regions link in a cognitive network mediating executive functions, attention, working memory, future planning, social interaction, and language itself. They link also to limbic (cingulate and para-hippocampal gyri), amygdala, caudate, and thalamus (Ross & Pearlson, 1996), and so play a major role in drive, mood, and personality. The heteromodal association cortex, pre-eminently a human evolutionary development, itself experiences late ontogenetic development, and is vulnerable to neurodevelopmental hazard genetically and from environmental influences, as in schizophrenia. Thus schizophrenia targets these regions, and results in profound alterations in personality and the essential humanness of the unfortunate patient. Paranoid-schizophrenic delusions typically involve complex conspiracies focused on the patient (Straube &

Oades, 1992), indicative of a breakdown of theory of mind, and of a malfunction of faculties for interpreting complex social relationships. Not surprisingly, hallucinations typically involve speech and language.

Autism and possibly also schizophrenia, both putative neurodevelopmental disorders impairing aspects of a theory of mind, are quintessentially *human* disorders; what would a chimpanzee look like with either condition? How would it behave or interact? And yet we have already seen evidence that chimpanzees possess at least some attributes of what we call a theory of mind. Without speech, of course, they cannot manifest the most obvious symptom of autism; nor can they tell us, except perhaps by sign, of any schizophrenic delusions. We can also speculate on the form that schizophrenic delusions of thought transfer, control, and mind reading might have taken hundreds of years ago before the electronic or information age, which gives a kind of face validity to the less extravagant claims of the schizophrenic. Maybe the religious experience of mystics and believers comes close to the core of schizophrenic mentation. Maybe religious belief or belief in the supernatural is not possible without the seeds of schizophrenia, which may be present in most of us. Temporal lobe pathology of course is implicated in schizophrenia, religiosity (Gruzelier & Flor-Henry, 1979; Hodoba, 1986; Schiff, Sabin, Geller et al., 1982), and paranormal feelings of for example *déjà vu* (Bancaud, Brunet-Bourgin, Chauvel, & Halgren, 1994).

There seems little doubt that social or Machiavellian intelligence was a major factor in the evolution of language as a sophisticated vocal-auditory channel (Dunbar, 1993), and rather than language evolution being a consequence of tool behavior, which we earlier rejected for a variety of reasons, it may *itself* have furthered the evolution of tool use and concrete culture (Wilkins & Wakefield, 1995). Animal *cognition* is therefore likely to be as relevant as animal *communication* as a possible precursor to the evolution of human language. All the evidence suggests that other species, whether or not they have introspective access to their desires and intentions, can nevertheless creatively urge us to do what they want:

> In the last analysis perhaps the best reason for thinking that some animals have minds like ours is simply that they seem to recognize that we have minds like theirs. (Cartmill, 1995b, p.77)

SELF-RECOGNITION IN MIRRORS AND SELF-AWARENESS

When chimpanzees first inspect their image in a mirror, they treat the reflection as if it were another animal; after several days, however, they start to exhibit self-directed activity, using the mirror for grooming and inspecting otherwise inaccessible parts of their bodies (for review, see e.g. Povinelli & Preuss, 1995) (see Fig. 9.2). If they are anaesthetized, and their

(a)

(b)

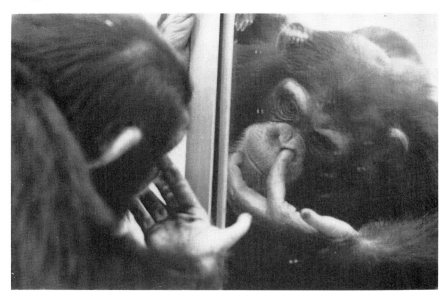

FIG. 9.2. Two examples (a, b) of a chimpanzee examining itself in a mirror in a fashion consistent with self-recognition. Materials kindly supplied by Daniel Povinelli; photograph by Donna T. Bierscwhale, University of Southwestern Louisiana/New Iberia Research Center.

171

foreheads are marked with a nonirritating dye, on recovery and seeing their reflection, they show interest in the marks, touching them afterwards and smelling their fingers. Such self-directed behavior guided by the mirror would therefore seem to demonstrate self-awareness, a state clearly related to possession of a theory of mind. There is debate as to whether other ape species may or may not behave similarly (Anderson, 1984; see also Westergaard & Hopkins, 1994). Monkeys and elephants apparently do not self-recognize, but they do readily learn to use mirrors to guide their own hand movements to obtain otherwise hidden food (Povinelli, 1989; Westergaard & Hopkins, 1994). Pigeons can be trained to use mirrors to locate dots placed on their bodies, whereas parrots, though not demonstrating clear self-exploratory behavior, may nevertheless use mirrors to discriminate among objects and to locate hidden objects in ways similar to those of marmosets, monkeys, dolphins, and children younger than 18 months, and similar to the initial responses of orangutans and young chimpanzees (Pepperberg, Garcia, Jackson, & Marconi, 1995). It is noteworthy that whereas chimpanzees do not show clear evidence of mirror self-recognition before about 3 years, children may do so at around 18 months; early exposure to mirrors may merely elicit behavior appropriate to meeting a conspecific (Parker, Mitchell, & Boccia, 1994), with self-directed behaviors emerging later. Though self-recognition can also be studied via videotapes or even photographs, it should also be noted that other forms of self-directed behavior may be elicited *without* "passing the spot test in the mirror", for example, using the mirror to examine the backside. Indeed, use of mirrors to locate otherwise inaccessible objects is considerably commoner than self-directed behavior. Conversely, mark-directed behavior with mirrors may still be accompanied by looking behind them, or calling the image the name of another animal.

Animals capable of mirror self-recognition have often been reared by humans and tend to score higher on other tests of social intelligence. They also tend to be capable of using symbols and tools and of imitating novel facial and gestural behaviors. One wonders how autistic children would behave under these circumstances, though there are suggestions that they can recognize their mirror images (Spiker & Ricks, 1984). Of course, the fact that you can make self-directed behavior of this sort does not conclusively prove self-awareness—you could still be touching those parts of your body that correspond to those of the image of the "other" creature in the mirror. Indeed, Hauser, Kralik, Botto-Mahan et al. (1995) note that New World monkeys (cotton-top tamarins) with extensive mirror exposure do exhibit self-directed mirror-guided behavior when the white head hair is extensively color-dyed so that it is particularly salient. These procedures perhaps overcome the animal's natural and innate initial tendency to respond aversively to an image of a potential competitor's face, and instead draw attention to it and its mirror properties. The authors conclude that prior failures to pass the mirror test may have been due to methodological problems, rather than to phylogenetic differences in the capacity for self-recognition; conversely, the mirror test may not be sufficient for assessing the concept of self and the awareness of mental states. Ultimately, of course, self- awareness in anyone but yourself can never be proven, as philosophers have long argued. Similarly, babies smiling in response to their mother's smile, or protruding their tongues in apparent imitation of a similar action by their mothers, may well be simply exhibiting hard-wired reflex behavior adaptive to mother–child bonding.

An interesting new twist to the standard Gallup mark test with chimpanzees was recently reported by Kitchen, Denton, and Brent (1996), who exposed their six chimpanzees to mirrors that produced distorted or multiplied self-images. Their reactions to their self-images, in terms of the usual kinds of mirror-guided self-referenced behaviors, indicated that the animals were able correctly to assess the sources of the mirror images. Their ability to recognize distorted self-images, furthermore, implied, according to the authors, an ability for abstraction, in that the distortion had to be rationalized before any self-recognition could occur.

CONSCIOUSNESS

Consciousness of the self—self-awareness—occupies the next level above the awareness of events and objects in the surrounding world, and both levels can of course only be inferred. Dog owners universally, it seems, believe that their pet understands everything said to it, being a hairy, four-legged person with a different language and view of life, but conscious withal (Lewin, 1994). The Skinnerian (Skinner, 1974) behaviorist tradition of discounting consciousness in animals (if it even exists, which is doubted) as at most an epiphenomenon, has recently given way to a widespread view (Griffin, 1992) that animals have minds as well as brains, and that some maybe attenuated or limited form of awareness extends well "down" the evolutionary "hierarchy". Thus we frequently see versatile, adaptive behavior in the face of obstacles, rather than inflexible response chains, together with evidence of "intentional" communication, deception, and (at least in apes) learned use of symbols. Most intriguingly, some of the characteristic electroencephalographic (EEG) patterns known in humans to be associated with conscious information processing, expectancy, and preparation, such as the P300, are found also in nonhuman species. Though such conscious information processing may therefore well be possessed by many species, it is interesting to speculate about the subjective experience and mental state of such processing when *self*-conscious monitoring or *self*-awareness is minimal. Our dream states, except perhaps for lucid dreams, may approximate to such a condition; the dreamer typically acts as an uncritical spectator, viewing or watching what only on waking recall may be remembered or interpreted as bizarre or improbable. During dreaming, such (necessarily self-conscious) interpretations or judgments of likelihood are typically suspended. Non-human species seem to be far less critical than we are of bizarre or improbable scenarios, but they are of course by no means totally unresponsive to event probabilities; monkeys "know" which alternatives are likely to be rewarded, and show surprise and frustration when unexpectedly "disappointed".

Though such considerations could imply that self-awareness in some form is likely to extend well "below" the level of the apes, Povinelli and Cant (1995) argue that the concept of the self evolved in apes as a psychological mechanism in large arboreal animals to facilitate planning and execution of unusually flexible locomotor patterns of a nonstereotyped nature. They claim that clambering in a fragile, unstable, and unpredictable habitat is underpinned by cognizance of one's actions and the need to see oneself in a three-dimensional context.

The work on self-recognition in mirrors indicates that humans are not unique in knowing that the image they face is that of themselves, and not merely that of another conspecific. Such knowledge may, as we saw, apparently fluctuate, be partial or inconsistent, in that the individual may *also* continue to exhibit those other forms of behavior normally consistent with seeing a conspecific, such as displaying or looking behind the mirror. Nevertheless, this situation is little different from the common human tendency to be able simultaneously to hold mutually inconsistent or conflicting views or values. Any response to the image in the mirror that indicates that it is seen as somehow personally special is at least consistent with an awareness of the existence of other minds. It is also consistent with a level of consciousness that transcends an awareness of others to an awareness of the self.

Much has been written on the nature of consciousness, particularly in relation to the mind–body problem, and whether it may be a special faculty, perhaps even localized to a particular structure or circuit, or "simply" an emergent property of a system that has reached a sufficient level of complexity, and that may therefore be "distributed" throughout that system (Dennett, 1992). It is clearly simplistic to invoke a homunculus in some kind of Cartesian "Theatre of the Mind" (Dennett, 1992) to monitor all brain activity (Donald, 1995), or even perhaps to appeal to a central executive localized to the prefrontal cortex. However, a major surgical technique, undertaken for the relief of otherwise intractable epilepsy, involves section of the forebrain commissures linking the two cerebral hemispheres, and can throw some light on the question. The procedure is designed to stop the spread of unwanted (epileptic) electrical activity from the affected to the hitherto intact hemisphere. It results, of course, in the more-or-less complete mutual isolation of the two cortical systems, the largely verbal left hemisphere from the spatially and attentionally specialized right. Does the operation result in two parallel, independent streams of consciousness (Wigan, 1844; Zangwill, 1976)? If consciousness corresponds to the monitoring of a chosen, selected action sequence performed at a nonautomatic level, given that it is an empirical finding that patients normally can only ever undertake a single such coherent sequence (Bradshaw & Mattingley, 1995), any other sequence being fragmentary and automatic, we may wish to conclude in favor of a single stream of consciousness even in the divided brain. In a real sense, of course, we are all of us a mosaic of modular minds, a vector of conflicting drives, feelings, and wills from a multiplicity of processors all operating in parallel, even though unifying attentional mechanisms may normally select only a single response at any one time. We only become conscious of those action sequences that are finally selected and monitored, requiring executive overview, and which cannot be run off automatically and in parallel with others.

Gray (1995) makes an essentially similar proposal in claiming that the contents of consciousness correspond to the outputs of a comparator that on a moment-by-moment basis compares the current state of one's perceptual world with the predicted state. Where can we find such a comparator? He invokes the septo-hippocampal system and associated limbic loop of Papez, a "behavioral-inhibitory" system, which is susceptible to the depressive effects of drugs and alcohol, with links to the temporal and frontal cortex, and which is modulated by ascending noradrenergic, dopaminergic, serotonergic, and cholinergic neurotransmitter systems. The sensorimotor filter of the basal ganglia is also connected to this system. As Gray observes, conscious experience is closely linked to action plans; one is conscious of motor program outputs, not of the program itself, and consciousness is closely linked to episodic or working memory in the dorsolateral prefrontal cortex, and is highly selective. At a less global level, that of visual awareness of discrete and meaningful objects, Vanni, Revonsuo, Saarinen, and Hari (1996) found that of the various brain regions activated when observers tried to discriminate such objects from disorganized and meaningless representations of nonobjects, only the right lateral occipital cortex showed significant activity correlating with accuracy of performance. Clearly, the different aspects of conscious awareness fractionate to incorporate multiple brain regions.

In the commissurotomy literature, there are occasional reports of alien-hand phenomena, usually the left hand grasping an object or "refusing" to release it; however such reports are rare and tend to be limited to the acute or immediately post-operative phase. We certainly cannot conclude with Sperry's (1968) original position that commissurotomy normally results in the production in everyday life of two independent wills or streams of consciousness (Bradshaw, 1989): There are just too many factors usually present that make for attentional unification. Conversely, as an apparently normal level of consciousness and volition is evident even after massive unilateral damage to either hemisphere, we must conclude that either hemisphere can subserve consciousness, and that normally subcortical mechanisms unify consciousness and volition.

It is the position taken in this book that Machiavellian or social intelligence, the need simultaneously to track the actions of others, played a major role in the evolution of both language and consciousness; though both phenomena nevertheless enjoyed a long prior evolutionary trajectory with antecedents in other species, consciousness must clearly be seen within the context of attention. Both introspectively and empirically we can distinguish perhaps three levels of attention—general vigilance, automatic orienting, and conscious selection. Posner and Raichle (1994) note that three networks can be identified, which perhaps relate more or less closely to the above three levels: the brain stem—midbrain ascending reticular activating system concerned with vigilance and wakefulness, and with its origin in the noradrenergic locus coeruleus; the posterior system involving the parietal cortex and the thalamic pulvinar, which mediates unconscious orienting; and, finally, the anterior system incorporating the anterior cingulate cortex, supplementary motor area, and dorsolateral prefrontal and premotor cortex. These last regions mediate conscious goal orientation, selective attention, declarative and working memory and executive functions; clearly there is no one center for consciousness. In keeping with what we know now about the neural mediation of language and praxis, consciousness too must be seen as multimodal and distributed, involving memory, perception, planning and action (Delacour, 1995). In addition to noradrenergic activation from the locus coeruleus, it probably also involves ascending cholinergic activation from the substantia innominata, excitatory glutamatergic activity in the cortex, probably dopaminergic and serotonergic activity modulating mood, drive, and reward states, with activity widespread in fronto-parietal and thalamic pathways.

Consciousness enables the success or failure of ongoing responses to be assessed or monitored. Indeed, the literature on human skills (see e.g., Schmidt, 1988) emphasizes that when unfamiliar or difficult tasks are performed, responses require conscious monitoring. Usually, in fact, only the attended task can be undertaken at any one time, though, later, increasing familiarity may permit a ballistic series of unmonitored responses to be run off, to match environmental demands. Such automaticity is achievable in the absence of conscious awareness, and indeed introspection may interfere. At this point other tasks may be simultaneously undertaken without affecting the original task. Conscious awareness may in fact correspond to the bottleneck of selective attention, which mediates response monitoring (LaBerge & Samuels, 1974). In Parkinson's disease, which affects the output of the basal ganglia to the supplementary motor area, when two tasks are simultaneously undertaken, one automatic and over-learned, and the other less practiced and under deliberate conscious control, it is the former, not the latter, which typically is most affected.

Frith and Dolan (1996) offer a useful synthesis of concepts such as consciousness, automaticity, and controlled or executive functioning. Lower-order cognitive processes are said to be automatic, routine (and, often, modular), whereas higher-order voluntary processes containing a novel element require controlled, strategic, executive (or non-modular) processes. The amount of mental effort seems more important than the complexity of the task, as with practice even complex processes can become automatized; they no longer require conscious oversight. Thus the higher cognitive functions, such as working memory, mental imagery and willed action, may all be associated with consciousness, involving processes that must be "held in the mind" for a period of time (Frith & Dolan, 1996). Such information, whether about incoming stimuli or response selection and execution, can be derived from the past or present, or can be generated for the future. Brain-imaging studies show that "holding something in mind" involves both anterior (dorsolateral prefrontal cortex) systems (working memory), and dedicated posterior regions, whose locations are determined by the exact nature of whatever is being processed. Automatic actions and/ or perceptions that do not involve consciousness are associated with activity in these relevant posterior areas, but not in the prefrontal cortex, irrespec-tive of whether the information is externally or internally generated. So how do we know whether what we experience derives from mental imagery or from real-life external events? A disconnection between prefrontal and posterior regions in schizophrenics may result in just such a breakdown and in hallucinations that are perceived as real (Frith & Dolan, 1996).

Conscious awareness clearly does not depend on language; thus the nonverbal right hemispheres of split-brain (commissurotomy) patients, appropriately interrogated nonverbally, seem to possess a normal range of human ambitions, desires, fears, emotions, and beliefs (Bradshaw & Mat-tingley, 1995). If indeed *Homo erectus* could not speak, could we regard the nonverbal right hemisphere of a split-brain patient today as a model for *erectus* thought? Nor indeed does the imaginative rationalization or ima-gination of the scientist or artist depend on language. Thus the introspec-tions and autobiographies of such people often describe the nonverbal imagery that is involved in creativity or problem-solving. Later, of course, the product or solution may be given verbal realization for posterity.

In conclusion, we may follow Rumbaugh and Savage-Rumbaugh (1990) in noting that human conscious awareness involves an understanding of the existence of behavioral alternatives, the concomitant knowledge of having chosen one rather than another of these alternatives, and an ongoing introspective monitoring of progress toward that alternative. With Dennett (1992) we see the brain as a hypothesis-making and testing machine, continually throwing up new "drafts" of what is occurring in the real world. Mental states achieve consciousness by winning in competition against others for domination in the control of behavior, and consciousness evolved from monitoring processes—monitoring the behavior of others, and the success of one's own actions.

SUMMARY AND CONCLUSIONS

There is no single definition, or measure of intelligence, which may in fact prove to be a slippery and illusory concept. Abilities, which may be more easily quantified, tend to a view of the intellect as consisting of a series of discrete, independent, "encapsulated" modules all operating in a quasi-autonomous fashion. Clinical neurology has in the past supported such conclusions with the demonstration of the discrete effects of lesions in generating such deficits as aphasia, agnosia, amnesia, and apraxia, on the one hand, and, on the other, the preservation of islands of ability in a general sea of intellectual inadequacy, as in the savant syndromes, autism, and so on. Nowadays, however, there is increasing emphasis on models of distributed processing and parallel interactive networks, and correspondingly less on strict localization of function.

At an ethological level we must be wary of equating proficient imitation or social learning with "truly intelligent" behavior, and must distinguish between copying a complex motor act by rote and finding a guiding rule for problem-solving. The archaeological record of tools and artefacts has been subjected to attempts at interpretational analysis based, for example, upon Piagettian principles of ontogenetic development, with varying levels of success. *Social*, as compared with *technical*, intelligence, may perhaps best be inferred from the observational studies of comparative ethology, but both aspects of intellect characterize *Homo sapiens sapiens* par excellence.

Only the great apes may approach us in empathy and levels of social understanding, in the ability to cooperate, request, and transmit information for mutual advantage, and ultimately in the awareness of the self. The theory of Machiavellian intelligence emphasizes the capacity to outwit one's peers and competitors, and to infer beliefs, desires, and intentions in others for one's own advantage, as perhaps the major evolutionary pressure in our order; increasingly, however, the other side of the coin is now being addressed—primates' remarkable capacities for apparent sympathy, care, reciprocity, and altruism. Both aspects seem to require the achievement of a "theory of mind", said to be present by five years of age in most children—and more or less absent in autism.

Various "markers" have been proposed for the possession of a "theory of mind", such as coaching and teaching conspecifics and offspring, pointing, and self-recognition in mirrors. The last, favored, approach, however, is itself fraught with methodological and interpretational difficulties. Nor may an individual animal always, or fully, understand that it is its own image that it sees and not that of another conspecific. Again the massively evolved (in humans) prefrontal cortex plays a vital role in social intelligence and theory-of-mind tasks. It mediates major social, supervisory, and executive roles, and may be the site where mental representations of others influence our own actions. It is also, along with the closely interconnected limbic structures of the mesial temporal cortex, particularly vulnerable to neuro-developmental insult in such theory-of-mind disorders as autism and schizophrenia.

Consciousness of the self should be distinguished from consciousness *per se*; it is, however, far from clear whether there may be "grades" of consciousness in "lower" animals, where or even whether it may be localized (or distributed) in the brain, whether it may be "simply" an emergent property of a sufficiently complex system or brain, what is its relationship to attention, will, action, and responsive monitoring, whether one can be simultaneously conscious of two (or more) incompatible situations, or even whether the two semi-autonomous and independently functioning sides of the brain, particularly after the commissurotomy (split-brain) operation, can maintain two separate streams of thought.

Conscious selective attention seems particularly to involve the anterior cingulate cortex, the supplementary motor area, and dorsolateral prefrontal and premotor cortex, regions that also mediate volitional action, working, and declarative (episodic) memory, and general executive functions. Consciousness must be seen as multimodal and distributed, involving memory, perception, planning, and action, via a range of diffuse ascending and activating neurotransmitter systems. Above all, it enables the success or failure of an ongoing chosen behavior-sequence to be monitored. In this respect it reflects (and reflects on) the operation of many of our higher cognitive functions. When did it appear in our evolutionary trajectory, and was its appearance gradual or sudden? Surely, as with praxis and language, we must appeal to a long process of continuous evolution.

FURTHER READINGS

Baron-Cohen, S. (1995). *Mindblindness: An essay on autism and theory of Mind*. Cambridge, MA: MIT Press.

Byrne, R.W. (1995). The thinking ape: Evolutionary origins of intelligence. Oxford: Oxford University Press.

Cairns-Smith, A.G. (1996). *Evolving mind: On the nature of matter and the origin of consciousness*. Cambridge: Cambridge University Press.

Calvin, W.H. (1994). The emergence of intelligence. *Scientific American, October*, 79–85.

Crick, F. (1994). *The astonishing hypothesis: The scientific search for the soul.* London: Simon & Schuster.

Dawkins, M.S. (1993). *Through our eyes only: The search for animal consciousness.* New York: Freeman.

Dennett, D.C. (1992). *Consciousness explained.* London: Allen Lane/The Penguin Press.

Denton, D. (1993). *The pinnacle of life: Consciousness and self awareness in humans and animals.* London: Allen & Unwin.

de Waal, F. (1996). *Good natured: The origins of right and wrong in humans and other animals.* Cambridge, MA: Harvard University Press.

Donald, M. (1991). *Origins of the modern mind.* Cambridge, MA: Harvard University Press.

Edelman, G. (1992). *Bright light, brilliant fire.* New York: Basic Books.

Gardner, H. (1983). *Frames of mind: The theory of multiple intelligence.* New York: Basic Books.

Greenfield, S.A. (1995). *Journey to the center of the mind.* New York: Freeman.

Griffin, D. (1992). *Animal minds.* Chicago, IL: Chicago University Press.

Hobson, R.P. (1993). *Autism and the development of the mind.* Hove, UK: Lawrence Erlbaum Associates Ltd.

Parker, S.T., Mitchell, R.W., & Boccia, M.L. (Eds.) (1994). *Self awareness in animals and humans: A developmental perspective.* Cambridge: Cambridge University Press.

Penrose, R. (1994). *Shadows of the mind: A search for the missing science of consciousness.* Oxford: Oxford University Press.

Povinelli, D.J. (1993). Reconstructing the evolution of mind. *American Psychologist, 48*, 493–509.

Povinelli, D.J., & Preuss, T.M. (1995). Theory of mind: Evolutionary history of a cognitive specialization. *Trends in Neurosciences, 18*, 418–424.

Tomasello, M., & Call, J. (1994). Social cognition in monkeys and apes. *Yearbook of Physical Anthropology, 37*, 273–305.

Wilson, D.S., Near, D., & Miller, R.R. (1996). Machiavellianism: A synthesis of the evolutionary and psychological literatures. *Psychological Bulletin, 119*, 285–299.

CHAPTER TEN

An overview

Matter and the Universe may have existed for between 8 and 16 billion years; it may be inadmissible to ask what there was before the Big Bang (or First Whimper, according to a minority view) if time, space, energy, and matter all came into being together. In this one instance science and received religion may be on an equal footing—either's explanations seem equally satisfactory, or unsatisfactory, according to one's point of view, and in many respects remarkably similar to each other. The Earth may have come into being around four and a half billion years ago, with life appearing maybe only one billion years later, almost as soon as conditions were conducive to its support and maintenance. Could it have somehow arrived in microscopic form from elsewhere in the Universe? Does such an "explanation" do anything more than merely push the problem back without actually explaining it further? Be that as it may, it was not until around 600 million years ago that multicellular animals became well established, possibly undergoing one or more major extinctions before the appearance of modern-looking life forms during the Cambrian explosion around 530 million years ago. Mass extinctions have continued to occur irregularly, the most recent being 65 million years ago.

Right from life's beginning, from whatever origin or source, principles of natural selection are likely to have operated on what were, and continue to be, self-organizing systems; random changes, if proving to be beneficial in the contemporary context, would tend to be preserved in future generations, and disadvantageous ones eliminated. Such evolutionary change would have been greatly accelerated with the advent of fully meiotic sexual reproduction, though evolution may have proceeded as much by relatively abrupt differentiation in locally stressed or peripheral populations, as by gradual genetic drift in the population as a whole.

With the Cambrian explosion and the attainment of full diversity of life forms, chordates, characterized by the possession of a supporting notochord adjacent to the nerve cord that runs the length of the animal's body, also made their appearance. From these two structures developed the cord and vertebral column of true vertebrates (or "craniates", as some would prefer), the first of whom, the ostracoderms, have been dated to 460 million years ago, though an agnathan or jawless vertebrate resembling the hagfish or lamprey may go back to 500 million years ago. Indeed, the genetic principles that determine segmentation and anterior–posterior sequential development and structure are very ancient, being virtually identical in arthropods and chordates.

Some time around 375 million years ago a transition (or transitions—there may have been more than one) occurred between jawed fishes like *Panderichthys* and the first tetrapod amphibians like *Acanthostega* and *Ichthyostega*, though with respect to "amphibian" we should be careful in using what is now seen cladistically as a rather loose and ambiguous term. This transition involved not just fins to limbs, but changes in respiration and the appearance of the amniote egg. Though the archetypal tetrapod is commonly conceived of as possessing five digits on each limb, this was not necessarily the case at the time of their first appearance, and had we possessed six fingers on each hand, this might have had profound consequences for praxis, music, and even arithmetic.

Mammal-like dicynodont therapsid reptiles appeared around 260 million years ago, with the first true mammals, the triconodonts, following maybe 60 million years later in the Triassic. One hundred million years ago in the Cretaceous the eutherian placentals may have diverged from the monotremes (egg-laying mammals) and the marsupials; primates may have made an early appearance perhaps as insectivores during the contemporaneous spread of the flowering plants. New World platyrrhine (Ceboidea) and Old World catarrhine (Cercopithecoidea) lineages, both belonging to the suborder Haplorhini, separated more than 35 million years ago. The Cercopithecoidea include the anthropoid primates (monkeys, apes, and humans), and in turn gave rise to the Hominoidea (apes—Pongidae, and humans—Hominidae). However, anthropoid origins (more than 45 million years ago) and evolution are still a matter of debate. What is clear, however, from molecular biology is that chimpanzees and humans are more closely related to each other than either is to gorillas, the latter having diverged from the common chimpanzee-human lineage about 8 million years ago, chimpanzees and humans splitting some time before 5 million years ago. Bipedalism may have appeared before 4 million years ago with *Australopithecus anamensis* (or maybe even as early as 4.4 million years ago with *Ardipithicus ramidus*). Bipedal *Australopithecus afarensis* around 4 million years ago is generally, but not universally, agreed to have lain on our evolutionary lineage and to have been followed by *Homo habilis* (2.2 million years ago). However, *Homo rudolfensis* may precede the latter, and *Homo ergaster* follow it, before the advent of *Homo erectus* (nearly 2 million years ago), and the existence, integrity, and relevance to ourselves of all these taxa continue to be debated. However, it does seem to be the case that the Neanderthals, who became extinct shortly before 30,000 years ago, were our evolutionary cousins and members of *Homo sapiens*, whether or not they and our ancestors could have, or even possibly did, interbreed. Much if not most of hominid evolution appears to have taken place in Africa and to have been driven largely by climatic and ecological changes.

Though bipedalism appeared early, increases in brain size, a correlate of intellectual capacity, followed considerably later; strangely, changes in tool manufacture (and presumably tool use) and in brain size were also largely decoupled. Bipedalism is as energy efficient as quadrupedal locomotion, no more and no less, and its chief evolutionary advantage is its flexibility, allowing us to walk, run, climb, and swim, individually perhaps no better than any other species, but unlike the latter to be reasonably efficient at all such modes of progression. It also, with consequent major redesign of the rest of the skeleton, permitted lifting, levering, digging, carrying, clubbing, and throwing, preadapting our ancestors for tool use. Consequent circulatory and other changes may have improved cooling and heat dispersal and removed a constraint on brain growth. Though it may have been preadapted for by brachiation, we should be very wary of seeking unifactorial causal explanations in evolution, as many factors, individually or in concert, may have selected for an upright bipedal posture. Moreover, the latter may for some time have coexisted with the retention of considerable arboreal or climbing capacities, capacities that indeed we have ourselves certainly not totally lost. Early evidence for bipedalism comes from trackways, dated to 3.6 million years ago, and analyses of foot and lower limb bones may put the date back even further; the configuration of the bony labyrinth, our balance organ, may possibly throw further light on this issue when appropriate data are available.

One undeniable consequence, however, of an upright posture, is modification of the pelvis, with its impact upon childbirth. The pattern of the latter in humans is unique, involving a tortuous rotating pathway and a baby's head that is large compared with the rest of the body. An upright, bipedal pelvis adapted for running, bending, carrying, and childbirth involves numerous compromises, and the latter must extend to include relative maturity of the offspring at birth, and head size. Thus, unlike the situation in other primates including apes, growth continues after birth for 1 year in humans, so that our gestation is effectively 21 months.

The first increase in brain size from that of the chimpanzee may have coincided with the appearance of our putative ancestor, *Homo habilis*, around 2.2 million years ago. Increase was especially marked in the frontal and parietal lobes, regions connected with our intrinsic humanness. Indeed, articulate speech may have been a possibility, and frontal development would have been consistent with strategic planning and goal-directed behavior. *Homo habilis* may also have been the first regular manufacturer of stone tools (the Oldowan tradition), and their nature, wear, and distribution suggest early indication of such essentially human characteristics as food-sharing, division of labor, reciprocity, and cooperation.

Homo erectus, appearing nearly two million years ago and with a yet larger brain, is traditionally thought of as the next in line, after *Homo habilis*, in our evolutionary lineage, and the first to have left Africa. There are, however, suggestions that *Homo habilis* might also have reached Asia, and that *Homo erectus* is Asian with *Homo ergaster*, its African equivalent, instead our predecessor. There is also debate as to whether the cranial capacity of *Homo erectus*, which was certainly greater than that of *Homo habilis*, continued to increase during its existence. Suffice to say that whereas the Oldowan stone tool tradition continued with early *Homo erectus*, the more advanced and aesthetically pleasing bifaces of the Acheulian technology equate with later *Homo erectus*. The Acheulian industry was not replaced by the Mousterian (typically Neanderthal) tradition in Europe until 200,000 years ago. *Homo erectus* may have pioneered the use of fire, and microscopic edge-wear analysis of stone tools indicates use for cutting, shredding, butchering, and whittling of meat, hide, bone, antler, wood, and plant material. Whether or not it lay directly on our lineage, fully humanlike behaviors are seen to be increasingly emerging.

Archaic forms of *Homo sapiens*, perhaps to be identified with *Homo heidelbergensis*, and which may have given rise to the Neanderthals about 230,000 years ago, are known from Europe 500,000 years ago, and probably earlier (700,000 years ago) in Africa. For more than 100,000 years there may have been overlap between archaic *Homo sapiens* and late-surviving *Homo erectus* in Asia, a situation reminiscent of the overlap, between 100,000 and 35,000 years ago, between Neanderthals and anatomically modern *Homo sapiens sapiens* in the Near East. In both cases one can speculate about the possibility or otherwise of interbreeding. Archaic *Homo sapiens* possessed a larger cranium—modern, in fact, in size, though not in configuration—than that of *Homo erectus*, and directly or indirectly gave rise to the Neanderthals, the last truly primitive members of the genus *Homo*. The Neanderthals may have possessed an impoverished capacity for speech—the evidence is debated—and seem shortly before their demise to have borrowed technology during the Châtelperronian from newly arrived anatomically modern *Homo sapiens sapiens* in western Europe. Why indeed they did disappear is unknown, but a competitive disadvantage with our ancestors in terms of flexibility of behavior, toolkit, language, and culture seems likely.

Anatomically modern *Homo sapiens sapiens*, according to the generally preferred "out-of-Africa" account, first arose in Africa maybe 200,000 years ago, migrating there from around 100,000 years ago and eventually replacing prior archaic aboriginals. (According to the minority "multiregional" viewpoint, all modern peoples evolved from local pre-existing populations, though some migration and/or hybridization is acknowledged to have probably occurred.) Molecular (genetic) studies of modern populations, whether they involve nuclear or mitochondrial DNA, together with independent archaeological data, support the above dates. Thus many traits show higher levels of variation in populations from sub-Saharan Africa, and genetic distances show the latter populations are the most divergent.

There is a resistance among many archaeologists against accepting an aesthetic sense among humans prior to the (western European) Upper Palaeolithic "creative explosion" around 35,000 years ago, coinciding with the arrival of anatomically modern *Homo sapiens sapiens* in that region. However, in the Acheulian Lower Palaeolithic, ochre, a pigment commonly used nowadays in tribal societies for decoration, seems to have been collected, and an awareness of symmetry and possibly of aesthetics is apparent in the shape and construction of the Acheulian bifaces of *Homo erectus*. A scoria pebble in the naturally occurring shape of a female figure from Acheulian horizons, and apparently intentionally engraved geometrical designs on bone, though rare, are further intriguing hints of a developing aesthetic sense. However, it is not until we reach the Mousterian Middle Palaeolithic of the Neanderthals that the record becomes richer. These peoples employed adhesives to haft their tools, made bone points, awls, and oval ochred bone plaques, and incised lines and zig-zags, and drilled teeth for pendants. They may even have created wooden domestic implements, and have enjoyed significant levels of symbolism, language, social structure, conceptual ability, technology, and possibly art. Whether they employed ritual, as in burial practices, or cared for their injured or sick, is a matter of debate. They seem to show evidence of planning, forethought, abstraction, learning, and many basic human characteristics, though their lifestyle seems to have been spartan, primitive, and basic, and their behavior appears somehow intangibly and subtly different from our own. Such factors may indeed have contributed to their competitive demise.

With the European Upper Palaeolithic there seems to have been an explosive appearance, concomitant with the arrival of anatomically modern peoples some time after 40,000 years ago, of art, culture, and aesthetics, though precursors, in the form of a well-developed and complex bone-tool industry, are now apparent 90,000 years ago in Africa. Nor should the indigenous cultures of Australia, which date back at least 60,000 years, be ignored in this context, and there is always the possibility of a *two*-way flow of ideas, during the Châtelperronian, between the Neanderthals and the newly arriving immigrants.

The European Upper Palaeolithic is noteworthy not only for its tools and personal ornaments, sculptures, and stone carvings, but above all perhaps for the galleries of cave or parietal art on rock walls. We do not know why it was done, though possibilities include recording one's presence or that of significant family members, clan symbols, commemorating significant events, fertility or shamanistic rituals, graffiti or doodling. The awkward inaccessibility of many of the loci, and the likely light-and-sound effects that would naturally occur, do suggest some aspect of ritual. Conversely, shadows and silhouettes naturally occurring under such conditions, and which invoke images of animals seen outside, may be the stimulus for the production of such art, often incorporating natural features or convexities into the end product. Thus there may be endless opportunities for the perceiver to impose an interpretive meaning upon such natural phenomena, just as we see images in clouds and smoke or grained wood panels. Gestalt principles of form and closure may do the rest. In this respect there is little evidence that Upper Palaeolithic humans differed perceptually or cognitively from ourselves—though apes, with their strong and spontaneous interest in painting, also can introduce formally relevant and aesthetic variations, and exhibit a sense of order, rhythm, and balance. We may ask to what extent there may, therefore, be commonalities between art and language in terms of abstraction, symbolism, imagery, and visual categorization, with perhaps co-evolution of the two faculties.

Migration from an African origin has left its trace in the molecular biology of modern peoples around the world; a tree constructed according to such data very closely resembles that based on linguistic classification. Language and genes have co-evolved along similar lines and according to similar principles of diversification and differentiation. Indeed, linguistic differences may themselves have acted to isolate populations genetically. Comparative linguistics permits us to trace ancestry of a group of related extant or recorded languages back to their common origin, and while such reconstructive procedures have been particularly well established for Indo-European of 6000 or more years ago, similar procedures for other such hypothetical ancestral tongues as Altaic, Uralic, and Dravidian point to a likely common antecedent, Nostratic, of twice that antiquity; indeed, a vocabulary of several hundred words has been proposed. There are even claims on behalf of a single original tongue, the common ancestor of all the world's languages, dating to 35,000 years ago.

Language is more than speech, and includes such additional modalities as writing, sign, and, maybe in certain contexts, gesture. In addition to speech and language we communicate emotions nonverbally by facial and vocal expressions and gestures, many of which we share with other primates. Though the production of speech is unique to our species, apes can be taught to comprehend both sign and gesture, and may come naturalistically to understand spoken speech in certain instances. The distinction between propositional communication on the one hand, which is discrete, categorical, and discontinuous, and has to be learned usually in infancy, and nonverbal, emotional expression on the other, which is innate and largely under subcortical or limbic control, is an important one, which can nevertheless be overstated. Both cortical and subcortical mechanisms can be involved in both modalities, and both, though admittedly to varying extents, involve aspects of innate inheritance and learned acquisition; both, moreover, can share common channels or signaling mechanisms. Not only is the gulf between ourselves and other nonhuman species rapidly closing in the contexts of communication, tool behavior, and consciousness, but the evidence is compelling for some degree of evolutionary continuity between human speech and language, and earlier primate systems of communication. Nor are the relationships, or boundaries, between thought and language clear, as evidenced by nonverbal problem-solving and the cognition of global aphasics.

Language requires learned use of arbitrary symbols in a fashion mutually agreed with others to represent objects, events, or states that may no longer be present. Much of such communication depends deeply on mutually shared common sense or tacit knowledge or assumptions. These aspects are particularly salient in the pragmatic aspects or the practical use to which we put language, as with jokes, irony, sarcasm, or metaphor, and where context plays an important role. Prosodic or suprasegmental aspects, which do not change denotative meaning, may provide the necessary extra, interpretive, or connotative information. Such aspects, which may involve frontal or right-hemisphere mechanisms, should be contrasted with the more purely mechanical aspects of speech production—phonology and morphology—and the syntactic rules and semantic lexicon, all of which involve major left-hemisphere mediation.

Such considerations, and the apparent uniqueness of our speech-production system, both centrally and peripherally, may suggest a Chomskian discontinuity from our primate forebears, with speech as an innate, encapsulated Fodorian module isolated from other perhaps more general-purpose processing mechanisms. However, an increase in size of a structure, perhaps merely in pace with other structures that have developed or increased in size to subserve other functions unrelated to speech and language, may lead to apparently qualitative changes of function, increased specialization or functional differentiation. Indeed, frontal regions previously subserving sequential, praxic behavior, or conditionality rules or judgments, may singly or jointly have been "co-opted" to subserve related functions in speech, and, hence, speech itself. In accord with Chomskian uniqueness of speech, we see an apparently innate drive to acquire language of some form, spoken or signed, within certain critical developmental periods; however, such periods are not unique in perceptual or cognitive development, and schema theory or concept formation can accommodate our tendency to generalize and operate according to rules. Nor can we invoke the apparent heritability of certain language deficits, or the phenomenon of abnormal language development or hyperlexia in the face of general intellectual deficit, in support of a unique language organ; thus "islands" of preserved—or lost—cognitive function are by no means rare. Even the phenomenon of categorical perception, one of the corner-stones of the Chomskian view of language uniqueness, is now known to extend to other primate and even nonprimate species. There may therefore be no such special speech-specific mechanisms, merely certain invariant properties of the mammalian auditory system, with speech production possibly evolving to match them. Even the spectral energy peaks (formants) of speech, thought fundamentally to underlie speech recognition, may be experimentally deleted, with remaining temporal envelope cues permitting a fair degree of intelligibility. Finally, other primate and even nonprimate species are now known to be capable of adaptively signaling a range of environmental events; birds show similar, to us, patterns of innate capacities and dependence on learning from a model, in acquiring birdsong before the expiry of critical developmental periods; and at least one African Grey Parrot has learned correctly to use more than 100 English words referentially, to categorize and abstract, to make and refuse requests, and to count.

Language, therefore, neither is mediated by a unique Chomskian module, nor is simply part of a general information processor. It is best seen as mediated by an archetypal distributed system or network interconnecting a series of relatively specialized subregions, with (at last in the young) considerable power of reserve function or substitution in the event of localized damage. Such networks are known in other contexts—memory, object recognition, and praxis—and have been observed, directly by neuroimaging, and as a function of clinical damage, to be capable of dynamic reorganization. Language is thus seen as "just" another—if very highly developed—complex, procedural skill with both innate and acquired aspects, but which can be flexibly realized by a network of contributing structures.

Apes' inability to speak may partly stem from limitations in vocal tract anatomy, and from an apparent (and presumably central) inability to produce multiple, sequential discontinuities during a vocalized exhalation. They can learn to communicate fairly readily with us along other channels, and the bonobo at least may naturalistically acquire, in infancy, the capacity to comprehend quite complex spoken English. Surprisingly little, however, seems to be known about the capacity for information transmission in their own really very varied natural cries and calls.

Homologs of our temporal-lobe speech-perception areas have been claimed in nonhuman primates, and sectors of the monkeys' likely homolog of our (speech-production) Broca's area are reciprocally connected with their anterior cingulate (limbic) vocalization area. Indeed, a recent challenging hypothesis proposes that speech evolved when a continual mouth open–close alternation (lip-smacks, a facio-visual communicative gesture) was superimposed on traditional, larynx-based phonation. Thus speech, rather than originating in primate call systems, may have developed from orofacial communicative gestures, which later became associated with sounds and, ultimately, phonemes. The likely monkey homolog of our Broca's area is active during the observation of others' hand and mouth actions, and may be the basis for understanding such events in others. Such a homolog may therefore have evolved into our Broca's area as a system for recognizing articulatory actions and gestures, though we should be wary of invoking gesture as a major precursor to language proper.

Language consequently seems to have recruited, mosaic fashion, circuits that previously subserved somewhat different, though maybe related, functions in our primate ancestors. Nor is communication its sole role, as it is a unique tool for modeling reality; nor did it evolve in lock-step with praxis, and neither praxis (in the form of tool use) nor language (communicatory, or reality modeling) provided, in a complex, multifactorial, interactive world, the primary impetus for an increase in brain size. Indeed, culture, in the form of social or Machiavellian intelligence, may have played a more important role in the latter context.

Our supralaryngeal vocal tract appears quantitatively if not qualitatively unique to our species, and parallel control of multiple articulators to their target positions permits our very rapid rate of information transmission in speech. The wide range of speech sounds that we can achieve are partly a consequence of our lowered larynx, whose cost is our ever-present danger of choking. Though apes cannot achieve such a range for a variety of possible reasons, it is not clear from soft-tissue reconstructions from fossil material whether our hominid ancestors or cousins, notably *Homo erectus* and the Neanderthals, could achieve such a range. Of course, parrots and human laryngectomies with grossly altered vocal tracts *can* produce quite intelligible speech, though much may depend upon the listener, in a quiet environment, filling in missing information. While the apparent presence of perisylvian speech-related areas in the natural brain-casts of *Homo habilis* suggest that it *could* speak, we do not of course know whether the other necessary structures and functions, central and peripheral, were also in place. We now know from aphasia studies that irreducible components of the speech network are Broca's anterior speech area on the left, which formulates utterances at the phonological and syntactic level, and Wernicke's posterior speech area, also on the left, which plays more of a semantic role. The latter, along with subcortical structures, monitors formulated propositions before their utterance, releasing them when appropriate.

Praxic tool use, as much as speech, characterizes our apparent human uniqueness. Though grasping is not limited to primates or even mammals, more than 35 million years ago higher primates evolved the ability to control individual digits on the hand, and some even developed an opposable thumb. Though the precision grip is essential for tool manipulation, food processing (fruits, nuts, and seeds) may have preadapted our ancestors for tool behavior. Indeed, the apes are noteworthy for their complex, food-related behaviors, many of which are learned from adults by careful, intuitive observation, rather than by rote. By the time of *Homo erectus* the hand has become specifically adapted with a powerful thumb for tool use, though even (maybe especially) the New World monkeys, such as the capuchin, are capable of considerable sophistication in the latter regard. However, their tool behavior, though flexible, adaptive and nonstereotyped, may not be insightful so much as the product of enormous persistence, imitation, and trial-and-error behavior. Thus chimpanzees succeed in similar tasks with far fewer trials through prior planning, modeling, insight, and abstraction, with apparently clear concepts of cause and effect, and of a final goal. They use the same tool in a wide range of contexts, and can use various alternatives, sometimes in sequence, for a particular context. They may even coach their young in the best use and positioning of anvil, nut, and hammer in nut cracking. However, though there is debate as to whether the Oldowan tools of *Homo habilis* of nearly 2.5 million years ago exhibit evidence of shared knowledge of design, apes never quite seem *naturally* able (though they can be taught) to achieve even that level of skill. Moreover, it was not until Acheulian times and *Homo erectus* that tools became standardized and symmetrical, with the makers apparently possessing a clear sense of intention and aesthetics. However we can still ask why even anatomically modern *Homo sapiens sapiens* apparently took so long to *behave* in a fully "modern" way, to judge from the tool record. One might invoke the advent of language in this regard, but the apparent parallelism and commonalities, in the syntactic and serial structure of both behaviors, can be overemphasized; hierarchical organization and embedding, so characteristic of language, is far less evident in serial tool behavior. More-over, the latter is better learned by direct modeling or observation than by verbal coaching.

Many brain regions contribute to efficient tool behavior. The prefrontal cortex, enormously enlarged in our species, plays a major executive and supervisory role in the intelligent deployment of behavior. The premotor cortex selects movement sequences that are contextually appropriate, and along with the basal ganglia releases them, via the primary motor cortex, whereas the cerebellum handles the automatized and timed coordination of individual muscles. Damage to such regions results in characteristic movement disorders. Deliberate voluntary action involves centers distributed between the parietal (where spatial and spatio-temporal aspects are elaborated) and anterior (frontal, prefrontal) cortices. Whereas the patient with basal ganglia disease typically still knows what should be done, the apraxic patient with disorders of skilled voluntary action may now seem to suffer from amnesia for the action itself. Many aphasics are also apraxic, though not all apraxics are also aphasic. Indeed, any mutual association between the two conditions may stem from anatomical contiguity between mediating centers, rather than from a common underlying mechanism. Just as with language, an elaboration of pre-existing circuits seems likely in the evolution of tool-using behaviors, rather than the sudden appearance, *ab initio*, of a special organ. Also, as a very broad generalization, just as occurs with language, the left hemisphere may mediate the more sequential or time-dependent aspects, and the right hemisphere the more spatial or contextual aspects.

Evolution is, of course, no guarantee of ever-increasing complexity, or capacity; nevertheless, from reptiles to archaic mammals, to modern mammals, to primates and particularly within the hominoids, there has indeed been a progressive increase in cranial capacity (and probable information-processing power), both in absolute terms and, in particular, when allometrically corrected for body mass. Such developments permitted exploitation of a wider range of environments and a reduced reproductive rate, though altered patterns of internal connectivity, and altered functional activity itself, may be no less important.

Embryological neurogenetic processes ultimately determine both target adult brain and body sizes, the former directly and the latter indirectly. The human brain grows as if in a giant ape's body, though partly because of decoupled growth in different brain regions (enormous prefrontal enlargement), it ultimately regulates body growth as though it were the size of a chimpanzee brain. As body size increases, so too does the basic metabolic rate, and metabolically very expensive brains may ultimately only become as big as the body can support further such increases in metabolic rate. Large brains also have a lower tolerance for temperature extremes, and pose obstetric problems whose solution may compromise locomotion. They may therefore only be "profitable" if associated with a very considerable increase in behavioral complexity, over a lengthy lifetime, and will be associated with additional adaptations in duration of gestation, and length of period before weaning and reproductive maturity. Our large brains are mainly achieved by an unusually lengthy postnatal period of brain growth, though the "final" shape of the developing brain in childhood may reflect pruning of excess cells or connections.

Though (allometrically corrected) brain size and cognitive function clearly correlate to some extent interspecifically, at an intraspecific level a small human brain is not necessarily associated with intellectual deficit. Indeed, the average human brain possesses enormous spare capacity, as is evident in the face of childhood hemidecortication. It is also likely at an evolutionary level that internal brain organization and local growth may determine intellectual capacity; an overall brain enlargement would then occur secondarily to selective reorganization and enlargement of just one or two individual structures. A cascade of such consequent changes could occur remotely, owing to embryonic coupling rather than via direct selection for such remote regions. New cognitive potentialities could then follow.

Intelligence is not easily definable; we may see it as the ability to solve novel problems or to manipulate several disparate concepts simultaneously, or to deal adaptively with a complex and changing environment. Nor is there agreement on how best to assess it, except that "crystallized" intelligence, reflecting our learned skills, and perhaps residing in more posterior regions, differs from "fluid", novel problem-solving capacities and strategic aspects, which may reside in our enormously enlarged prefrontal structures. It is here that flexible, insightful, intuitive (as compared with rote or imitative) problem-solving behavior may be mediated. Is it such behavior that has been selected for in human evolution, perhaps involving tool behavior and abstract concepts, or have the more social behaviors, also mediated in these prefrontal regions, provided the real driving force? Ethological observation of primate social behavior, and the apparent disconnection between complexity of tool kits and cranial capacity in the hominid fossil record, suggests the importance of social or Machiavellian intelligence, though both problem-solving behaviors may well have interacted in our evolution.

Group membership involves the constant need to reassess one's standing with one's peers, to form alliances, and to switch tactics when necessary during intense social competition. Manipulation and deceit may become the order of the day, with insight necessary into what significant others may be thinking about oneself or those with one. This is the basis for a "theory of mind", the drawing of inferences about other's desires, intentions, and beliefs. Such an awareness may not develop in children after the first few years of life and may never be present in autistic individuals. The degree of its presence in other primates is currently a matter of some debate, with much of the evidence necessarily anecdotal.

Relative to apes, we certainly have improved capacities not just in problem-solving, praxis, and communication, but also in social-event perception, shared attention, imitation, pantomime, cooperation, deception, and reciprocal communication of intentions. Should we perhaps emphasize the positive aspects of trust, care, altruism, reciprocity, and cooperation no less than the negative ones of expediency, manipulation, and selfish advancement? May the former perhaps involve *group* selection (itself a hotly debated concept) rather than selection at the level of the individual? Group selection may indeed occur when groups, rather than individuals, are in mutual competition, and it is under such circumstances that apparent altruism may seem to make sense, though of course it is always open to exploitation by cheats or freeloaders.

Evidence from neuroimaging studies involving theory-of-mind tasks, and from the neuropathology associated with brain lesions and autism, implicates the disproportionately enlarged (in humans) prefrontal structures. Such regions mediate executive functions, attention, set, working memory, and future planning, both in abstract cognitive tasks and behaviors, and, now, in the social context. Did both aspects co-evolve, or did one, perhaps social intelligence, drive the other and the growth of the prefrontal cortex? Whatever the case, may be, animal cognition seems as relevant as animal communication as precursors of human language and intellect.

An awareness of other minds would seem to imply an awareness or consciousness of the self, and an ability to self-recognize. Self-recognition in mirrors is another hotly debated issue, and may be restricted to the apes and humans. What can such studies tell us about consciousness itself? Neurological studies, perhaps not surprisingly, have failed to locate any one "center" for consciousness, which is clearly multimodal and distributed, and in the surgically divided brain it is not clear whether there is more than one stream of consciousness; we should, however, remember ourselves as in many ways a mosaic of modular minds, of conflicting drives and desires, though we may only *choose* one response option at a time, and become consciously aware of that which was selected and acted on. Conscious awareness may therefore correspond to the bottleneck of selective attention whereby we choose our action sequences.

Consciousness enables the success or failure of ongoing responses to be assessed or monitored, particularly when they are difficult or nonautomatic. Indeed, automaticity is typically achievable in the absence of conscious awareness, and introspection may prove interfering or detrimental to overlearnt skills. Conscious awareness does not depend upon language, and nonverbal imagery may be fundamental to much creative or problem-solving behavior. There is no reason to suppose its absence in the higher primates, and indeed the lesson from evolution, and the theme of this book, is continuity with other species in communication, praxis, consciousness, and intellect. From these observations we may choose to draw certain moral conclusions as to how we should interact and deal with individuals of other species—or even of other races, ethnic, or social groups. So far, our record has been poor at all levels. Indeed, we can speculate on the very possibility of the long-term coexistence of two (or more) substantially different groups of individuals endowed with similar levels of sentience and conscious self-awareness. Several million years ago there may have been more than one species of *Homo*, along perhaps with *Paranthropus*, but we do not know how they interacted, if at all. The demise of the Neanderthals with the arrival of anatomically modern people in Europe is probably significant. Science fiction paints a gloomy picture of what might happen should we encounter somewhere in the Universe another "civilization". Had a smart species of dinosaur survived the terminal Cretaceous extinctions, it is very doubtful whether the Earth would have supported a reptilian intelligence equivalent and additional to our own. Of course, none of this is to suggest that evolution is progressive. We just happen to have the most complex (so far) central nervous system in the geological record, which we view from our own parochial, if privileged, and precarious, standpoint.

In this book we have examined human evolution against a backdrop of the evolution of living things, of tetrapods, mammals, primates, and hominids, while trying to avoid giving an impression of inexorable "upward" progress towards ever-increasing complexity, whether by the blind forces of natural selection, or through the influence of a directing force or agency. The question "Where do we go from here?" can be answered in two ways, relating either to the future of the species, or to future directions for research. Species, like civilizations, do not endure for ever; they either give rise to new species, necessarily (by definition) qualitatively different from their predecessors, or they just become extinct. As we observed in Chapter 1, the direction of evolution is massively underdetermined; we cannot predict either the nature of future selective pressures, nor the adaptations that will appear and the likely consequences. However, now that we are no longer reproductively isolated in a world of mass travel, further speciation may be unlikely. To ask what are the likely directions for future research in human evolution is akin to asking what will be the likely technical developments of the next century—or how psychology will itself develop. If we knew, and had the technology, we would be doing it now. One clue is perhaps to ask in what areas the study of evolutionary psychology currently exhibits the greatest gaps.

The field of evolutionary psychology is new and still emerging (and see Cosmides, Tooby, & Barkow, 1992); it seeks to explain human behavior, particularly where it seems qualitatively or quantitatively different from other species, in terms of adaptive responses to selective pressures. In neuropsychological textbooks, in addition to chapters on language and praxis, consciousness and cognition, and disorders of thought and movement, we typically encounter chapters on object recognition (and its breakdown, in the agnosias), and memory (and the amnesias). In this book we have addressed from a neuropsychological perspective those faculties that have either in the past been seen as uniquely human, or which nowadays may be regarded as more prominently, or aberrantly, developed in ourselves, despite having in many cases a very long evolutionary tradition in other primate or mammalian species. After four or more score years of continuous exposure to trivia of every imaginable kind—objects, individuals, faces, scenes, and events—we still retain an amazing quantity of information, acquired often decades ago, and can recall or recognize with surprising fidelity; moreover, our ability to acquire new knowledge, unless we unfortunately develop a dementing disorder, is relatively undiminished. We really know very little about how such information is encoded (on experiencing it), stored, maintained, retrieved, or rendered inaccessible, temporarily (as with the familiar and frustrating tip-of-the-tongue state of feeling-of-knowing) or permanently (as with certain forms of amnesia). We know that at a macro level the temporal lobes (with adjacent limbic and mesial occipital regions) are involved in object recognition and object, person, face, and event memories; at a finer level, areas of synchronized activity across networks, which are perhaps functionally established on an *ad hoc* basis for each object or scene, are probably important. At a yet finer level, we must look to the synapse (and changed probabilities of transmission), as Hebb (1949) argued so many years ago, and below that to semipermanent changes within the cell chemistry itself during the process of memory consolidation. Bailey, Bartsch, and Kandel (1996), for example, propose that the storage of long-term memory is associated with a cellular program of gene expression, altered protein synthesis and the growth of new synaptic connections; the molecular switch required for consolidation involves the activation of an adenosine $3':5'$-cyclic phosphate (cAMP) induced cascade of genes, with associated protein transcription. The mechanisms seem essentially similar even in invertebrates. We have no reason to believe that our present nearest primate relatives differ substantially from us in their capacity to recognize objects (as long as they are somehow meaningful to them), though future research may well plot the limits, quantitative and qualitative, of object recognition and object memory in nonhuman primates.

Because of the difficulties in "getting into" the mind of another (human, not to say of a chimpanzee), it will be much more difficult to determine whether apes recall events ("episodic memory") in the way we do; do they, for example, ever daydream or reflect on past events? Are such capacities dependent on a level of consciousness that perhaps is unavailable to our nearest relatives? New brain-imaging techniques (PET, and functional magnetic resonance imaging: fMRI) are revealing, in humans, those brain areas that are *active* (though this may not necessarily imply that they are *essential*) during a host of relatively "everyday" tasks, which are far more "ecologically valid" than the controlled, and contrived, experiments of cognitive psychology. So far, such work has not extended to other primates, and it would be fascinating to plot homologies in this fashion. Of course, the problem remains of verifying that the animal is doing, mentalistically, just what you want it to do. Even (maybe especially) humans can achieve the same apparent physical endpoint via a range of mental strategies.

Cognitive psychology has long made the useful (but not always watertight) distinction between episodic and semantic memory. Though the contents of the former are essentially trivial—events and experiences—they are of course the bases of our personal histories, and probably depend preeminently upon some form of conscious awareness, a faculty that we have seen is disputed in infrahuman species. Indeed, episodic memory and consciousness of the *self* may be inextricably interconnected, though clearly individuals of most mammalian species can recognize objects previously experienced as meaningful. However, such *meaningful* objects (or events) partake more of the qualities of semantic memory, memory for objects or events that belong within an organized or systematic body of knowledge (language, mathematics, certain aspects of topography). Though we may think of such bodies of knowledge as highly evolved, we are not conscious, in a strict sense, of their contents, and the organized, systematic foraging behavior of a gorilla, according to seasons, time of day and place, would seem to imply possession of a well-developed semantic memory. The otherwise-useful distinction between episodic and semantic is not always easy to uphold; nor, again except perhaps by brain imaging (or inductive observation!), can we easily or usefully assess nonhuman capacities in these respects. Suffice it to say that though there is every reason to ascribe to our primate relatives a reasonably developed network of semantic associations, the question of episodic memory is bound up in the domain of consciousness.

Consciousness also supervenes in the domain of working memory, largely mediated, as we saw, by the dorsolateral prefrontal cortex, a structure that is highly developed in our species. It is working memory that enables us to perform all our various problem-solving operations, deductive and inductive reasoning. By its very nature, it should be readily accessible to brain imaging in the case of nonhuman primates, as input, task, and requisite responses can be readily controlled. It will be a fascinating challenge to determine the extent of involvement of similar structures, temporal, occipital and frontal, in object recognition, semantic, episodic and working memory, in other species.

Postscript

The Universe as we know it has existed for maybe 16 thousand million years, the Earth for just over one-third of that time span, vertebrates for maybe one-tenth of the Earth's existence, and hominids for maybe one one-hundred-and-seventieth as long as vertebrates have inhabited the Earth. Throughout the aeons of life on Earth there have been dramatic climatic changes occasioned by solar and tectonic activity, and repeated cycles of extinction due to meteoric and cometary impact. During the past 25,000 years of evolution—which must proceed incrementally even during so brief a time span—human populations in different parts of the globe have continued to be subjected to a great variety of geographical and climatic conditions, and many different faunal and floral associations. In response to these diverse environmental conditions, a variety of local population adaptations have been selected, which include relatively minor variations in body build (somatotypes), limb configuration, pigmentation, facial features (in response to cold, wind, and sun), hair type and distribution, blood groups, biochemical and physiological functions, and disease resistance (Freedman, 1995). Many commentators have been concerned that technological "progress" is outstripping our inherited ability as Upper Palaeolithic hunter-gatherers, newly out of Africa, to adapt individually or selectively as a species, to all the new demands that we have ourselves called into being. We have created an ecological niche for ourselves, which is proving in many ways less and less comfortable, and one for which at our (and its) current rate of change we shall be progressively less fitted. Such positive feedback in a dynamic system leads to increasing instability, an instability that is becoming all too obvious in its different manifestations around an ever smaller and less happy world. As Freedman (1995) observes, our previously selected flexibility and adaptability as generalists, and lack of narrow specialization, may be our best, or indeed only, prospect for an increasingly uncertain future. Within 150 years of population growth and technology we have progressed from Darwin's (1859, p. 490) exalted optimism and wonder at the ever-continuing evolution, "from so simple a beginning [of] endless forms most beautiful and most wonderful . . . a grandeur in this view of life", to Dawkins' (1995, p. 67) bleak and profound pessimism concerning selfish genes, blind physical forces and chance, an absence of justice, rhyme or reason, "a universe of pitiless indifference". Maybe in the end our technology *will* save us from the otherwise inevitable, sooner or later, extinction from cosmic events. Or maybe we too shall first become victims of the house that we have built.

References

Abitbol, M.M. (1995). Lateral view of *Australopithecus afarensis*: Primitive aspects of bipedal positional behavior in the earliest hominids. *Journal of Human Evolution, 28*, 211–229.

Aboitiz, F. (1996). Does bigger mean better? Evolutionary determinants of brain size and structure. *Brain, Behaviour and Evolution, 47*, 225–245.

Ahlberg, P.E., Clack, J.A., & Lukševičs, E. (1996). Rapid brain case evolution between *Panderichthys* and the earliest tetrapods. *Nature, 381*, 61–63.

Ahlberg, P.E., & Milner, A.R. (1994). The origin and early diversification of tetrapods. *Nature, 368*, 507–514.

Aiello, L.C. (1994). Thumbs up for our early ancestors. *Science, 265*, 1540–1541.

Aitken, P.G. (1981). Cortical control of conditioned and spontaneous vocal behavior in rhesus monkeys. *Brain and Language, 13*, 171–184.

Akazawa, T., Muhesen, S., Dodo, Y., Kondo, O., & Mizoguchi, Y. (1995). Neanderthal infant burial. *Nature, 377*, 585–586.

Aldhous, P. (1996). Wrong laugh leaves chimps speechless. *New Scientist, 20 January*, 5.

Alpagut, B., Andrews, P., Fortelius, M., Kappelman, J., Temizsoy, I., Celebi, H., & Lindsay, W. (1996). A new specimen of *Ankarapithecus meteai* from the Sinap Formation of central Anatolia. *Nature, 382*, 349–351.

Anderson, A., Holmes, B., & Else, L. (1996). Zombies, dolphins and blindsight. *New Scientist, 4 May*, 20–27.

Anderson, J.R. (1984). Development of self-recognition: A review. *Developmental Psychobiology, 5*, 297–305.

Anderson-Gerfaud, P. (1990). Aspects of behaviour in the Middle Palaeolithic: Functional analysis of stone tools from south west France. In P. Mellars (Ed.), *The emergence of modern humans: An archaeological perspective* (pp. 389–413). Edinburgh: Edinburgh University Press.

Andrews, P. (1995). Ecological apes and ancestors. *Nature, 376*, 555–556.

Andrews, P., & Pilbeam, D. (1996). The nature of the evidence. *Nature, 379*, 123–124.

Arendt, D., & Nübler-Jung, K. (1994). Inversion of dorsoventral axis? *Nature, 371*, 26.

Arensburg, B., Tillier, A.M., Vandermeersch, B., Duday, H., Schepartz, L.A., & Rak, Y. (1989). A Middle Palaeolithic human hyoid bone. *Nature, 338*, 758–760.

Armstrong, D.F., Stokoe, W.C., & Wilcox, S.E. (1995). *Gesture and the nature of language.* Cambridge: Cambridge University Press.

Arsuaga, J.L., Martinez, I., Gracia, A., Carretero, J.-M., & Carbonell, E. (1993). Three new human skulls from Sima de Los Huesos Middle Pleistocene site in Sierra de Atapuerca, Spain. *Nature, 362*, 534–537.

Averof, M., & Cohen, M. (1997). Evolutionary origin of insect wings from ancestral gills. *Nature, 385*, 627–630.

Ayala, F.J. (1995). The myth of Eve: Molecular biology and human origins. *Science, 270*, 1930–1936.

Ayala, F.J., Escalante, A., O'hUigin, C., & Klein, J. (1994). Molecular genetics of speciation and human origins. *Proceedings of the National Academy of Sciences, 91*, 6787–6794.

Bahn, P.G., & Vertut, J. (1988). *Images of the ice age.* Leicester: Windward.

Bailey, C.H., Bartsch, D., & Kandel, E.R. (1996). Toward a molecular definition of long-term memory storage. *Proceedings of the National Academy of Sciences, 93*, 13445–13452.

Baker, S.C., Rogers, R.D., Owen, A.M., Frith, C.D., Dolan, R.J., Frackowiak, R.S.J., & Robbins, T.W. (1996). Neural systems engaged by planning: A PET study of the Tower of London task. *Neuropsychologia, 34*, 515–526.

Balter, M. (1996). Looking for clues to the mystery of life on Earth. *Science, 273*, 870–872.

Bancaud, J., Brunet-Bourgin, F., Chauvel, P., & Halgren, E. (1994). Anatomical origin of déjà vu and vivid "memories" in human temporal lobe epilepsy. *Brain, 117*, 71–90.

Barber, T.X. (1996). Restrictive vs open paradigms in comparative psychology. *American Psychologist, 1*, 58–59.

Barinaga, M. (1995). Brain researchers speak a common language. *Science, 270*, 1437–1438.

Barinaga, M. (1996). Guiding neurons to the cortex. *Science, 274*, 1100–1101.

Baron-Cohen, S. (1995). *Mindblindness: An essay on autism and theory of mind.* Cambridge, MA: MIT Press.

Baron-Cohen, S., Campbell, R., Karmiloff-Smith, A., Grant, J., & Walker, J. (1995). Are children with autism blind to the mentalistic significance of the eyes? *British Journal of Developmental Psychology, 13*, 379–398.

Barton, R.A., Purvis, A., & Harvey, P.H. (1995). Evolutionary radiation of visual and olfactory brain systems in primates, bats and insectivores. *Philosophical Transactions of the Royal Society of London B, 348*, 381–392.

Bar-Yosef, O., & Vandermeersch, B. (1993). Modern humans in the Levant. *Scientific American, April*, 64–70.

Bates, E., & Elman, J. (1996). Learning rediscovered. *Science, 274*, 1849–1850.

Bauman, M.L. (1992). Neuropathology of autism. In A.B. Joseph & R.R. Young (Eds.), *Movement disorders in neurology and neuropsychiatry* (pp. 662–666). Oxford: Blackwell Scientific.

Beard, K.C., Tong, Y., Dawson, M.R., Wang, J., & Huang, X. (1996). Earliest complete dentition of an anthropoid primate from the Late Middle Eocene of Shanxi Province, China. *Science, 272*, 82–85.

Bechara, A., Damasio, H., Tranel, D., and Damasio, A.R. (1997). Deciding advantageously before knowing the advantageous strategy. *Science, 275*, 1293–1296.

Beck, B.B. (1980). *Animal tool behavior: The use and manufacture of tools by animals.* New York: Garland STPM Press.

Bednarik, R. (1995). Concept mediated marking in the Lower Pleistocene. *Current Anthropology, 36*, 605–634.

Begun, D.R. (1992). Miocene fossil hominids and the chimp–human clade. *Science, 257*, 1929–1933.

Begun, D.R. (1994). Relations among the great apes and humans: New interpretations based on the fossil great ape *Dryopithecus. Yearbook of Physical Anthropology, 37*, 11–63.

Belitzky, S., Goren-Inbar, N., & Werker, E. (1991). A Middle Pleistocene wooden plank with man-made polish. *Journal of Human Evolution, 20*, 349–353.

Benefit, B.R., & McCrossin, M.L. (1995). Miocene hominoids and hominid origins. *Annual Review of Anthropology, 24*, 237–256.

Benson, D.F. (1993). Prefrontal abilities. *Behavioural Neurology, 6*, 75–81.

Benton, M.J. (1995). Diversification and extinction in the history of life. *Science, 268*, 52–58.

Berardelli, A., Hallett, M., Rothwell, J.C., & Marsden, C.D. (1996). Single joint rapid arm movements in normal subjects and in patients with motor disorders. *Brain, 119*, 661–674.

Berge, C. (1994). How did the australopithecines walk? A biomechanical study of the hip and thigh of *Australopithecus afarensis. Journal of Human Evolution, 26*, 259–273.

Beynon, P., & Rasa, O.A.E. (1989). Do dwarf mongooses have a language? Warning vocalizations transmit complex information. *South African Journal of Science, 85*, 447–450.

Bickerton, D. (1990). *Language and species.* Chicago, IL: University of Chicago Press.

Bickerton, D. (1995). *Language and human behavior.* Seattle: University of Washington Press.

Bishop, D.V.M. (1992). The underlying nature of specific language impairment. *Journal of Child Psychology and Psychiatry, 16*, 333–366.

Blinkov, S.M., & Glezer, I.I. (1968). *The human brain in figures.* New York: Basic Books.

Blumenschine, R.J., & Cavallo, J.A. (1992). Scavenging and human evolution. *Scientific American, October*, 70–76.

Boaz, N.T. (1988). Status of *Australopithecus afarensis. Yearbook of Physical Anthropology, 31*, 85–113.

Boëda, E., Connan, J., Dessort, J., Muhesen, S., Mercier, N., Valladas, H., & Tisnérat, N. (1996). Bitumen as a hafting material on Middle Palaeolithic artifacts. *Nature, 380*, 336–338.

Boehm, C. (1989). Methods for isolating chimpanzee vocal communication. In P.J. Heltne & L.A. Marquardt (Eds.), *Understanding chimpanzees* (pp. 2–21). Cambridge, MA: Harvard University Press.

Boesch, C. (1991). Teaching among wild chimpanzees. *Animal Behaviour, 41*, 530–532.

Boesch, C. (1996). The question of culture. *Nature, 379*, 207–208.

Bolte, M., & Hogan, C.J. (1995). Conflict over the age of the Universe. *Nature, 376*, 399–402.

Bolter, M. (1995). Did *Homo erectus* tame fire first? *Science, 268*, 1570.

Bowring, S.A., Grotzinger, J.P., Isachsen, C.E., Knoll, A.H., Pelechaty, S.M., & Kolosor, P. (1993). Calibrating rates of Early Cambrian evolution. *Science, 261*, 1293–1298.

Boysen, S.T., Berntson, C.G., & Prentice, J. (1987). Simian scribbles: A reappraisal of drawing in the chimpanzee (*Pan troglodytes). Journal of Comparative Psychology, 101*, 82–89.

Bradshaw, J.L. (1989). *Hemispheric specialization and psychological function.* Chichester: Wiley.

Bradshaw, J.L. (1995). Another far more ancient tongue. *Behavioral and Brain Sciences, 18*, 385–400.

Bradshaw, J.L. (1996). Gail D. – Poizner, Klima and Bellugi's (1987) deaf agrammatic signer: Form and function in the left cerebral hemisphere for speech and language. In C. Code, C.-W. Wallesch, Y. Joanette, & A.-R. Lecours (Eds.), *Classic cases in neuropsychology.* Hove: Psychology Press.

Bradshaw, J.L., & Mattingley, J.B. (1995). *Clinical neuropsychology: Behavioral and brain sciences.* San Diego, CA: Academic Press.

Bradshaw, J.L., & Rogers, L.J. (1993). *The evolution of lateral asymmetries, language, tool use and intellect.* San Diego, CA: Academic Press.

Bressler, S.L. (1995). Large-scale cortical networks and cognition. *Brain Research Reviews, 20,* 288–304.

Bressler, S.L., Coppola, R., & Nakamura, R. (1993). Episodic multiregional cortical coherence at multiple frequencies during visual task performance. *Nature, 366,* 153–156.

Brewer, S.M., & McGrew, W.C. (1990). Chimpanzee use of a tool set to get honey. *Folia Primatologica, 54,* 100–104.

Briggs, D.E.G., Erwin, D.H., & Collier, F.J. (1994). *The fossils of the Burgess Shale.* Washington: Smithsonian Institute Press.

Bromage, T.G., & Schrenk, F. (1995). Biogeographic and climatic basis for a narrative of early hominid evolution. *Journal of Human Evolution, 28,* 109–111.

Brooks, D.J. (1995). The role of the basal ganglia in motor control: Contributions from PET. *Journal of the Neurological Sciences, 128,* 1–13.

Brown, S.L. (1994). Animals at play. *National Geographic, 186(6),* 2–35.

Bunney, S. (1993). On the origins of the midwife. *New Scientist, 22 May,* 18.

Bunney, S. (1994). Did modern culture begin in prehistoric caves? *New Scientist, 15 January,* 16.

Burling, R. (1993). Primate calls, human language and nonverbal communication. *Current Anthropology, 34,* 25–53.

Butovskaya, M.L., & Kozintsev, A.G. (1996). A neglected form of quasi-aggression in apes: Possible relevance for the origins of humor. *Current Anthropology, 37,* 716–717.

Byrne, R.W. (1995a). The smart gorilla's recipe book. *Natural History, 10,* 12–15.

Byrne, R.W. (1995b). *The thinking ape: Evolutionary origins of intelligence.* Oxford: Oxford University Press.

Call, J., & Tomasello, M. (1994). Production and comprehension of referential pointing by orangutans (*Pongo pygmaeus*). *Journal of Comparative Psychology, 108,* 307–317.

Calvin, W.H. (1994). The emergence of intelligence. *Scientific American, October,* 79–85.

Campbell, D.G. (1996). Splendid isolation in Thingvallavatn. *Natural History, 6,* 48–55.

Cann, R.L., Stoneking, M., & Wilson, A.C. (1987). Mitochondrial DNA and human evolution. *Nature, 325,* 31–36.

Carbonell, E., Bermudez de Castro, J.M., Arsuaga, J.L., Diez, J.C., Rosas, A., Cuenca-Bescós, G., Sola, R., Mosquera, M., & Rodriguez, X.P. (1995). Lower Pleistocene hominids and artifacts from Atapuerca-TD6 (Spain). *Science, 269,* 826–830.

Carbonell, E., & Castro-Curel, Z. (1992). Palaeolithic wooden artifacts from the Abric Romani (Capellades, Barcelona, Spain). *Journal of Archaeological Science, 19,* 707–719.

Cardon, L.R., Smith, S.D., Fulker, D.W., Kimberling, W.J., Pennington, B.F., & DeFries, J.C. (1994). Quantitative trait locus for reading disability on chromosome 6. *Science, 266,* 276–279.

Caro, T.M., & Hauser, M.D. (1992). Is there teaching in nonhuman animals? *The Quarterly Review of Biology, 67,* 151–174.

Carroll, R. (1995). Between fish and amphibian. *Nature, 373,* 389–390.

Carroll, R. (1996). Revealing the patterns of macroevolution. *Nature, 381,* 19–20.

Carroll, S.B. (1995). Homeotic genes and the evolution of arthropods and chordates. *Nature, 376,* 479–485.

Cartmill, M. (1995a). Aping language. *Nature, 373,* 206.

Cartmill, M. (1995b). Significant others. *Natural History, 6,* 74–77.

Cavalli-Sforza, L.L., Menozzi, P., & Piazza, A. (1993). Demic expansions and human evolution. *Science, 259,* 639–646.

Cavalli-Sforza, L.L., Menozzi, P., & Piazza, A. (1994). *The History and Geography of Human Genes.* Princeton,NJ: Princeton University Press.

Cavalli-Sforza, L.L., Minch, E., & Mountain, J.L. (1992). Coevolution of genes and languages revisited. *Proceedings of the National Academy of Sciences, 89,* 5620–5624.

Chaboyer, B., Demarque, P., Kernan, P.J., & Krauss, L.M. (1996). A lower limit to the age of the Universe. *Science, 271*, 957–961.

Chase, P.G., & Dibble, H.L. (1987). Middle Palaeolithic symbolism: A review of current evidence and interpretations. *Journal of Anthropological Archaeology, 6*, 263–296.

Chauvet, J.M., Deschamps, E.B., & Hillaire, C. (1996). *Chauvet cave: Discovery of world's oldest paintings*. London: Thames & Hudson.

Chen, J.-Y., Dzik, J., Edgecombe, G.D., Ramskold, L., & Zhou, G.-Q. (1995). A possible Early Cambrian chordate. *Nature, 377*, 720–722.

Cheney, D.L., & Seyfarth, R.M. (1990). *How monkeys see the world: Inside the mind of another species*. Chicago, IL: Chicago University Press.

Chevalier-Skolnikoff, S. (1990). Tool use by wild *Cebus* monkeys at Santa Rosa National Park, Costa Rica. *Primates, 3*, 375–383.

Chomsky, N. (1980). Rules and representations. *Behavioral and Brain Sciences, 3*, 1–61.

Ciaranello, A.L., & Ciaranello, R.D. (1995). The neurobiology of infantile autism. *Annual Review of Neuroscience, 18*, 101–128.

Clack, J.A. (1994). Earliest known tetrapod braincase and the evolution of the stapes and the fenestra ovalis. *Nature, 369*, 392–394.

Clarke, R.J., & Tobias, P.V. (1995). Sterkfontein member 2 foot bones of the oldest South African hominid. *Science, 269*, 521–524.

Coates, M.I., & Clack, J.A. (1990). Polydactyly in the earliest known tetrapod limbs. *Nature, 347*, 66–69.

Coates, M.I., & Clack, J.A. (1995). Romer's gap: Tetrapod origins and terrestriality. *Bulletin du Museum National d'Histoire Naturelle: Section C, Sciences de la Terre Paleontologie, Geologie, Mineralogie, 17*, 373–388.

Cohen, P. (1996). Are proteins real key to life? *New Scientist, 10 August*, 16.

Comings, D.E. (1995). Tourette's syndrome: A behavioral spectrum disorder. In W.J. Weiner & A.E. Lang (Eds.), *Behavioral neurology of movement disorders: Advances in neurology, Vol. 65* (pp. 293–303). New York: Raven Press.

Como, P.G. (1995). Obsessive-compulsive disorder in Tourette's syndrome. In W.J. Weiner & A.E. Lang (Eds.), *Behavioral Neurology of Movement Disorders; Advances in Neurology, Vol. 65* (pp. 281–291). New York: Raven Press.

Cooper, S.F. (1996). Origins: The backbone of evolution. *Natural History, 6*, 31–43.

Corballis, M.C. (1991). *The lopsided ape*. New York: Oxford University Press.

Cosmides, L., Tooby, J., & Barkow, J.H. (1992). Introduction: Evolutionary psychology and conceptual integration. In J.H. Barkow, L. Cosmides, & J. Tooby (Eds.), *The adapted mind: Evolutionary psychology and the generation of culture* (pp. 3–18). Oxford: Oxford University Press.

Culotta, E. (1995a). Asian anthropoids strike back. *Science, 270*, 918.

Culotta, E. (1995b). Anthropologists overturn old ideas about new developments. *Science, 268*, 364–365.

Cummings, J.L. (1993). Frontal-subcortical circuits and human behavior. *Archives of Neurology, 50*, 873–879.

Cutting, J. (1990). *The right cerebral hemisphere and psychiatric disorder*. Oxford: Oxford University Press.

Damasio, H. (1996). Human neuroanatomy relevant to decision making. In A.R. Damasio, H. Damasio, & Y. Christen (Eds.), *Neurobiology of decision making* (pp. 1–11). New York: Springer.

Damasio, A.R., & Anderson, S.W. (1993). The frontal lobes. In K.M. Heilman & E. Valenstein (Eds.), *Clinical neuropsychology* (3rd Edn, pp. 409–460). Oxford: Oxford University Press.

Damasio, H., Grabowski, T.J., Tranel, D., Hichwa, R.D., & Damasio, A.R. (1996). A neural basis for lexical retrieval. *Nature, 380*, 499–505.

Darwin, C. (1859). *On the origin of species by means of natural selection, or the preservation of favoured races in the struggle for life*. London: John Murray.

Davidson, E.H., Peterson, K.J., & Cameron, R.A. (1995). Origin of bilaterian body plans: Evolution of developmental regulatory mechanisms. *Science, 270*, 1319–1325.

Davidson, I. (1990). Bilzingsleben and early marking. *Rock Art Research, 7*, 52–56.

Davidson, I. (1991). The archaeology of language origins: A review. *Antiquity, 65*, 39–48.

Dawkins, R. (1995). God's utility function. *Scientific American, November*, 62–67.

Dawkins, R. (1996). *The selfish gene*. Oxford: Oxford University Press.

Deacon, T.W. (1986a). Human brain evolution: 1. Evolution of language circuits. In H.J. Jerison & I. Jerison (Eds.), *Intelligence and evolutionary biology* (pp. 363–380). New York: Springer.

Deacon, T.W. (1986b). Human brain evolution: 11. Embryology and brain allometry. In H.J. Jerison & I. Jerison (Eds.), *Intelligence and evolutionary biology* (pp. 381–415). New York: Springer.

Deacon, T.W. (1989). The neural circuitry underlying primate calls and human language. *Human Evolution, 4*, 367–401.

Deacon, T.W. (1990). Problems of ontogeny and phylogeny in brain-size evolution. *International Journal of Primatology, 11*, 237–282.

Dean, D., & Delson, E. (1994). *Homo* at the gates of Europe. *Nature, 373*, 472–473.

Delacour, J. (1995). An introduction to the biology of consciousness. *Neuropsychologia, 33*, 1061–1074.

Della Sala, S., Marchetti, C., & Spinnler, H. (1994). The anarchic hand: A fronto-mesial sign. In F. Boller & J. Grafman (Eds.), *Handbook of neuropsychology, Vol. 9* (pp. 233–255). New York: Elsevier.

Dennell, R. (1997). The World's oldest spears. *Nature, 385*, 767–768.

Dennett, D.C. (1992). *Consciousness explained*. London: Allen Lane/The Penguin Press.

DePaolo, D.J. (1994). Strange bedfellows. *Nature, 372*, 131.

Deregowski, J.B. (1995). Perception–depiction–perception and communication: A skeleton key to rock art and its significance. *Rock Art Research, 12*, 3–10.

Dettwyler, K.A. (1991). Can paleopathology provide evidence for compassion? *American Journal of Physical Anthropology, 84*, 375–384.

de Waal, F. (1996). *Good natured: The origins of right and wrong in humans and other animals*. Cambridge, MA: Harvard University Press.

Diamond, M. (1988). *Enriching environment: The impact of the environment on the anatomy of the brain*. New York: The Free Press.

Dingwall, W.O. (1988). The evolution of human communicative behavior. In F.J. Newmeyer (Ed.), *Linguistics: The Cambridge Survey, Vol. III, Language: Psychological and biological aspects* (pp. 274–313). New York: Cambridge University Press.

Divac, I. (1995). Monotremunculi and brain evolution. *Trends in Neurosciences, 18*, 2–4.

Dolgopolsky, A. (1995). Linguistic prehistory. *Cambridge Archaeological Journal, 5*, 268–271.

Donald, M. (1995). The neurobiology of human consciousness: An evolutionary approach. *Neuropsychologia, 33*, 1087–1102.

Dorit, R.L., Akashi, H., & Gilbert, W. (1995). Absence of polymorphism at the ZFY locus on the human Y chromosome. *Science, 268*, 1183–1185.

Dorman, C. (1991). Microcephaly and intelligence. *Developmental Medicine and Child Neurology, 33*, 267–272.

Dorozynski, A. (1993). Possible Neandertal ancestor found. *Science, 262*, 991.

Douglas-Hamilton, I., & Douglas-Hamilton, O. (1975). *Among the elephants*. London: Collins.

Dronkers, N.F. (1996). A new brain region for coordinating speech articulation. *Nature, 384*, 159–161.

Duchin, L.E. (1990). The evolution of articulate speech: Comparative anatomy of the oral cavity in *Pan* and *Homo*. *Journal of Human Evolution, 19*, 687–697.

Dunbar, R.I.M. (1993). Coevolution of neocortical size, group size and language in humans. *Behavioral and Brain Sciences, 16*, 681–735.

Dunbar, R.I.M. (1996). *Grooming, gossip and the evolution of language*. London: Faber & Faber.

Early, T.S. (1993). Left globus pallidus hyperactivity and right sided neglect in schizophrenia. In R.L. Cromwell & C.R. Snyder (Eds.), *Schizophrenia: Origins, processes, treatment and outcomes* (pp. 17–30). Oxford: Oxford University.

Falk, D. (1989). Primate tool use: But what about their brains? *Behavioral and Brain Sciences, 12*, 595–596.

Falk, D. (1990). Brain evolution in *Homo*: The radiator theory. *Behavioral and Brain Sciences, 13*, 333–381.

Falk, D. (1993). Meningeal arterial patterns in great apes: Implications for hominid vascular evolution. *American Journal of Physical Anthropology, 92*, 81–101.

Finlay, B.L., & Darlington, R.B. (1995). Linked regularities in the development and evolution of mammalian brains. *Science, 268*, 1578–1583.

Fischman, J. (1994). Putting our oldest ancestors in their proper place. *Science, 265*, 2011–2012.

Fischman, J. (1995a). Why mammal ears went on the move. *Science, 270*, 1436.

Fischman, J. (1995b). Arms and the man. *Science, 268*, 364–365.

Fletcher, P. (1996). Linguistic leaps and bounds. *Nature, 379*, 504–505.

Fodor, J.A. (1983). *The modularity of the mind: An essay on faculty psychology*. Cambridge, MA: MIT Press.

Forey, P., & Janvier, P. (1994). Evolution of the early vertebrates. *American Scientist, 82*, 554–565.

Freedman, L. (1995). Evolution and human behaviour: A human biological perspective. *South African Journal of Science, 91*, 443–449.

Friedman-Hill, S.R., Robertson, L.C., & Treisman, A. (1995). Parietal contributions to visual feature binding: Evidence from a patient with bilateral lesions. *Science, 269*, 853–857.

Frith, U. (1989). *Autism: Explaining the enigma*. Oxford: Blackwell.

Frith, C., & Dolan, R. (1996). The role of the prefrontal cortex in higher cognitive functions. *Cognitive Brain Research, 5*, 175–181.

Fromkin, V., Krashen, S., Curtiss, S., Rigler, D., & Rigler, M. (1974). The development of language in Genie: A case of language acquisition beyond the critical period. *Brain and Language, 1*, 81–107.

Fullagar, R.L.K., Price, D.M., & Head, L.M. (1996). Early human occupation of northern Australia: Archaeology and thermoluminescence dating of Jinmium rock shelter, Northern Territory. *Antiquity, 70*, 751–773.

Gabunia, L., & Vekua, A. (1994). A Plio-Pleistocene hominid from Dmanisi, East Georgia, Caucasus. *Nature, 373*, 509–512.

Gallese, V., Fadiga, L., Fogassi, L., & Rizzolatti, G. (1996). Action recognition in the premotor cortex. *Brain, 119*, 593–609.

Gao, J.-H., Parsons, L.M., Bower, J.M., Xiong, J., Li, J., & Fox, P.T. (1996). Cerebellum implicated in sensory acquisition and discrimination, rather than motor control. *Science, 272*, 545–547.

Gardner, H. (1983). *Frames of mind: The theory of multiple intelligence*. New York: Basic Books.

Gargett, R.H. (1989). Grave shortcomings: The evidence for Neanderthal burial. *Current Anthropology, 30*, 157–177.

Gazzaniga, M.S. (1992). *Nature's mind: The biological roots of thinking, emotions, sexuality, language and intelligence*. New York: Basic Books.

Gebo, D.L. (1992). Plantigrady and foot adaptation in African apes: Implications for hominid origins. *American Journal of Physical Anthropology, 89,* 29–58.

Gebo, D.L. (1996). Climbing, brachiation and terrestrial quadrupedalism: Historical precursors of hominid bipedalism. *American Journal of Physical Anthropology, 101,* 55–92.

Gee, H. (1993). Why we still love Lucy. *Nature, 366,* 207.

Geschwind, N. (1965). Disconnexion syndromes in animals and man. *Brain, 88,* 585–644.

Gibbons, A. (1990). Our chimp cousins get that much closer. *Science, 250,* 376.

Gibbons, A. (1993a). Pleistocene population explosions. *Science, 262,* 27–28.

Gibbons, A. (1993b). Empathy and brain evolution. *Science, 259,* 1250–1251.

Gibbons, A. (1994a). Anthropologists take the measure of humanity. *Science, 264,* 350–351.

Gibbons, A. (1994b). Rewriting—and redating—prehistory. *Science, 263,* 1087–1088.

Gibbons, A. (1995a). The mystery of humanity's missing mutations. *Science, 267,* 35–36.

Gibbons, A. (1995b). When it comes to evolution humans are in the slow class. *Science, 267,* 1907–1908.

Gibbons, A. (1995c). Language's last stand. *Science, 267,* 1272.

Gibbons, A. (1996). Did Neanderthals lose an evolutionary "arms" race? *Science, 272,* 1586–1587.

Goel, V., Grafman, J., Sadato, N., & Hallett, M. (1995). Modeling other minds. *NeuroReport, 6,* 1741–1746.

Goldman-Rakic, P.S. (1992). Working memory and the mind. *Scientific American, March,* 72–79.

Goldstein, D.B., Ruiz-Linares, A., Cavalli-Sforza, L.L., & Feldman, M.W. (1995). Genetic absolute dating based on microsatellites and the origin of modern humans. *Proceedings of the National Academy of Sciences, 92,* 6723–6727.

Goldin-Meadow, S., McNeill, D., & Singleton, J. (1996). Silence is liberating: Removing the handcuffs on grammatical expression in the manual modality. *Psychological Review, 103,* 34–55.

Gomez, J.C. (1991). Visual behavior as a window for reading the mind of others in primates. In A. Whiten (Ed.), *Natural theories of mind: Evolution, development and simulation of everyday mindreading* (pp. 195–207). Oxford: Blackwell.

Goodall, J. (1989). Gombe: Highlights and current research. In P.G. Heltne & L.A. Marquardt (Eds.), *Understanding chimpanzees* (pp. 2–21). Cambridge, MA: Harvard University Press.

Goodall, J. van Lawick (1968). The behaviour of free living chimpanzees in the Gombe Stream Reserve (Tanzania). *Animal Behaviour Monographs, 1,* 161–311.

Goodglass, H. (1993). *Understanding aphasia.* San Diego, CA: Academic Press.

Goodman, R.A., & Whitaker, H.A. (1985). Hemispherectomy: A review (1928–1981) with special reference to the linguistic abilities and disabilities of the residual right hemisphere. In C.T. Best (Ed.), *Hemispheric function and collaboration in the child* (pp. 121–155). New York: Academic Press.

Goren-Inbar, N., Lewy, Z., & Kislev, M.E. (1991). The taphonomy of a bead-like fossil from the Acheulian of Gesher Benot Ya'aqov, Israel. *Rock Art Research, 8,* 83–87.

Goren-Inbar, N., & Peltz, S. (1995). Additional remarks on the Berekhat Ram figurine. *Rock Art Research, 12,* 131–132.

Gould, S.J. (1991). Eight (or fewer) little piggies. *Natural History, 1,* 22–29.

Gould, S.J. (1992). Foreword to D'Arcy Wentworth Thompson's *On growth and form.* Cambridge: Cambridge University Press.

Gould, S.J. (1994). The evolution of life on earth. *Scientific American, October,* 63–69.

Gould, S.J. (1995a). Of it, not above it. *Nature, 377,* 681–682.

Gould, S.J. (1995b). Evolution by walking. *Natural History, 3,* 10–15.

Gould, S.J., & Eldredge, N. (1993). Punctuated equilibrium comes of age. *Nature, 366,* 223–227.

Graf, W., & Vidal, P.-P. (1996). Semicircular canal size and upright stance are not interrelated. *Journal of Human Evolution, 30,* 175–181.

Grafton, S.T., Hazeltine, E., & Ivry, R. (1995). Functional mapping of sequence learning in normal humans. *Journal of Cognitive Neuroscience, 7,* 497–510.

Gray, J.A. (1995). The contents of consciousness: A neuropsychological conjecture. *Behavioral and Brain Sciences, 18,* 659–722.

Greenfield, P.M. (1991). Language, tools and the brain: The ontogeny and phylogeny of hierarchically organized sequential behavior. *Behavioral and Brain Sciences, 14,* 531–595.

Griffin, D.R. (1992). *Animal minds.* Chicago, IL: University of Chicago Press.

Grotzinger, J.P., Bowring, S.A., Saylor, B.Z., & Kaufman, A.J. (1995). Biostratigraphic and geochronological constraints on early animal evolution. *Science, 270,* 598–604.

Gruzelier, J., & Flor-Henry, P. (1979). *Hemispheric asymmetries of function in psychopathology.* Amsterdam: Elsevier.

Gutin, J. (1995). Do Kenya tools root birth of modern thought in Africa? *Science, 270,* 1118–1119.

Hale, W.R. (1991). Superior posterior. *New Scientist, 1 June,* 3.

Hallett, M. (1995). The plastic brain. *Annals of Neurology, 38,* 4–5.

Halpern, D.F. (1986). *Sex differences in cognitive abilities.* Hillsdale, NJ: Erlbaum.

Halverson, J. (1992a). The first pictures: Perceptual foundations of Paleolithic art. *Perception, 21,* 389–404.

Halverson, J. (1992b). Paleolithic art and cognition. *The Journal of Psychology, 126,* 221–236.

Hammer, M.F. (1995). A recent common ancestry for human Y chromosomes. *Nature, 378,* 376–378.

Happé, F., Ehlers, S., Fletcher, P., Frith, U., Johansson, M., Gillberg, C., Dolan, R., Frackowiak, R., & Frith, C. (1996). "Theory of Mind" in the brain. Evidence from a PET scan study of Asperger syndrome. *NeuroReport, 8,* 197–201.

Harpending, H.C., Sherry, S.T., Rogers, A.R., & Stoneking, M. (1993). The genetic structure of ancient human populations. *Current Anthropology, 34,* 483–496.

Harré, R., & Reynolds, V. (1984). *The meaning of primate signals.* Cambridge: Cambridge University Press.

Harrington, D.L., & Haaland, K.Y. (1992). Motor sequencing with left hemisphere damage. *Brain, 115,* 857–874.

Harrison, G.A., Tanner, J.M., Pilbeam, D.R., & Baker, P.T. (1988). *Human biology: An introduction to human evolution, variation, growth and adaptability* (3rd Edn). Oxford: Oxford University Press.

Harvey, P.H. (1986). Allometric analysis and brain size. In H. J. Jerison & I. Jerison (Eds.), *Intelligence and evolutionary biology* (pp. 199–210). New York: Springer.

Hauser, M. (1988). Invention and social transmission: New data from wild vervet monkeys. In R. Byrne & A. Whiten (Eds.), *Machiavellian intelligence: Social expertise and the evolution of intellect in monkeys, apes and humans* (pp. 327–343). Oxford: Oxford University Press.

Hauser, M. (1993). Review of *Language and species.* Edited by D. Bickerton. Chicago: Chicago University Press (1990). *Animal Behaviour, 46,* 829–833.

Hauser, M., Kralik, J., Botto-Mahan, C., Garrett, M., and Oser, J. (1995). Self recognition in primates: Phylogeny and the salience of species-typical creatures. *Proceedings of the National Academy of Sciences, 99,* 10811–10814.

Hausler, M., & Schmid, P. (1995). Comparison of the pelves of Sts 14 and AL 288-1: Implications for birth and sexual dimorphism in australopithecines. *Journal of Human Evolution, 29,* 363–383.

Hayden, B. (1993). The cultural capacities of Neandertals: A review and re-evaluation. *Journal of Human Evolution, 24,* 113–146.

Hayes, J.M. (1996). The earliest memories of life on Earth. *Nature, 384,* 21–22.

Hebb, D.O. (1949). *Organization of behavior.* New York: Wiley.

Herman, L.M. (1991). What the dolphin knows, or might know, in its natural world. In K. Pryor & K. Norris (Eds.), *Dolphin societies: Discoveries and puzzles* (pp. 349–363). Berkeley, CA: University of California Press.

Hewes, G.W. (1976). The current status of the gestural theory of language origin. *Annals of the New York Academy of Sciences, 280*, 482–504.

Hewes, G.W. (1977). Language origin theories. In D.M. Rumbaugh (Ed.), *Language learning by a chimpanzee: The Lana project* (pp. 3–53). New York: Academic Press.

Heyes, C. (1995). Knowing minds. *Nature, 375*, 290.

Hill, A., Ward, S., Deino, A., Curtis, G., & Drake, R. (1992). Earliest *Homo*. *Nature, 355*, 719–722.

Hodoba, D. (1986). Paradoxic sleep facilitation by interictal epileptic activity of right temporal origin. *Biological Psychiatry, 21*, 1267–1278.

Holden, C. (1991). Brains: Is bigger better? *Science, 254*, 1584.

Holden, C. (1996). Art stirs uproar down under. *Science, 274*, 33–34.

Holden, C. (1997). Tooling around: Dates show early Siberian settlement. *Science, 275*, 1268.

Holloway, M. (1994). Family matters. *Scientific American, May*, 15–21.

Holloway, R.L. (1995). Toward a synthetic theory of human brain evolution. In J.-P. Changeux & J. Chavaillon (Eds.), *Origins of the human brain* (pp. 42–54). Oxford: Clarendon Press.

Horai, S., Hayasaka, K., Kondo, R., Tsugane, K., & Takahata, N. (1995). Recent African origin of modern humans revealed by complete sequences of hominid mitochondrial DNAs. *Proceedings of the National Academy of Sciences, 92*, 532–536.

Houghton, P. (1993). Neandertal supralaryngeal vocal tract. *American Journal of Physical Anthropology, 90*, 139–146.

Hoyle, F. (1981). *Evolution from space*. London: Dent.

Hublin, J.-J., Spoor, F., Braun, M., Zonneveld, F., & Condemi, S. (1996). A late Neanderthal associated with Upper Palaeolithic artefacts. *Nature, 381*, 224–226.

Humphrey, N.K. (1976). The social function of intellect. In P.P.G. Bateson & R.A. Hinde (Eds.), *Growing Points in Ethology* (pp. 307–317). Cambridge: Cambridge University Press.

Hunt, G.R. (1996). Manufacture and use of hook-tools by New Caledonian crows. *Nature, 379*, 249–251.

Hunt, K.D. (1994). The evolution of human bipedality: Ecology and functional morphology. *Journal of Human Evolution, 26*, 183–202.

Ingold, T. (1994). Tool using, tool making and the evolution of language. In D. Quiatt & J. Itani (Eds.), *Hominid culture in primate perspective* (pp. 279–314). Niwot, CO: University of Colorado Press.

Iriki, A., Tanaka, M., & Iwamura, Y. (1996). Coding of modified body schema during tool use by macaque postcentral neurons. *NeuroReport, 7*, 2325–2330.

Jablonski, N.G., & Chaplin, G. (1993). Origin of habitual terrestrial bipedalism in the ancestor of the Hominidae. *Journal of Human Evolution, 24*, 259–280.

James, S.R. (1989). Hominid use of fire in the Lower and Middle Pleistocene. *Current Anthropology, 30*, 1–26.

Jeannerod, M., Arbib, M.A., Rizzolatti, G., & Sakata, H. (1995). Grasping objects: The cortical mechanisms of visuomotor transformation. *Trends in Neurosciences, 18*, 314–320.

Jerison, H.J. (1982). The evolution of biological intelligence. In R. Sternberg (Ed.), *Handbook of Intelligence* (pp. 723–791). Cambridge: Cambridge University Press.

Jerison, H.J. (1986). Evolutionary biology of intelligence: The nature of the problem. In H.J. Jerison & I. Jerison (Eds.), *Intelligence and evolutionary biology* (pp. 1–12). New York: Springer.

Johnson, E.W., Briggs, D.E.G., Suthren, R.J., Wright, J.L., & Tunnicliff, S.P. (1994). Non-marine arthropod traces from the subaerial Ordovician Borrowdale Volcanic Group, English Lake District. *Geological Magazine, 131*, 395–406.

Jones, S., Martin, R., & Pilbeam, D. (Eds.) (1992). *Cambridge encyclopedia of human evolution* (pp. 246–257). Cambridge: Cambridge University Press.

Joubert, D. (1991). Eyewitness to an elephant wake. *National Geographic, 179(5)*, 39–41.

Kappelman, J., Swisher, C.C., Fleagle, J.G., Yirga, S., Brown, T.M., & Feseha, M. (1996). Age of *Australopithecus afarensis* from Fejej, Ethiopia. *Journal of Human Evolution, 30*, 139–146.

Karten, H.J. (1991). Homology and evolutionary origins of the neocortex. *Brain, Behaviour and Evolution, 38*, 264–272.

Katz, L.C., & Shatz, C.J. (1996). Synaptic activity and the construction of cortical circuits. *Science, 274*, 1133–1138.

Kauffman, S. (1996). Even peptides do it. *Nature, 382*, 496–497.

Kawai, M. (1965). Newly acquired pre-cultural behavior of the natural troop of Japanese monkeys on Koshima islet. *Primates, 6*, 1–30.

Kay, R.F., Ross, C., & Williams, B.A. (1997). Anthropoid origins. *Science, 275*, 797–804.

Kendon, A. (1991). Some correlations for a theory of language origins. *Man, 26*, 199–221.

Kerr, R.A. (1993). Evolution's big bang gets even more explosive. *Science, 261*, 1274–1275.

Kerr, R.A. (1995). Did Darwin get it all right? *Science, 267*, 1421–1422.

Kien, J. (1991). The need for data reduction may have paved the way for evolution of language ability in hominids. *Journal of Human Evolution, 29*, 157–165.

Kim, H.-S., & Takenaka, O. (1996). A comparison of TSPY genes from Y-chromosomal DNA of the great apes and humans: Sequence, evolution and phylogeny. *American Journal of Physical Anthropology, 100*, 301–309.

Kimbel, W.H., Walter, R.C., Johanson, D.C., Reed, K.E., Aronson, J.L., Assefa, Z., Marean, C.W., Eck, G.G., Bobe, R., Hovers, E., Rak, Y., Vondra, C., Yemane, T., York, D., Chen, Y., Evensen, N.M., & Smith, P.E. (1996). Late Pliocene *Homo* and Oldowan tools from the Hadar Formation (Kada Hadar Member), Ethiopia. *Journal of Human Evolution, 31*, 549–561.

Kimberg, D.Y., & Farah, M.J. (1993). A unified account of cognitive impairments following frontal lobe damage: The role of working memory in complex, organized behavior. *Journal of Experimental Psychology, 122*, 411–428.

Kimura, D. (1976). The neural basis of language *qua* gesture. In H. Whitaker & H.A. Whitaker (Eds.), *Studies in neurolinguistics, Vol. 1* (pp. 145–156). New York: Academic Press.

Kimura, D. (1982). Left hemisphere control of oral and brachial movements and their relation to communication. *Philosophical Transactions of the Royal Society of London B, 298*, 135–149.

Kimura, D. (1993). *Neuromotor mechanisms in human communication.* Oxford: Oxford University Press.

Kimura, D., & Harshman, R.A. (1984). Sex differences in brain organization for verbal and nonverbal functions. *Progress in Brain Research, 61*, 423–444.

Kirzinger, A., & Jürgens, U. (1982). Cortical lesion effects and vocalization in the squirrel monkey. *Brain Research, 233*, 299–315.

Kitchen, A., Denton, D., & Brent, L. (1996). Self-recognition and abstraction abilities in the common chimpanzee studied with distorting mirrors. *Proceedings of the National Academy of Sciences, 93*, 7405–7408.

Klein, J., Takahata, N., & Ayala, F.J. (1993). MHC polymorphism and human origins. *Scientific American, December*, 46–51.

Klein, R.G. (1989). *The human career: Human biological and cultural origins.* Chicago, IL: University of Chicago Press.

Klein, R.G. (1993). Culture in the Paleolithic. *Science, 262*, 1751–1752.

Knoll, A.H. (1994). Proterozoic and early Cambrian protists: Evidence for accelerating evolutionary tempo. *Proceedings of the National Academy of Sciences, 91*, 6743–6750.

Kozlowski, J.K. (1990). A multiaspectual approach to the origins of the Upper Palaeolithic in Europe. In P. Mellars (Ed.), *The emergence of modern humans: An archaeological perspective* (pp. 419–439). Edinburgh: Edinburgh University Press.

Kuhl, P.K. (1988). Auditory perception and the evolution of speech. *Human Evolution, 3,* 19–43.

Kuhl, P.K., Williams, K.A., Lacerda, F., Stevens, K.N., & Lindblom, B. (1992). Linguistic experience alters phonetic perception in infants by 6 months of age. *Science, 255,* 606–608.

LaBerge, D., & Samuels, S.J. (1974). Toward a theory of automatic information processing in reading. *Cognitive Psychology, 6,* 293–323.

Lahr, M.M. (1994). The multiregional model of modern human origins: A reassessment of its morphological basis. *Journal of Human Evolution, 26,* 23–56.

Laitman, J.T., Reidenberg, J.S., Marquez, S., and Gannon, P.J. (1996). What the nose knows: New understanding of the Neanderthal upper respiratory tract specializations. *Proceedings of the National Academy of Sciences, 93,* 10543–10545.

Laplane, D., Talairach, J., Meninger, V., Bancaud, J., & Orgogozo, J.M. (1977). Clinical consequences of corticectomies involving the supplementary motor cortex in man. *Journal of Neurological Science, 34,* 301–314.

Leakey, M.D., & Hay, R.L. (1979). Pliocene footprints in the Laetolil beds at Laetoli, northern Tanzania. *Nature, 278,* 317–323.

Leakey, M.G., Feibel, C.S., McDougall, I., & Walker, A. (1995). New four-million-year-old hominid species from Kanapoi and Allia Bay, Kenya. *Nature, 376,* 565–571.

Leavens, D.A., Hopkins, W.D., & Bard, K.A. (1996) Indexical and referential pointing in chimpanzees *(Pan troglodytes)*. *Journal of Comparative Psychology, 110,* 346–353.

Lee, D.H., Granja, J.R., Martinez, J.A., Severin, K. & Ghadiri, M.R. (1996). A self-replicating peptide. *Nature, 382,* 525–528.

Lenain, T. (1995). Ape painting and the problem of the origin of art. *Human Evolution, 10,* 205–215.

Leslie, A.M. (1990). Pretence, autism and the basis of "theory of mind". *The Psychologist, 3,* 120–123.

Leslie, A.M. (1991). The "theory of mind" impairment in autism: Evidence for a modular mechanism of development? In A. Whiten (Ed.), *Neural theories of mind: Evolution, development and simulation of everyday mindreading* (pp. 63–78). Oxford: Blackwell.

Lewin, R. (1991). Neanderthals puzzle the anthropologists. *New Scientist, 20 April,* 17.

Lewin, R. (1992). Secret life of the brain: The great brain race. *New Scientist, 5 December,* 2–4.

Lewin, R. (1993). *Human evolution: An illustrated introduction* (3rd Edn.). Oxford: Blackwell Scientific.

Lewin, R. (1994). I buzz therefore I think. *New Scientist, 15 January,* 29–33.

Lewin, R. (1995a). Little foot stumbles into the crossfire. *New Scientist, 5 August,* 14.

Lewin, R. (1995b). Adam makes a date with Eve. *New Scientist, 3 June,* 14.

Lewin, R. (1995c). Birth of a tool maker. *New Scientist, 11 March,* 38–41.

Lewin, R. (1996). Evolution's new heretics. *Natural History, 5,* 12–16.

Lichtheim, L. (1885). On aphasia. *Brain, 7,* 433–484.

Lieberman, D.E. (1995). Testing hypotheses about recent human evolution from skulls. *Current Anthropology, 36,* 159–197.

Lieberman, D.E., Wood, B.A., & Pilbeam, D.R. (1996). Homoplasy and early *Homo*: An analysis of the evolutionary relationships of *Homo habilis, sensu stricto,* and *Homo rudolfensis. Journal of Human Evolution, 30,* 97–120.

Lieberman, P. (1985). On the evolution of human syntactic ability: Its pre-adaptive bases— motor control and speech. *Journal of Human Evolution, 14,* 657–668.

Lieberman, P. (1989). The origins of some aspects of human language and cognition. In P. Mellars & C. Stringer (Eds.), *The human revolution: Behavioral and biological perspectives on the origins of modern humans* (pp. 391–414). Princeton, NJ: Princeton University Press.

Lieberman, P. (1991). *Uniquely human: The evolution of speech, thought and selfless behavior.* Cambridge, MA: Harvard University Press.

Lieberman, P. (1994). Hyoid bone position and speech: reply to Dr Arensburg et al. (1990). *American Journal of Physical Anthropology, 94,* 275–278.

Lieberman, P., Laitman, J.T., Reidenberg, J.S., & Gannon, P.J. (1992). The anatomy, physiology, acoustics and perception of speech: Essential elements in analysis of the evolution of human speech. *Journal of Human Evolution, 23,* 447–467.

Limongelli, L., Boysen, S.T., & Visalberghi, E. (1995). Comprehension of cause–effect relations in a tool-using task by chimpanzees (*Pan troglodytes*). *Journal of Comparative Psychology, 109,* 18–26.

Locke, J.L. (1994). Phases in the child's development of language. *American Scientist, 82,* 436–445.

Long, J.A. (1995). *The rise of the fishes: 500 million years of evolution.* Sydney: University of New South Wales Press.

Lovejoy, C.O. (1988). Evolution of human walking. *Scientific American, November,* 82–89.

Lynn, R.L. (1993). Brain size and intelligence in Man: A correction to Peters. *Canadian Journal of Psychology, 47,* 748–750.

MacNeilage, P.F. (1987). The evolution of hemispheric specialization for manual function and language. In S.P. Wise (Ed.), *Higher brain functions: Recent explorations of the brain's emergent properties* (pp. 285–309). New York: Wiley.

MacNeilage, P.F. (1990). Grasping in modern primates: The evolutionary context. In M.A. Goodale (Ed.), *Vision and action: The control of grasping* (pp. 1–13). Norwood, NJ: Ablex Publishing.

MacNeilage, P.F. (in press). The frame/content theory of evolution of speech production. *Behavioral and Brain Sciences.*

MacNeilage, P.F., Studdert-Kennedy, M.G., & Lindblom, B. (1984). Functional precursors of language and its lateralization. *American Journal of Physiology: Regulatory, Integrative and Comparative Physiology, 15(246:R),* 912–914.

MacNeilage, P.F., Studdert-Kennedy, M.G., & Lindblom, B. (1993). Hand signals. *The Sciences, January/February,* 32–37.

Maddox, J. (1995). More muddle over the Hubble constant. *Nature, 376,* 291.

Markson, L., and Bloom, P. (1977). Evidence against a dedicated system for word learning in children. *Nature, 385,* 813–815.

Marshack, A. (1988). *The Neanderthals and the human capacity for symbolic thought: Cognitive and problem-solving aspects of Mousterian symbol.* Paper presented at the international colloquium "L'Homme de Néandertal", Liege.

Marshack, A. (1989a). Evolution of the human capacity: The symbolic evidence. *Yearbook of Physical Anthropology, 32,* 1–34.

Marshack, A. (1989b). Methodology in the analysis and interpretation of Upper Palaeolithic image: Theory versus contextual analysis. *Rock Art Research, 6,* 17–38.

Marshack, A. (1991). Deliberate engravings on bone artifacts of *Homo erectus.* Further comment: A reply to Davidson on Mania and Mania. *Rock Art Research, 8,* 47–58.

Marshall, J.C. (1980). On the biology of language acquisition. In D. Caplan (Ed.), *Biological studies of language processes* (pp. 106–148). Cambridge, MA: MIT Press.

Marzke, M.W. (1997). Precision grips, hand morphology, and tools. *American Journal of Physical Anthropology, 102,* 91–110.

Maurus, M., Barclay, D., & Streit, K.-M. (1988). Acoustic patterns common to human communication between monkeys. *Language and Communication, 8,* 87–94.

McCune, L., Vihman, M.M., Roug-Hellichius, L., Delery, D.B., & Gogate, L. (1996). Grunt communication in human infants (*Homo sapiens*). *Journal of Comparative Psychology, 110,* 27–37.

McDermott, L. (1996). Self-representation in Upper Paleolithic female figures. *Current Anthropology, 37,* 227–275.

McDonald, S., & Pearce, S. (1996). Clinical insights into pragmatic theory: Frontal lobe deficits and sarcasm. *Brain and Language, 53,* 81–104.

McGlone, J. (1986). The neuropsychology of sex differences in human brain organization. In G. Goldstein & R.E. Tarter (Eds.), *Advances in clinical neuropsychology, Vol. 3* (pp. 1–30). New York: Plenum Press.

McGrew, W. (1992). *Chimpanzee material culture: Implications for human evolution.* Cambridge: Cambridge University Press.

McGuire, P.K. (1995). The brain in obsessive compulsive disease. *Journal of Neurology, Neurosurgery and Psychiatry, 59,* 457–459.

McHenry, H.M. (1994). Tempo and mode in human evolution. *Proceedings of the National Academy of Sciences, 91,* 6780–6786.

Meighan, C.W. (1996). Human nature and rock art production. *Rock Art Research, 13,* 68–70.

Mellars, P. (1996). *The Neanderthal legacy: An archaeological perspective from Western Europe.* Princeton, NJ: Princeton University Press.

Meltzer, D.J. (1995a). Clocking the first Americans. *Annual Review of Anthropology, 24,* 21–45.

Meltzer, D.J. (1995b). Stones of contention. *New Scientist, 24 June,* 31–35.

Merzenich, M.M. (1987). Dynamic neocortical processes and the origins of higher brain functions. In J.-P. Changeux & M. Konishi (Eds.), *The neural and molecular bases of learning* (pp. 337–358). Chichester: Wiley.

Mesulam, M.-M. (1990). Large-scale neurocognitive networks and distributed processing for attention, language, and memory. *Annals of Neurology, 28,* 597–613.

Miller, G. (1981). *Language and speech.* San Francisco: Freeman.

Milner, A. (1996). Early amphibian globetrotters. *Science, 381,* 74–75.

Milton, K. (1993). Diet and primate evolution. *Scientific American, August,* 70–77.

Mishkin, M., Ungerleider, L.G., & Macko, K.A. (1983). Object vision and spatial vision: Two cortical pathways. *Trends in Neurosciences, 6,* 414–417.

Mojzsis, S.J., Arrhenius, G., McKeegan, K.D., Harrison, T.M., Nutman, A.P., and Friend, C.R.L. (1996). Evidence for life on Earth before 3,800 million years ago. *Nature, 384,* 55–58.

Morrell, V. (1994). Will primate genetics split one gorilla into two? *Science, 265,* 1661.

Morrell, V. (1995). The earliest art becomes older—and more common. *Science, 267,* 1908–1909.

Morris, S.C. (1997). Molecular clocks: Defusing the Cambrian explosion. *Current Biology, 7,* 71–74.

Moyà-Solà, S., & Köhler, M. (1996). A *Dryopithecus* skeleton and the origins of great-ape locomotion. *Nature, 379,* 156–159.

Mulvaney, K. (1996). What to do on a rainy day: Reminiscences of Mirriuwung and Gadjerong artists. *Rock Art Research, 13,* 3–30.

Näätänen, R., Lehtokoski, A., Lennes, M., Cheour, M., Huotilainen, M., Livonen, A., Vainio, M., Alku, P., Ilimoniemi, R.J., Luuk, A., Allik, J., Sinkkonen, J., & Alho, K. (1997). Language-specific phoneme representations revealed by electric and magnetic brain responses. *Nature, 385,* 432–433.

Nei, M. (1995). Genetic support for the out-of-Africa theory of human evolution. *Proceedings of the National Academy of Sciences, 92,* 6720–6722.

Neisser, U., Boodoo, G., Bouchard, T.J., Boykin, A.W., Brody, N., Ceci, S.J., Halpern, D.F., Loehlin, J.C., Perloff, R., Sternberg, R.J., & Urbina, S. (1996). Intelligence: Knowns and unknowns. *American Psychologist, 51,* 77–101.

Nisbet, E.G., & Fowler, C.M.R. (1996). Some liked it hot. *Nature, 382,* 404–406.

Noble, S.B. (1990). *The emergence of human intelligence and of civilization.* Volendam, Netherlands: Language Origins Society.

Noble, W., & Davidson, I. (1996). *Human evolution, language and mind: A psychological and archaeological enquiry.* Cambridge: Cambridge University Press.

Nottebohm, F. (1979). Origins and mechanisms in the establishment of cerebral dominance. In M.S. Gazzaniga (Ed.), *Handbook of Behavioral Neurobiology, Vol. 2, Neuropsychology* (pp. 295–344). New York: Plenum Press.

Novacek, M.J. (1994). A pocketful of fossils. *Natural History, 4,* 41–43.

Nübler-Jung, K., & Arendt, D. (1996). Enteropneusts and chordate evolution. *Current Biology, 6,* 352–353.

Oakley, K.P. (1981). Emergence of higher thought, 3.0–0.2 Ma B.P. *Philosophical Transactions of the Royal Society of London B, 292,* 205–211.

Ochipa, C., Rothi, J.G., & Heilman, K.M. (1994). Conduction apraxia. *Journal of Neurology, Neurosurgery and Psychiatry, 54,* 1241–1244.

Oliwenstein, L. (1995). New foot steps into walking debate. *Science, 269,*476–477.

Orgel, L.E. (1994). The origin of life on the earth. *Scientific American, October,* 53–61.

Ozonoff, S., & Miller, J.N. (1996). An explanation of right hemisphere contributions to the pragmatic impairments of autism. *Brain and Language, 52,* 411–431.

Palmer, D. (1996). Ediacarans in deep water. *Nature, 379,* 114.

Parker, S.T., & Gibson, K.R. (1977). Object manipulation, tool use and sensorimotor intelligence as feeding adaptations in cebus monkeys and great apes. *Journal of Human Evolution, 6,* 623–641.

Parker, S.T., & Gibson, K.R. (1979). A developmental model for the evolution of language and intelligence in early hominids. *Behavioral and Brain Sciences, 2,* 367–408.

Parker, S.T., Mitchell, R.W., & Boccia, M.L. (1994). Expending dimensions of the self: through the looking glass and beyond. In S. T. Parker, R. W. Mitchell, & M. L. Boccia (Eds.), *Self awareness in animals and humans* (pp. 3–19). Cambridge: Cambridge University Press.

Parsons, P. (1996). Dusting off panspermia. *Nature,* 383, 221–222.

Passingham, R.E. (1993). *The frontal lobes and voluntary action.* Oxford: Oxford University Press.

Patel, T. (1995). Ancient masters put painting in perspective. *New Scientist, 17 June,* 5.

Paulesu, E., Harrison, J., Baron-Cohen, S., Watson, J.D.G., Goldstein, L., Heather, J., Frackowiak, R.S.J., & Frith, C.D. (1995). The physiology of colored hearing: A PET activation study of color–word synaesthesia. *Brain, 118,* 661–676.

Pääbo, S. (1995). The Y chromosome and the origin of all of us (men). *Science, 268,* 1141–1142.

Pepperberg, I.M. (1989). Tool use in birds: An avian monkey wrench? *Behavioral and Brain Sciences, 12,* 604–605.

Pepperberg, I.M. (1990). Some cognitive capacities of an African Grey parrot (*Psittacus erithacus*). *Advances in the Study of Behavior, 19,* 357–409.

Pepperberg, I.M., Garcia, S.E., Jackson, E.C., & Marconi, S. (1995). Mirror use by African grey parrots (*Psittacus erithacus*). *Journal of Comparative Psychology, 109,* 182–195.

Perani, D., Cappa, S., Bettinardi, V., Bressi, S., Gorno-Tempini, M., Matarrese, M., & Fazio, F. (1995). Different neural systems for the recognition of animals and man-made tools. *NeuroReport, 6,* 1637–1639.

Pickford, M. (1986). The evolution of intelligence: A palaeontological perspective. In H.J. Jerison & I. Jerison (Eds.), *Intelligence and evolutionary biology* (pp. 175–198). New York: Springer.

Pinker, S. (1994). *The language instinct.* New York: William Morrow.

Poizner, H., Clark, M.A., Merians, A.S., Macauley, B., Rothi, L.J.G., & Heilman, K.M. (1995). Joint coordination deficits in limb apraxia. *Brain, 118,* 227–242.

Pope, G.G. (1991). Evolution of the zygomatico-maxillary region in the genus *Homo* and its relevance to the origin of modern humans. *Journal of Human Evolution, 21,* 189–213.

Posner, M.I., & McCandliss, B.D. (1993). Converging methods for investigating lexical access. *Psychological Science, 4,* 305–309.

Posner, M.I., & Raichle, M.E. (1994). *Images of mind.* New York: Scientific American Library.

Povinelli, D.J. (1989). Failure to find self-recognition in Asian elephants (*Elephas maximus*) in contrast to their use of mirror cues to discover hidden food. *Journal of Comparative Psychology, 103,* 122–131.

Povinelli, D.J., & Cant, J.G.H. (1995). Arboreal climbing and the evolution of self conception. *Quarterly Review of Biology, 70,* 393–421.

Povinelli, D.J., & Davis, D.R. (1994). Differences between chimpanzees (*Pan troglodytes*) and humans (*Homo sapiens*) in the resting state of the index finger: Implications for pointing. *Journal of Comparative Psychology, 108,* 134–139.

Povinelli, D.J., & Eddy, T.J. (1996). Factors influencing young chimpanzees' (*Pan troglodytes*) recognition of attention. *Journal of Comparative Psychology, 110,* 336–345.

Povinelli, D.J., Parks, K.A., & Novack, M.A. (1992). Role reversal by rhesus monkeys, but no evidence of empathy. *Animal Behaviour, 44,* 269–281.

Povinelli, D.J., & Preuss, T.M. (1995). Theory of mind: Evolutionary history of a cognitive specialization. *Trends in Neurosciences, 18,* 418–424.

Premack, D. (1988). "Does the chimpanzee have a theory of mind?" revisited. In R. Byrne & A. Whiten (Eds.), *Machiavellian intelligence: Social expertise and the evolution of intellect in monkeys, apes and humans* (pp. 160–179). Oxford: Oxford University Press.

Price, C.J., Wise, R.J.S., Watson, J.D.G., Patterson, K., Howard, D., & Frackowiak, R.S.J. (1994). Brain activity during reading: The effects or exposure duration and task. *Brain, 117,* 1255–1269.

Provine, R.R. (1996). Laughter. *American Scientist, 84,* 38–45.

Rauschecker, J.P., Tian, B., & Hauser, M. (1995). Processing of complex sounds in the macaque nonprimary auditory cortex. *Science, 268,* 111–114.

Raymond, J.L., Lisberger, S.G., & Mauk, M.D. (1996). Thecerebellum: A neuronal learning machine. *Science, 272,* 1126–1131.

Rees, M. (1997). *Before the beginning: Our universe and others.* New York: Simon & Schuster.

Relethford, J.H. (1995). Genetics and modern human origins. *Evolutionary Anthropology, 4,* 53–63.

Renfrew, C. (1994). World linguistic diversity. *Scientific American, 1,* 104–110.

Renner, M.J., & Rosenzweig, M.R. (1987). *Enriched and empoverished environments: Effects on brain and behavior.* New York: Springer-Verlag.

Ridley, M. (1996). *The origins of virtue.* New York: Viking Press.

Rigaud, J.-P., Simek, J.F., & Thierry, G. (1995). Mousterian fires from Grotte XVl (Dordogne, France). *Antiquity, 69,* 902–912.

Rightmire, G.P. (1990). *The evolution of Homo erectus: Comparative anatomical studies of an extinct human species.* Cambridge: Cambridge University Press.

Rightmire, G.P. (1995). Geography, time and speciation in Pleistocene Homo. *South African Journal of Science, 91,* 450–454.

Ristau, C.A. (1991). Before mindreading: Attention, purposes and deception in birds. In A. Whiten (Ed.), *Natural theories of mind: Evolution, development and simulation of everyday mindreading* (pp. 195–207). Oxford: Blackwell.

Rizzolatti, G., Fadiga, L., Gallese, V., & Fogassi, L. (1996). Premotor cortex and the recognition of motor actions. *Cognitive Brain Research, 3,* 131–141.

Rizzolatti, G., Fadiga, L., Matelli, M., Bettinardi, V., Paulesu, E., Perani, D., & Fazio, F. (1996). Localization of grasp representations in humans by PET: 1. Observation versus execution. *Experimental Brain Research, 111,* 246–252.

Roberts, R.G., Jones, R., Spooner, N.A., Head, M.J., & Murray, A.S. (1994). The human colonisation of Australia: Optical dates of 53,000 and 60,000 years bracket human arrival at Deaf Adder Gorge Northerm Territory. *Quaternary Science Review, 13*, 575–583.

Roosevelt, A.C., da Costa, M.L., Machado, C.L., Michab, M., Mercier, N., Valladas, H., Feathers, J., Barnett, W., da Silveira, M.I., Henderson, A., Sliva, J., Chernoff, B., Reese, D.S., Holman, J.A., Toth, N., & Schick, K. (1996). Paleoindian cave dwellers in the Amazon: The peopling of the Americas. *Science, 272*, 373–376.

Rosenberg, K.R. (1992). The evolution of modern human childbirth. *Yearbook of Physical Anthropology, 35*, 89–124.

Rosenberg, K., & Trevathan, W. (1996). Bipedalism and human birth: The obstetrical dilemma revisited. *Evolutionary Anthropology, 5*, 161–168.

Ross, C., & Henneberg, M. (1995). Basicranial flexion, relative brain size and facial kyphosis in *Homo sapiens* and some fossil hominids. *American Journal of Physical Anthropology, 98*, 575–593.

Ross, C.A., & Pearlson, G.D. (1996). Schizophrenia, the heteromodal association neocortex and development: Potential for a neurogenetic approach. *Trends in Neurosciences, 19*, 171–176.

Roush, W. (1995). Arguing why Johnny can't read. *Science, 267*, 1896–1898.

Roush, W. (1996). New neurons use "lookouts" to navigate the nervous system. *Science, 271*, 1807–1808.

Rubens, A. B. (1975). Aphasia with infarction in the territory of the anterior cerebral artery. *Cortex, 11*, 239–250.

Ruff, C. (1995). Biomechanics of the hip and birth in early *Homo*. *American Journal of Physical Anthropology, 98*, 527–574.

Ruhlen, M. (1994). *On the origin of languages*. Stanford, CA: Stanford University Press.

Ruhlen, M. (1995). Linguistic evidence for human prehistory. *Cambridge Archaeological Journal, 5*, 268–271.

Rumbaugh, D.M., Hopkins, W.D., Washburn, D.A., & Savage-Rumbaugh, E.S. (1991). Comparative perspectives of brain, cognition and language. In N.A. Krasnegor, D.M. Rumbaugh, R.L. Schiefelbusch, & M. Studdert-Kennedy (Eds.), *Biological and behavioral determinants of language development* (pp. 145–164). Hillsdale, NJ: Lawrence Erlbaum.

Rumbaugh, D.M., & Savage-Rumbaugh, E.S. (1990). Chimpanzees, competence for language, and numbers. In W.C. Stebbins & M.A. Berkley (Eds.), *Comparative perception, Vol. II: Complex signals* (pp. 409–439). New York: Wiley.

Rushton, J.P., & Ankney, E. (1996). Brain size and cognitive ability: Correlations with age, sex, social class and race. *Psychonomic Bulletin and Review, 3*, 21–36.

Ruvolo, M., Disotell, T.R., Allard, M.W., Brown, W.M., & Honeycutt, R.L. (1991). Resolution of the African hominoid trichotomy by use of a mitochondrial gene sequence. *Proceedings of the National Academy of Sciences, 88*, 1570–1574.

Ruvolo, M., Pan, D., Zehr, S., Goldberg, T., Disotell, T.R., & von Dornum, M. (1994). Gene trees and hominid phylogeny. *Proceedings of the National Academy of Sciences, 91*, 8900–8904.

Sadato, N., Pascual-Leone, A., Grafman, J., Ibawez, V., Delber, M.-P., Dold, G., & Hallett, M. (1996). Activation of the primary visual cortex by Braille reading in blind subjects. *Nature, 380*, 526–528.

Saffran, J.R., Aslin, R.N., and Newport, E.L. (1996). Statistical learning by 8-month-old infants. *Science, 274*, 1926–1928.

Saint-Cyr, J.A., Taylor, A.E., & Nicholson, K. (1995). Behavior and thebasal ganglia. In W.J. Weiner & A.E. Lang (Eds.), *Behavioral Neurology of Movement Disorders: Advances in Neurology, Vol. 65* (pp. 1–28). New York: Raven Press.

Sarich, V. (1992). All about Eve. *Scientific American, September*, 6.

Savage-Rumbaugh, E.S. (1994). Hominid evolution: Looking to modern apes for clues. In D. Quiatt & J. Itani (Eds.), *Hominid culture in primate perspective* (pp. 7–49). Niwot, CO: University of Colorado Press.

Savage-Rumbaugh, E.S., & Lewin, R. (1994). *Kanzi: The ape at the brink of the human mind.* New York: Wiley.

Savage-Rumbaugh, E.S., & McDonald, K. (1988). Deception and social manipulation in symbol-using apes. In R. Byrne & A. Whiten (Eds.), *Machiavellian intelligence: Social expertise and the evolution of intellect in monkeys, apes and humans* (pp. 224–237). Oxford: Oxford University Press.

Savage-Rumbaugh, E.S., Romski, M.A., Hopkins, W.D., & Sevcik, R.A. (1989). Symbol acquisition and use by *Pan troglodytes, Pan paniscus, Homo sapiens.* In P.G. Heltne & L.A. Marquardt (Eds.), *Understanding chimpanzees* (pp. 266-295). Cambridge, MA: Harvard University Press.

Schepartz, L.A. (1993). Language and modern human origins. *Yearbook of Physical Anthropology, 36*, 91–126.

Schiff, H.B., Sabin, T.D., Geller, A., Alexander, L., & Mark, V. (1982). Lithium in aggressive behavior. *American Journal of Psychiatry, 139*, 1346–1348.

Schmidt, R.A. (1988). *Motor control and learning* (2nd Edn). Champaign, IL: Human Kinetics Publishers.

Schopf, J.W. (1993). Microfossils of the Early Archean Apex Chert: New evidence of the antiquity of life. *Science, 260*, 640–646.

Schwartz, J.H., & Tattersall, I. (1996). Significance of some previously unrecognized apomorphies in the nasal region of *Homo neanderthalensis. Proceedings of the National Academy of Sciences*, 93, 10852–10854.

Sedvall, G., & Farde, L. (1995). Chemical brain anatomy in schizophrenia. *The Lancet, 346*, 743–749.

Semaw, S., Renne, P., Harris, J.W.K., Feibel, C.S., Bernor, R.L., Fesseha, N., & Mowbray, K. (1997). 2.5-million-year-old stone tools from Gona, Ethiopia. *Nature, 385*, 333–336.

Sergent, J., Zuck, E., Terriah, S., & MacDonald, B. (1992). Distributed neural network underlying musical sight-reading and keyboard performance. *Science, 257*, 106–109.

Shallice, T., & Burgess, P.W. (1991). Deficits in strategy application following frontal damage in man. *Brain, 114*, 727–741.

Shannon, R.V., Zeng, F.-G., Karnath, V., Wygonski, J., & Ekelid, M. (1995). Speech recognition with primarily temporal cues. *Science, 270*, 303–304.

Shaywitz, B.A., Shaywitz, S.E., Pugh, K.R., Constable, R.T., Skudlarski, P., Fulbright, R.K., Bronen, R.A., Fletcher, J.M., Shankweiler, D., Katz, L., & Gore, J.C. (1995). Sex differences in the functional organization of the brain for language. *Nature, 373*, 607–609.

Shevoroshkin, V. (1990). The mother tongue. *The Sciences, May/June*, 20–27.

Shreeve, J. (1996). New skeleton gives path from trees to ground an odd turn. *Science, 272*, 654.

Shu, D.-G., Morris, S.C., & Zhang, X.-L. (1996). A *Pikaia*-like chordate from the Lower Cambrian of China. *Nature, 384*, 157–158.

Shu, D.-G., Zhang, X., & Chen, L. (1996). Reinterpretation of Yunnanozoon as the earliest known hemichordate. *Nature, 380*, 428–430.

Shubin, N.H., & Alberch, P. (1986). A morphogenetic approach to theorigin and basic organization of the tetrapod limb. In M.K. Hecht, B. Wallace, & G.T. Prance (Eds.), *Evolutionary biology, Vol. 20* (pp. 319–387). New York: Plenum.

Shuren, J.E., Schefft, B.K., Yeh, H.-S., Privitera, M.D., Cahill, W.T., & Houston, W. (1995). Repetition and the arcuate fasciculus. *Journal of Neurology, 242*, 596–598.

Siegal, M., Carrington, J., & Rodel, M. (1996). Theory of mind and pragmatic understanding after right hemisphere damage. *Brain and Language, 53*, 40–50.

Silk, J. (1997). Infinite possibilities. *Nature, 385*, 786.

Sillen, A., & Brain, C.K. (1990). Old flame. *Natural History, 4*, 6–10.

Silverman, I., & Eals, M. (1992). Sex differences in spatial abilities: Evolutionary theory and data. In J.H. Barkow, L. Cosmides, & J. Tooby (Eds.), *The adapted mind: Evolutionary psychology and the generation of culture* (pp. 533–553). Oxford: Oxford University Press.

Simons, E.L. (1989). Human origins. *Science, 245*, 1343–1350.

Simons, E.L. (1995). Skulls and anterior teeth of *Catopithecus* (primates: Anthropoidea) from the Eocene and anthropoid origins. *Science, 268*, 1885–1892.

Singer, W. (1994). A new job for the thalamus. *Nature, 369*, 444–445.

Skinner, B.F. (1974). *About behaviorism*. New York: Alfred A. Knopf.

Smith, B.H., & Tompkins, R.L. (1995). Toward the life history of the hominidae. *Annual Review of Anthropology, 24*, 257–270.

Smith, M.P., Sansom, I.-J., & Repetski, J.E. (1996). Histology of the first fish. *Nature, 380*, 702–704.

Snowdon, C.T. (1990). Language capacities of nonhuman animals. *Yearbook of Physical Anthropology, 33*, 215–243.

Sperry, R.W. (1968). Mental unity following surgical disconnection of the cerebral hemispheres. *The Harvey Lectures, 62*, 293–323.

Spiker, D., and Ricks, M. (1984). Visual self recognition in autistic children: Developmental relationships. *Child Development, 55*, 214–225.

Spinney, L. (1996). Stone me, those crows make tools. *New Scientist, 20 January*, 16.

Spitzer, M., Kwong, K.K., Kennedy, W., Rosen, B.R., & Bellivean, J.W. (1995). Category-specific brain activation in fMRI during picture naming. *NeuroReport, 6*, 2109–2112.

Spoor, F., Wood, B., & Zonneveld, F. (1994). Implications of early hominid labyrinthine morphology for evolution of human bipedal locomotion. *Nature, 369*, 645–648.

Spoor, F., Wood, B., & Zonneveld, F. (1996). Evidence for a link between human semicircular canal size and bipedal behavior. *Journal of Human Evolution, 30*, 183–187.

Spuhler, J.N. (1988). Evolution of mitochondrial DNA in monkeys, apes and humans. *Yearbook of Physical Anthropology, 31*, 15–48.

Stanley, S.M. (1992). An ecological theory for the origin of *Homo*. *Paleobiology, 18*, 237–257.

Steg, G., & Johnels, B. (1993). Physiological mechanisms and assessment of motor disorders in Parkinson's disease. In H. Narabayashi, T. Nagatsu, N. Yanagisawa, & Y. Mizuno (Eds.), *Advances in neurology, Vol. 60* (pp. 358–365). New York: Raven Press.

Steriade, M., & Amzica, F. (1996). Intracortical and cortical coherency of fast spontaneous oscillations. *Proceedings of the National Academy of Sciences, 93*, 2533–2538.

Sternberg, R.J. (1985). *Beyond IQ: A triarchic theory of human intelligence*. Cambridge: Cambridge University Press.

Steudel, K. (1996). Limb morphology, bipedal gait, and the energetics of hominid locomotion. *American Journal of Physical Anthropology, 99*, 345–355.

Stoneking, M. (1993). DNA and recent human evolution. *Evolutionary Anthropology, 2*, 60–73.

Straube, E.R., & Oades, R.D. (1992). *Schizophrenia: Empirical research and findings*. San Diego, CA: Academic Press.

Straus, L.S. (1995). The Upper Paleolithic of Europe: An overview. *Evolutionary Anthropology, 4*, 4–16.

Stringer, C.B. (1990a). The emergence of modern humans. *Scientific American, December*, 68–74.

Stringer, C.B. (1990b). The Asian connection. *New Scientist, 17 November*, 23–27.

Stringer, C.B., & Gamble, C. (1993). *In search of the Neanderthals: Solving the puzzle of human origins*. London: Thames & Hudson.

Stringer, C., & McKie, R. (1996). *African exodus: The origins of modern humanity*. London: Cape.

Stromswold, K., Caplan, D., Alpert, N., & Rauch, S. (1996). Localization of syntactic comprehension by PET. *Brain and Language, 52*, 452–473.

Studdert-Kennedy, M. (1990). This view of language. *Behavioral and Brain Sciences, 13*, 758–759.

Stuss, D.T., Eskes, G.A., & Foster, J.K. (1994). Experimental neuropsychological studies of frontal lobe functions. In F. Boller & J. Grafman (Eds.), *Handbook of neuropsychology, Vol. 9* (pp. 149–185). New York: Elsevier.

Sugiyama, Y. (1994). Tool use by wild chimpanzees. *Nature, 367*, 327.

Susman, R.L. (1994). Fossil evidence for early hominid tool use. *Science, 265*, 1570–1573.

Sutton, D., Trachy, R.E., & Lindeman, R.C. (1981). Primate phonation: unilateral and bilateral cingulate lesion effects. *Behavioural Brain Research, 3*, 99–114.

Swisher, C.C., Curtis, G.H., Jacob, T., Getty, A.G., & Widiasmoro, A.S. (1994). Age of the earliest known hominids in Java, Indonesia. *Science, 263*, 1118–1121.

Swisher, C.C., Rink, W.J., Antón, S.C., Schwarcz, H.P., Curtis, G.H., & Widiasmoro, A.S. (1996). Latest *Homo erectus* of Java: Potential contemporaneity with *Homo sapiens* in Southeast Asia. *Science, 274*, 1870–1873.

Tanji, J., & Mushiake, H. (1996). Comparison of neuronal activity in the supplementary motor area and primary motor cortex. *Cognitive Brain Research, 3*, 143–156.

Tanvir, N.R., Shanks, T., Ferguson, H.C., & Robinson, D.R.T. (1995). Determination of the Hubble Constant from observations of Cepheid variables in the galaxy M96. *Nature, 377*, 27–31.

Tattersall, I. (1995). *The fossil trail*. Oxford: Oxford University Press.

Thieme, H. (1997). Lower Palaeolithic hunting spears from Germany. *Nature, 385*, 807–810.

Thomson, K.S. (1992). The challenge of human origins. *American Scientist, 80*, 519–522.

Tillier, A.-M. (1989). The evolution of modern humans: Evidence from young Mousterian individuals. In P. Mellars & C. Stringer (Eds.), *The human revolution: Behavioral and biological perspectives on the origins of modern humans* (pp. 286–297). Princeton, NJ: Princeton University Press.

Tishkoff, S.A., Dietzsch, E., Speed, W., Pakstis, A.J., Kidd, J.R., Cheung, K., & Bonné-Tamir, B. (1996). Global patterning of linkage disequilibrium at the CD4 locus and modern human origins.*Science, 271*, 1380–1387.

Tlemel, C., Quan, Y., & En, W. (1994). Antiquity of *Homo sapiens* in China. *Nature, 368*, 55.

Tobias, P.V. (1987). The brain of *Homo habilis*: A new level of organization in cerebral evolution. *Journal of Human Evolution, 16*, 741–761.

Tobias, P.V. (1995). The brain of the first hominids. In J.-P. Changeux & J. Chavaillon (Eds.), *Origins of the human brain* (pp. 61–81). Oxford: Clarendon Press.

Tokida, E., Tanaka, I., Takefushi, H., & Hagiwara, T. (1994). Tool using in Japanese macaques: Use of stones to obtain fruit from a pipe. *Animal Behaviour, 47*, 1023–1030.

Tomasello, M. (1990). Cultural transmission in the tool use and communicatory signaling of chimpanzees? In S.T. Parker & K.R. Gibson (Eds.), *Language and intelligence in monkeys and apes: Comparative and developmental perspectives* (pp. 274–311). Cambridge: Cambridge University Press.

Tomasello, M., & Call, J. (1994). Social cognition in monkeys and apes. *Yearbook of Physical Anthropology, 37*, 273–305.

Toth, N. (1985). Archaeological evidence for preferential right-handedness in the Lower and Middle Pleistocene, and its possible implications. *Journal of Human Evolution, 14*, 607–614.

Toth, N., Clark, D., & Ligabue, G. (1992). The last stone ax makers. *Scientific American, July*, 66–71.

Toth, N., & Schick, K.D. (1993). *Making silent stones speak: Human evolution and the dawn of technology.* New York: Simon & Schuster.

Trinkaus, E. (1994). Femoral neck-shaft angles of the Qafzeh-Skuhl early modern humans, and activity levels among immature Near Eastern Middle Paleolithic hominids. *Journal of Human Evolution, 25,* 393–416.

Turner, G. (1996). Intelligence and the X chromosome. *The Lancet, 347,* 1814–1815.

Tuttle, R.H. (1990). The pitted pattern of Laetoli feet. *Natural History, 3,* 61–64.

Tyson, N.D.G. (1995). The size and the age of the universe. *Natural History, 2,* 72–75.

van der Lely, H.K.J., & Stollwerck, L. (1996). A grammatical specific language impairment in children: An autosomal dominant inheritance. *Brain and Language, 52,* 484–504.

Van Essen, D.C. (1997). A tension-based theory of morphogenesis and compact wiring in the central nervous system. *Nature, 385,* 313–318.

Vanni, S., Revonsuo, A., Saarinen, J., & Hari, R. (1996). Visual awareness of objects correlates with activity of right occipital cortex.*NeuroReport, 8,* 183–186.

Vargha-Khadem, F., Watkins, K., Alcock, K., Fletcher, P., & Passingham, R. (1995). Praxic and nonverbal cognitive deficits in a large family with a genetically transmitted speech and language disorder. *Proceedings of the New York Academy of Sciences, 92,* 930–933.

Vermeij, G.J. (1996). Animal origins. *Science, 274,* 525–526.

Visalberghi, E. (1989). Primate tool use: Parsimonious explanations make better science. *Behavioral and Brain Sciences, 12,* 608–609.

Visalberghi, E. (1993). Capuchin monkeys: A window into tool use in apes and humans. In R.K. Gibson & T. Ingold (Eds.), *Tools, language and cognition in human evolution* (pp. 138–150). Cambridge: Cambridge University Press.

Visalberghi, E., & Fragaszy, D.M. (1990). Do monkeys ape? In S.T. Parker & K.R. Gibson (Eds.), *"Language" and intelligence in monkeys and apes: Comparative developmental perspectives* (pp. 247–273). Cambridge: Cambridge University Press.

Visalberghi, E., Fragaszy, D.M., & Savage-Rumbaugh, S. (1995). Performance in a tool-using task by common chimpanzees (*Pan troglodytes*), bonobos (*Pan paniscus*), an orangutan (*Pongo pygmaeus*), and capuchin monkeys (*Cebus apella*). *Journal of Comparative Psychology, 109,* 52–60.

Vogel, G. (1997). Scientists probe decisions behind decision-making. *Science, 275,* 1269.

Walsh, V. (1995). Reading between the laminae. *Current Biology, 5,* 1216–1217.

Wanpo, H., Ciochon, R., Yumin, G., Larick, R., Qiren, F., Schwarcz, H., Yonge, C., de Vos, J., & Rink, W. (1995). Early Homo and associated artefacts from Asia. *Nature, 378,* 275–278.

Warren, A.A., Jupp, R., & Bolton, B.R. (1986). Earliest tetrapod trackway. *Alcheringa, 10,* 183–186.

Waters, M.R., Forman, S.L., and Pierson, J.M. (1997). Diring Yuriakh: A Lower Palaeolithic site in central Siberia. *Science, 275,* 1281–1283.

Weiss, K.M. (1994/1995). What recapitulates what? Genetics and the evolution of development. *Evolutionary Anthropology, 3,* 216–222.

Westergaard, G.C., & Hopkins, W.D. (1994). Theories of mind and self-recognition. *American Psychologist, 8,* 761–762.

Westergaard, G.C., & Suomi, S.J. (1994). The use and modification of bone tools by capuchin monkeys. *Current Anthropology, 35,* 75–77.

Westergaard, G.C., & Suomi, S.J. (1996). Hand preference for stone artefact production and tool use by monkeys: Possible implications for evolution of right handedness in hominids. *Journal of Human Evolution, 30,* 291–298.

Wheeler, P. (1993). Human ancestors walked tall, stayed cool. *Natural History, 8,* 65–67.

White, R. (1992). Beyond art: Toward an understanding of the origins of material representation in Europe. *Annual Review of Anthropology, 21,* 537–564.

White, T.D., Suwa, S., & Asfaw, B. (1994). *Australopithecus ramidus*, a new species of early hominid from Aramis, Ethiopia. *Nature, 371*, 306–312.

White, T.D., Suwa, S., & Asfaw, B. (1995). *Australopithecus ramidus*, a new species of early hominid from Aramis, Ethiopia. *Nature, 375*, 88.

White, T.D., Suwa, S., Hart, W.K., Walter, R.C., WoldeGabriel, G., Heinzelin, J., Clark, J.D., Asfaw, B., & Vrba, E. (1993). New discoveries of *Australopithecus* at Maka in Ethiopia. *Nature, 366*, 261–265.

Whiten, A. (1991). The emergence of mindreading: Steps towards an interdisciplinary enterprise. In A. Whiten (Ed.), *Natural theories of mind: Evolution, development and simulation of everyday mindreading* (pp. 195–207). Oxford: Blackwell.

Wigan, A.L. (1844). *The duality of the mind*. London: Longman, Brown & Green.

Wilkins, W.K., & Wakefield, J. (1995). Brain evolution and neurolinguistic preconditions. *Behavioral and Brain Sciences, 18*, 161–226.

Williams, N. (1995). The trials and tribulations of cracking the prehistoric code. *Science, 269*, 923–924.

Williams, N. (1997). Evolutionary psychologists look for roots of cognition. *Science, 275*, 29–30.

Wilson, A.C., & Cann, R.L. (1992). The recent African genesis of humans. *Scientific American, April*, 22–33.

Wilson, D.S., Near, D., & Miller, R.R. (1996). Machiavellianism: A synthesis of the evolutionary and psychological literatures. *Psychological Bulletin, 119*, 285–299.

Wind, J. (1989). The evolutionary history of the human speech organs. In J. Wind & E. Pulleyblank (Eds.), *Studies in language origins* (pp. 173–197). Amsterdam: Benjamins.

Winstein, C.J., & Pohl, P.S. (1995). Effects of unilateral brain damage on the control of goal-directed hand movements. *Experimental Brain Research, 105*, 163–180.

Wolpoff, M.H. (1989). Multiregional evolution: The fossil alternative to Eden. In P. Mellars & C. Stringer (Eds.), *The human revolution: Behavioral and biological perspectives on the origin of modern humans* (pp. 62–108). Princeton: Princeton University Press.

Wolpoff, M., & Caspari, R. (1996). *Race and human evolution*. New York: Simon & Schuster.

Wood, B. (1992). Origin and evolution of the genus *Homo. Nature, 355*, 783–790.

Wood, B. (1994). The oldest hominid yet. *Nature, 371*, 280–281.

Wood, B., & Quinney, P.S. (1996). Assessing the pelvis of AL 288–1. *Journal of Human Evolution, 31*, 563–568.

Wray, G.A., Levinton, J.S., and Shapiro, L.H. (1996). Molecular evidence for deep Precambrian divergences among metazoan phyla. *Science, 274*, 568–571.

Wynn, T. (1989). *The evolution of spatial competence: Illinois studies in anthropology number 17*. Urbana and Chicago, IL: University of Illinois Press.

Wynn, T.G. (1991). The comparative simplicity of tool-use and its implications for human evolution. *Behavioral and Brain Sciences, 14*, 576–577.

Wynn, T.G., & McGrew, W.C. (1989). An ape's view of the Oldowan. *Man, 24*, 383–398.

Wynn, T., Tierson, F.D., & Palmer, G.T. (1996) Evolution of sex differences in spatial cognition. *Yearbook of Physical Anthropology, 39*, 11–42.

Yamada, J.E. (1991). *Laura: A case for the modularity of language*. Cambridge, MA: MIT Press.

Yellen, J.E., Brooks, A.S., Cornelissen, E., Mehlman, M.J., & Stewart, K. (1995). A middle stone age worked bone industry from Katanda, Upper Semliki Valley, Zaire. *Science, 268*, 553–555.

Zangwill, O.L. (1976). Thought and the brain. *British Journal of Psychology, 67*, 301–314.

Author Index

Subject Index